ROUTLEDGE LIBRARY EDITIONS:
SOCIAL AND POLITICAL THOUGHT IN THE
NINETEENTH CENTURY

Volume 5

LIBERTARIAN THOUGHT IN NINETEENTH CENTURY BRITAIN

LIBERTARIAN THOUGHT IN NINETEENTH CENTURY BRITAIN

Freedom, Equality and Authority

WILLIAM R. MCKERCHER

Routledge
Taylor & Francis Group

LONDON AND NEW YORK

First published in 1987 by Garland Publishing, Inc.

This edition first published in 2017
by Routledge
2 Park Square, Milton Park, Abingdon, Oxon OX14 4RN

and by Routledge
711 Third Avenue, New York, NY 10017

Routledge is an imprint of the Taylor & Francis Group, an informa business

British Library Cataloguing in Publication Data
A catalogue record for this book is available from the British Library

ISBN: 978-1-138-69658-7 (Set)
ISBN: 978-1-315-52405-4 (Set) (ebk)
ISBN: 978-1-138-68034-0 (Volume 5) (hbk)
ISBN: 978-1-138-68037-1 (Volume 5) (pbk)
ISBN: 978-1-315-56380-0 (Volume 5) (ebk)

Foreword

Nineteenth-century libertarian political thought encompasses a wide variety of ideas in the works of a heterodox and often quarrelsome group of writers. What unites them, despite their many differences, is their rejection of state coercion as a morally permissible basis of government and their belief in the inherent capacity of human beings to live fulfilling lives as autonomous individuals, guided by their conscience and free from the dictates of institutional authorities. They reject the claim that they have an obligation to obey those who presume the right to rule over them, and regard the instruments of surveillance, control and manipulation that those authorities use to exert their rule as illegitimate and immoral.

Today, in the in the early decades of the twenty-first century, even in what had once been liberal democracies there is constant stoking of public fear – of terrorism, crime, or some other currently dreaded menace – and relentless pressure on citizens to trade their personal freedom for the supposed benefits of enhanced security. At the same time, state and corporate authorities are in possession of technologically advanced instruments of surveillance that enable them to monitor and control human activity to a degree never before possible. Little wonder, therefore, that there is a revival of interest in libertarian thought.

Will McKercher came early to the realization that writers in the libertarian tradition raised profound questions about the ethical foundations of political order and that their ideas remain as challenging and relevant as when they were written. His thinking first found expression in his brilliant 1971 master's thesis at the University of Western Ontario, titled simply "Obedience in Anarchism." In it he focused principally on the works of the anarchist-socialists Alexander Berkman and Emma Goldman, but also wove into his discussion sharply insightful observations on the works of Tolstoy, Kropotkin, Proudon and others. I was privileged to be one of Will's teachers at that stage of his career, but in truth my role was an easy one: his remarkable talent for lucid exposition and analysis and his fluid, direct, first-person writing style were already in place and fully formed.

In his doctoral research at the LSE his interest turned in a new but related direction, away from the anarchist-socialist school of theorists and towards a rich but under-studied vein of nineteenth-century English political thought which he eventually defined as libertarian rather than anarchist. That body of writing incorporated a broader range of ideas than that found in anarchist thought and included works by authors whose views of anarchism were ambiguous and often contradictory. The task he set for himself was "to characterize and identify the intellectual heritage of the proponents of the libertarian tradition," and in particular to elucidate their understanding of the concepts of freedom and authority. The result was a study distinguished by extraordinary depth of research and masterful exposition – perhaps best exemplified in his discussion of the works of William Morris, which alone is a noteworthy contribution to original scholarship.

Today, the label 'libertarian' has been largely appropriated by a school of theorists whose philosophy is on the opposite end of the ideological scale from that of the nineteenth-century anarchists and libertarians – who were all, in one way or another, on the political left. Right-wing libertarianism has intellectual roots that may be traced to the writings of Friedrich Hayek, Ludwig von Mises and other economists of the Austrian school, and has been widely popularized by modern American advocates, including, most notably, the philosopher Robert Nozick. While divided over certain matters, the core belief of right-wing libertarians is that freedom can only be fully realized under a system of unregulated free-market capitalism, with a minimal state whose functions are limited to little more (or nothing more) than protecting private property and enforcing contracts. Their narrow construction of liberty leaves no room to consider the consequences of extreme inequality or structures of economic domination that such a system would inevitably generate.

The re-issue of William R. McKercher's *Libertarian Thought in Nineteenth Century Britain* is a timely reminder that there is an older, alternative tradition of left-libertarian thought that now, perhaps more than ever, deserves our most serious attention. Readers of this book will find themselves treated to a guided tour through the literature of that tradition by a scholar who is deeply engaged with his subject and who approaches it in a manner that is unfailingly respectful and sympathetic but by no means uncritical. There is much that is original and thought-provoking in the following pages. Read on and enjoy.

Sid Noel
London, Ontario, 2016

LIBERTARIAN THOUGHT IN NINETEENTH CENTURY BRITAIN

Freedom, Equality and Authority

William R. McKercher

Garland Publishing, Inc., New York & London
1987

Library of Congress Cataloging-in-Publication Data

McKercher, William Russell, 1944–
Libertarian thought in nineteenth century Britain.

(Political theory and political philosophy)
Based on the author's thesis (doctoral)—London
School of Economics and Political Science.
Bibliography: p.
1. Libertarianism—Great Britain—History—19th
century.   I. Title.   II. Series.
JC599.G7M38   1987   320.5′12′0941   86-27028
ISBN 0-8240-0826-X

All volumes in this series are printed
on acid-free, 250-year-life paper.

Printed in the United States in America

LIBERTARIAN THOUGHT IN 19TH CENTURY BRITAIN:

FREEDOM, EQUALITY AND AUTHORITY

William Russell McKercher

To Henry Wilmer McKercher

ACKNOWLEDGEMENTS

This book is based upon a doctoral thesis completed at the London School of Economics and Political Science and written under the guidance of Maurice Cranston and Fred Rosen.

The research was partially funded by the Canada Council, and completed with the generous assistance of awards from King's College, at the University of Western Ontario.

Colleagues, professional associates, and friends played an instrumental part in the completion of this work. I wish to thank them all for their support. In particular, may I express my gratitude to S.J.R. Noel, Robert Sansom, Sharon Lannon, Barry Bartmann, Tozun Bahcheli, Jerry Mulcahy, Marie Fleming, Cathy Mendler and Carol McDonald.

W.R. McKercher
London, Ontario
1986.

On September 7, 1872, the anarchist-socialist Mikhail Bakunin was driven out of the First International by Marx and his followers at a meeting (from which Bakunin was absent) of the General Council at The Hague. This divisive split between the 'Bakuninists' and the 'Marxists' characterized the dramatic difference between the anti-state socialists and the so called 'Scientific Socialists' the latter of whom were the founders of most present-day Marxist political parties. While the followers of Bakunin called for the revolutionary destruction of the state and the establishment of federal communities, the Marxists proposed using the power of the state to smash capitalism and centralize the power of the industrial proletariat. The goals of both groups were essentially the same, but the means towards their achievement were irreconcilably different.

In the ensuing decades an ideological battle raged between these two factions with the state socialist followers of Marx pursuing their goal of state power through party politics and subversive action. The anti-state socialists led by Peter Kropotkin and William Morris rallied themselves around the slogan "educate, organize, agitate" and vainly continued to propose an alternative vision of the social revolution. Their brand of socialism was ultimately rejected by most radicals as either too anarchistic or utopian. The strength of their movement was sapped by the early success of the Russian Revolution when most members of the Left converted to the ideas of Marx and Lenin.

The rise of the modern totalitarian state, the legal-rational bureaucracies of Western Europe, the hegemony of the nuclear powers, and the one party states common in Eastern Europe, Asia, and Africa give credence to the early libertarian fears about the coercive nature of the state. In the last decade neo-Marxists and New Left critics have become increasingly aware of the fact that the power of the state has itself presented a problem for those who seek to restructure their societies in conformance with their ideological beliefs. Those writers who deal with questions of alienation, freedom, the role of authority, and state power owe an intellectual debt to the socialist opponents of Marx, a group of men and women who, from the time of Bakunin's ejection from the First International, contributed to what I have characterized as the libertarian tradition.

Libertarian thought is to many an eclectic area of discourse and one which has not been thoroughly scrutinized within the context of nineteenth-century British political philosophy. One of the primary purposes of this book is to characterize and identify the intellectual heritage of the proponents of the libertarian tradition. To set this within a theoretical framework, these ideas will be examined by using the pragmatic and conceptual formulations of freedom and authority, two notions which are central to any understanding of political philosophy in the twentieth century.

In examining the proponents of libertarian thought, their ideas, and their theories, I have drawn from sources which are not widely available. They take the form of pamphlets and journals, newspapers, magazines, broadsheets, manifestos, public records, diaries, and organizational propaganda published by various 'radical' political groups. To this list may be added a variety of famous and infamous books ranging from the fictitious to those of pure philosophical speculation, biographies and autobiographies, and the odd anonymous and pseudonymous work. Most of these have been preserved by the British Library, the British Library of Political and Economic Science, and the International Institute of Social History in Amsterdam. Thus the select bibliography in this volume represents a unique collection of the primary sources of libertarian literature which, in itself, helps to define the scope of libertarian thought.

In the identification of libertarian ideas, especially those relating to the central concept of freedom, I have chosen in Chapter One to deal with John Stuart Mill's notion of liberty as expounded in his influential essay On Liberty. My purpose is not only to interpret and clarify some of Mill's ideas on the subject of liberty but also to provide a critical analysis which is pertinent to an understanding of any libertarian critique of the state. Here I have set out Mill's perceptions of the individual in 'civilized' society along with his notions pertaining to the role of law in 'developed' states. As a parallel to these ideas, I present those of the libertarians which are shown to be sharply at variance with most of Mill's conceptual formulations and the a priori assumptions upon which they rest. The chapter ends with an attempt to clarify the distinctions between libertarian thought and such partially derivative ideologies as anarchism and socialism.

In Chapter Two, I turn my attention to William Morris in the belief that he is very much the epitome of a consistent libertarian thinker. Since Morris at various times called himself a socialist and a communist, many, especially in the American school of libertarianism, might feel somewhat dubious about concentrating on the ideas of Morris. I would, however, characterize the modern American libertarian movement as primarily individualist. I argue that the British libertarian tradition was dominated by those who believed that the freedom of the individual was impossible without a community of equals.

As a 'socialist' commentator, Morris was nonetheless aware of the fact that he was "spurred to action" after having read such conservative writers as Carlyle and Ruskin. By the early 1880's he had become politicized and had come to the conclusion that the products of one's labour bore a direct relation to one's attitudes towards work and the conditions under which this work was performed. Morris felt that only when work was both pleasurable and useful could it be said to be acceptable and contributory to the spiritual and physical well-being of the producing individual. To this end, he believed that all work ought to be the expression of one's labour as shown in the satisfaction one receives in performing any task. Morris would call the products of such satisfaction 'art.' During the last sixteen years of his life, and especially when he was involved with the Socialist League (which he founded), we are able to see the mature development of his ideas. These ideas, and particularly those relating to the expansion and expression of personal freedom, place Morris firmly within what I have characterized as the libertarian tradition of nineteenth-century Britain.

The scope of the debate is broadened somewhat in Chapter Three where I have made extensive use of what are often thought to be ephemeral sources--namely newspapers and journals. Here I investigate how information and ideas were disseminated at a time when the printed word was of paramount importance. By way of specific example I make use of three journals which were in publication during the 1880's: The Anarchist, Commonweal, and Freedom. Those involved in the production of these propaganda organs were acquainted with one another and with radical circles in Europe and the United States. Many were instrumental in creating an environment for the nascent socialist and labour movements in Britain. The investigation provided in this chapter enables us to achieve a better understanding of their ideas, and also assesses their personal achievements in relation to one another and to the causes for which they had lent their support. Thus, having identified and discussed the literature which evolved from these circles, I develop a theoretical analysis of libertarian thought as it pertains to the central concepts of authority and freedom.

When one discusses the oppressive nature of the state and the role of coercion in society, the concept of authority cannot be ignored. In Chapter Four, I identify the varying conceptual interpretations in terms of their general usage within the writings of notable political theorists of the post-sixteenth century. I argue that the libertarians can be seen to possess two distinct notions of authority. The first notion is the object of much of their critical comment regarding the role of institutions and the law in western society. It is the form of authority which anarchists commonly wish to see abolished since they see it as being by its very nature, coercive. I have called this form of authority 'command-authority,' for it is most obvious in relationships of an institutionalized form maintained by compliant behaviour subject to the sanction of physical force or the threat of physical force.

The second form of authority I have called 'belief-authority.' My argument defends the notion that the libertarians accept such a relationship in practice even though this is obscured by the fact that they do not refer to it as 'authority.' This is, I believe, the factor which allows for social cohesion in a libertarian society, for it is complementary to certain conceptions of freedom.

Belief-authority is basically the relationship which arises from a person legitimizing the influence that any other person has upon them. Thus, in the case of belief-authority, unlike command-authority, it is the person who is being influenced who defines the nature of the relationship. This person is ostensibly able to make a choice, that is, to be free and at liberty to act as one will, given that one accepts the consequences of one's actions.

The argument is carried forward in Chapter Five where I deal first with the concept of liberty and secondly, with that of freedom. Unlike political theorists such as Isaiah Berlin or Maurice Cranston, I argue that they are very distinct concepts. Here I maintain that the words themselves allow us to recognize a crucial juxtaposition within libertarian thought. Liberty is understood mainly in terms of a lack of restraint or impediment, usually of a physical nature. This is to suggest that in the best of circumstances, one must be 'at liberty' fully to express one's freedom, or be free. Freedom is thus choice. Having the ability to make a choice is seen to be worthwhile or necessary to the person who makes it, regardless of the opinions of others. As such, freedom is not in conflict with what I view as belief-authority.

In the Conclusion I briefly reinforce the argument that in libertarian terms the individual and society are complementary to one another for reasons analogous to those which led to the view that belief-authority and freedom are not in conflict. This, of course, runs contrary to the views of most present-day libertarians, especially in the United States, as well as many recent writers who have studied libertarian thinkers and contributed to modern libertarian thought. An obsessive reliance upon the rights of individual, or the "Ego and Its Own" as Max Stirner characterized the individualist spirit, was not a major factor in the British libertarian movement. The individualism of modern libertarian parties is, in essence, a mixture of the ideas derived from the individualist anarchists including Godwin, Stirner, Tucker, and Warren, or those whom I would call the 'state minimalists' such as Proudhon, Spencer, Nietzsche, and a host of other minor characters referred to in this study. The strength of the contribution by the non-individualist libertarians is to be seen in the state critics of the Left, who have challenged the Marxist version of the necessity for the revolutionary seizure of state power to serve the ends of a particular world view.

TABLE OF CONTENTS

CHAPTER ONE

A LIBERTARIAN CRITIQUE OF THE ESSAY 'ON LIBERTY'

An Introduction to Mill

In this chapter I shall compare John Stuart Mill's ideas on liberty with those expressed by libertarian thinkers. Although Mill's views are the subject of controversy, I have chosen to concentrate on his most famous and widely known work, the essay, On Liberty.

The topic of liberty has many facets, and the concept itself is not a static one, but both Mill and the libertarian thinkers share a concern with several of the same main issues. These are, firstly, the problems which relate to the individual in society; that is, one man dealing with another, with groups of all kinds, or with the whole of society. As Mill's initial solution was to accept, or take for granted, certain 'rules of conduct,' my second line of inquiry will deal with two limits on liberty - opinion and the law. Thirdly, I shall deal with the relationship between the rulers and the ruled, or more specifically, between those who make law and impose opinion and those who are obliged to obey or suffer the consequences.

By looking at what Mill said on these subjects, I shall then be able to comment on the implications of these opinions. Any criticism will, in a complementary fashion, be set against what could be called a libertarian critique of Mill's ideas.

Throughout my analysis, the liberal opinion of Mill will be used as a foil and a reference point from which to identify more clearly the basis of the libertarian criticism of political and social life in the later nineteenth century. This method ought to give the reader an insight into two lines of argument, while at the same time clarifying the nature and scope of libertarian thought.

In the 'Introductory' to the essay <u>On Liberty</u>, John Stuart Mill claimed that he would discuss a fundamental problem of political philosophy which was in need of fresh expression. The problem arose from the time-honoured conflict between liberty and authority. However, the nature of the problem had changed; the increasing trend towards democracy in the 'civilized' nations of the world led Mill to the conclusion that a re-examination of this conflict was imperative to the understanding of man as a social animal living in nineteenth-century England.

His main concern, therefore, was twofold; regarding authority as opposed to liberty in the broad sense, he wanted to ascertain what were the proper bounds of that authority. Such a discussion meant that boundaries must be designated; there would have to be limitations on the liberty of individuals, and so rules of conduct would have to be made which would give to the individual, and to society, 'its proper share' of liberty, one in relation to the other.

As a result, Mill's first premise incorporates the fact that certain rules of conduct were necessary to make 'existence valuable.' These rules of conduct were the means of restraint, and were to be carried through by the use of two particular devices - opinion and the law. Therefore, as restraining devices, opinion and the law were the only legitimate implements which could be used to impose upon the freedom of the individual, or to protect him from the excesses of society. But law and opinion could themselves only operate within certain limitations, and it was these limitations which Mill set out to clarify and justify.

Mill initially stipulated that justifications for these limitations could only be made if one followed a guiding principle. In this way one could judge the propriety or impropriety of government or public interference. Regarding the liberty of action Mill wrote,

> That principle is, that the sole end for which mankind are warranted individually or collectively, in interfering with the liberty of action of any of their number, is self-protection.[1]

The freedom of the individual to look after his own interests seemed absolute. "Over himself, over his own body and mind the individual is sovereign."[2]

In the first instance, therefore, the individual is pitted against society, or rather, both the individual and society are posited as being in need of constant vigilance for their own self-protection. Mill feared the tyranny of opinion, as well as the 'tyranny of the majority.' He had already accepted that governments all too easily became despotic institutions.[3] But he still thought that limits on action by individuals ought to be imposed by the government through the law and by society itself through the exercise of opinion or oral disapprobation. So it is therefore necessary to examine those limitations that Mill would put upon these to very different legitimate forms of restriction.

The distinction between the individual and society must be clarified because it is central to the discussion of limitation and the justifications for it. As the argument about limitations is also basic to libertarian doctrine, a fruitful discussion and criticism of Mill's ideas in On Liberty will go a long way to explain why the two theories are so different even though they do, for the most part, address themselves to the same problems.

The Individual and Society

Mill believed that the progress of mankind and the development of civilization were very much the result of individual effort. Individual diversity contributed to the progress of society. In many notable instances the 'dissidents' of an age made the most lasting social and cultural contributions. According to Mill in On Liberty, it was the responsibility of those who were 'in advance of society' to question whether or not accepted values and opinions were either true or useful. Mill claimed that questions regarding 'the rights of the individual against society' had only been challenged 'on broad grounds of principle' in the area of religious belief.[4] There were certain restrictions put upon the individual. Yet rather than deal with the 'acceptable' restrictions which could be put on freedom of thought and belief, I shall limit this discussion to the limitations on the behaviour of the individual in society; that is, we shall deal with liberty of action and the ways in which it can be legitimately restricted. Here we can set the ideas of Mill, in On Liberty, parallel with similar problems in libertarian thought.

When counteracting the weight of the whole of society, the individual seemed, to Mill, to be facing a formidable foe. An uncontrolled society could result in the most all-pervasive form of despotism possible. With reference to the mass, or a society whose opinion could decide on all issues, Mill did not mince his words when he said,

> It practices a social tyranny more formidable than many kinds of political oppression...enslaving the soul itself.[5]

To prevent such a situation from coming into being, what was needed was a limit "...to the legitimate interference of collective opinion with individual independence."[6] Mill, therefore, sought to establish that dissent was necessary and that it ought to be one of the rights of the individual. Thus men 'in advance of society' would be protected from the overwhelming force of majority or unified opinion.

Mill, from the beginning, recognizes that there must be principles to protect the individual from both 'collective opinion' and 'political despotism.' This entails addressing oneself to the problem of "...how to make the fitting adjustment between individual independence and social control."[7]

The libertarian faces the same problem, to some degree, although he is not nearly as pessimistic about the role of public opinion as he is about 'political despotism.' Yet the libertarian is as concerned about freedom and the individual as the liberal is, albeit for quite different reasons. These reasons relate particularly to the liberal notions of law and private property, and it will suffice to say at the moment that the libertarians disagree with the liberals most conspicuously on these points.

With regard to the rights of the individual, Mill regarded utility 'as the ultimate appeal on all ethical questions' although he did stress that "...it must be utility in the largest sense, grounded on the permanent interests of a man as a progressive being."[8] This is, in effect, a guiding principle which could be said to be the measure of all other standards. And we ought to remember that utility is the grand principle upon which the ultimate belief in Mill's liberal society is to stand or fall.

In reference to the proper limits of restricting individual, as opposed to societal freedom, Mill believed that the notion of self-protection was to be the basic standard upon which an appeal could be grounded. Yet 'self-protection' is a particular standard and, it seems, one which is already subsumed under the larger and more general utilitarian schema. Self-protection was itself part of the notion of utility.

We begin, therefore, with an examination of Mill's objectives in the essay On Liberty in order that we may establish the type of relationships he envisioned between the individual and society. He begins with a very clear statement of intent.

> The object of this essay is to assert one very simple principle, as entitled to govern absolutely the dealings of society with the individual in the way of compulsion and control, whether the means used be physical force in the form of legal penalties, or the moral coercion of public opinion. That principle is, that the sole end for which mankind are warranted, individually or collectively interfering with the liberty of action of any of their number, is self-protection.[9]

Mill accepts that because there must be 'rules of conduct', people must also establish methods of enforcement. Thus people may be compelled to act in a certain fashion so that the interests of others will be protected. In a civilized society (and Mill certainly believed he was in one), the use of force could be justified only 'for the security of others.' Therefore, one is free to do what one wants as long as it does not threaten the security of others, or actually infringe upon their independent rights.

It would be difficult to find a libertarian who would disagree with such 'liberal' sentiments as these. Numerous writers of the libertarian persuasion regard self-preservation and self-protection to be of the utmost importance. In fact, they only justify the use of violence, in most cases, for this very reason.

Guy Aldred, who described himself as 'a kind of anarchist,' linked self-preservation with progress. He wrote, in a paper entitled The Possibility and Philosophy of Anarchist Communism, that,

> Underlying all social progress is the first law of Nature, the law of self-preservation.[10]

An American libertarian, Jay Fox, who published in England at the turn of the century, considered self-preservation as a means for justifying 'selfishness.' He suggested, in a paper on Trade Unionism and Anarchism that high regard should be paid to this selfish virtue.

> He [the anarchist] knows that selfishness - self-preservation - is the strongest force in man, that it cannot be eliminated, and should not if it could; for such a condition would reduce mankind to mere machines.[11]

If 'self-preservation' is seen to be selfish by Fox, to Mill it is the only possible way to live in a civilized manner. The individual, first and foremost, must have security in order to make life worth living. That the individual must preserve his own independence and life, is not then, an issue between Mill and the libertarians. The libertarians, in fact usually refer to the notion of self-preservation as a defensive action in the same way as Mill does, or as legitimate justification for using compulsion in one form or another. We must realize, however, that there is no agreement upon what can be legitimately protected so as to give the individual the greatest amount of freedom, nor indeed is there agreement as to methods of protection.

Mill justifies restrictions on liberty that ultimately rest upon legal or moral coercion. It was society's responsibility to determine its own rules of conduct, guided by the broad notion of utility. As it turns out, utility as Mill understood it, demanded that conduct be regulated by either law or opinion. Society was bound to protect the individual, and the individual was obliged to comply with those dictates which could be justified as conforming to the principle of self-protection.

The notion of 'society' for Mill seemed at first to refer to all those people who were gathered under one state umbrella. Society includes all, but its interests are often interpreted by segments of it, as in the case of the legislators who make the law, or the magistrates who act upon and interpret it. The individual has to compete against these interests which exist at the behest of a broader concept of society. As a representative of the legislative powers of society, the government can make law to enforce compliance "...only in respect of those actions of each which concern the interest of other people."[12] Society, through opinion rather than law, can also punish or elicit obedience by 'general disapprobation.' The question which is of importance is 'Who defines the rights and interests of the society?'

The libertarians would say that no community or society "...has any rights at all beyond the individual rights voluntarily combined of those composing it."[13] The typical anarchist would say that "...an individual has an absolute right to do exactly as he pleases just so long as he doesn't invade another's right."[14] This may sound like Mill without qualifications but, in fact, the libertarians do themselves qualify such statements.

Henry Seymour, Editor of The Anarchist and follower of Proudhon, Tucker, and Kropotkin, identified anarchy with liberty and suggested that liberty was in itself an absolute moral value. Seymour stated in 'The Anarchists' Catechism':

> How can morality be thus defined? If an individual trespasses on the equal right of another, he commits a crime. There are consequently, degrees of crime, only varying according to the extent to which one's liberty is infringed.[15]

Thus, the libertarians, like Mill, are seeking to reconcile the liberty of the individual with membership in society. To Mill this meant that the individual must, if necessary, be compelled to submit to the broader interests of society. To the libertarians, who are optimists on this question, the individual by virtue of the options open to him will, himself, be an expression of those interests; this is so because the libertarians substitute cooperation for competition.

Only by distinguishing between Mill's individual and what Mill considers society, and the libertarian individual and what he understands as society, will any clear distinction emerge. This distinction is important because it cannot be stressed too much that when the words 'individual' and 'society' are used, the libertarians have a different conception not only from Mill's but from the one usually taken as the common view. In many ways the words of Mill are filled with pessimism because he believes that man cannot be free and secure without a comprehensive system of law to restrict the bad side of human nature. Yet Mill is very optimistic in his belief that legislators will be able to construct a system of law which will allow the individual (of which the legislator is but a particular case) to pursue his own self-development in concert with the rest of society. We cannot doubt that Mill believed coercion to be necessary to prevent even greater evils; and this coercion was, as we know, to be enforced by groups within the society, which were by various means designated as spokesmen for the society in general.

Just as Mill used historical examples to show the stultifying effects of custom and the potential despotism of various kinds of governments so, for similar historical reasons, were the libertarians sceptical about the role of government and its agencies. As far as the libertarian belief in some forms of utilitarian optimism was concerned, Henry Seymour commented (in 1885) that,

> ...this 'Utilitarian' nonsense is preached today as the new philosophy of life; a philosophy which should have been buried with its cleverest expositors, Bentham and Mill (good and wise men in some other respects nonetheless).[16]

But as pessimistic as the libertarians were about giving great power to certain groups because of its corrupting influence, they had what at first appears as a naive view regarding the humanitarian qualities of men living under a system devoid of law. Mill, too, disliked the improper use of power,[17] but the libertarians went much further in their condemnation of it. They believed that, in moral terms, law was as 'evil' as liberty was 'good.' To them, power and corruption went hand in hand. The powerful individual or group was not in a position of equal liberty with the rest of the individuals in the society; there was no equal liberty which was the foundation of the 'good' society.

Mill's initial conception of liberty is not what could be called a wholly positive one. The individual is free, or at liberty to do something within particular bounds. These bounds are to be defined by the rules of conduct. And still Mill sometimes does have a more positive notion of liberty. This is expressed in his references to that positive law which, in effect, tends to enhance one's area of choice. This 'positive' view extends to Mill's optimistic belief in individual self-development. But as Mill begins to develop these notions, we find that his original <u>guiding</u> principle, that of self-protection, becomes an all-encompassing maxim.

In the 'Introduction' to <u>On Liberty</u>, the consequences of what is involved, or subsumed, under the original 'principle' of self-protection begin to change. This change occurs as soon as Mill begins discussing the circumstances under which an individual may be coerced to act against his will. We begin, according to Mill, with the "...subjugation of individual spontaneity to external control, only in respect to those actions of each which concern the interest of other people."[18] This is, in effect, the same as the libertarian notion about 'equal liberty for all with respect to one another's rights.' It soon becomes apparent, however, that the 'interest' which Mill has in mind goes beyond the bounds of 'self-preservation' or acts 'hurtful to others,' for he goes on to say in the same paragraph that,

> There are also many positive acts for the benefit of others, which he may rightfully be compelled to perform; such...things which whenever it is obviously a man's duty to do, he may rightfully be made responsible to society for not doing.[19]

In other words, society, or a segment of it can hold an individual responsible for not doing those things which society itself deems in its own interest. Furthermore, Mill believes that society can also be hurt by <u>inaction</u>, while to be in conformance to his principle of self-protection, this ought not to be. The individual man may, by doing nothing, 'cause evil to others.' This, says Mill, can be seen as exceptional in most circumstances, but that nonetheless inaction and its consequences should be judged by society in the light of the individual case. In all these situations the intentions of the individual seem to make no difference.

The justifications for compulsion under the wider heading of self-protection can be seen as an important turning point in the whole discussion. We are told that a person may be compelled to perform positive acts which are defined as being 'necessary to the interest of the society of which he enjoys the protection.'[20] What this appears to mean is that an individual, simply by being physically present in a certain area, is presumed to seek or need the protection of society. Such an assumption of unsolicited membership and obligation is somewhat reminiscent of Locke's notion of 'tacit consent.' It was the catch-all condition for all those who had not been seen to 'actually' consent. Mill does however have more subtle qualifications and certain beliefs which entail them. These qualifications revolve around the role of law in society and the relationship of the individual with that law and its makers. It is law which protects the individual from the protectors, and it is this assumption which the libertarians simply do not find either desirable or acceptable. Given these considerations, it is evident that libertarian thought is not the logical extension of liberalism.

It would be unfair to suggest, on the other hand, that Mill considered either society or the individual responsible _per se_ for its or his salvation. If law was the ultimate protector and was necessary, it would be easy to conclude that Mill's views on the distinctive roles delineated in respect of both society and the individual were coloured by his own particular preferences.

In the chapter, 'Of Individuality, As One of the Elements of Well-Being,' Mill expressed grave doubts as to the validity and worth of mass opinion.[21] He felt that most people did not desire, and often did not even think about liberty,[22] and that if they continued to "...conform to custom merely as custom..."[23] they would cease to have 'character,' which was one of the elements of individuality in a progressive and civilized society. He more than once cited China as being the obvious example of what happens when character was but a function of custom.[24]

"The despotism of custom is everywhere the standing hindrance to human advance,..."[25] he said, as he bemoaned the fate of a society which would not put its energies into creating the individuality of all its members.[26]

> The greatness of England is now all collective; individually small, we only appear capable of anything great by our habit of combining; ... But it was men of another stamp than this that made England what it had been; and men of another stamp will be needed to prevent its decline.[27]

In his ideas regarding the individual at odds with the rest of society, Mill's desire was to see dissent and eccentricity established,[28] because he meant to protect what he termed 'men of genius.'[29] He did not mean that any and every man could not express his own individuality, but he particularly wanted to guarantee that men of originality would be heard above the din of mass opinion.

Thus it is that the individualism of Mill is, in effect, the expression of a certain cultivated individuality. This individualism must of course be in conformance with the law, and sometimes (such as in cases of obvious self-regarding behaviour) with opinion. Opinion, in reference to moral disapprobation, is more likely to be that kind which is spoken by friends, family, or community, rather than the mass of custom-ridden opinions of the majority of society. Mill's ideas as to what constituted individuality are, however, of two sorts.

First, there is the individuality which is identified with the person of energetic capacity. This is the person who has strong impulses.[30] That is, "...one person's desires and feelings are stronger and more various than those of another."[31] This individual capacity, or energy, is, according to Mill, a thing which can be used for either good or evil purposes.[32] Mill, of course, believed that these energies should be made to serve a good end, in effect, the interests of society. Indeed, should this not turn out to be the case, and the energetic individual took the 'bad' course, then he ought to be punished. Nonetheless, with regard to the individual's good qualities,

> It is through the cultivation of these that society both does its duty and protects its interests.[33]

It is therefore clear that, within limits, what society cannot accomplish through education and persuasion, it must do by compulsion, through law. Thus will the individualism of Mill, as one form of pursuit of individuality, guarantee 'good' and productive members of society.[34]

Mill's second form of individuality is more a concern of self than it is of the relations with the rest of society, but the rest of society, he assures us, will benefit.[35] This individuality is self-development, or what Mill refers to as 'character.'[36] It is not gained by mere dissent or erascibility but through more positive acts which give "...fair play to the nature of each...to lead different lives."[37] Here we have an individuality which Mill believed had been harnessed by civilization, one which would if it would not bow to custom or general conformity, nonetheless conform to the dictates of 'law and ordinance.'[38] Individuality which is more concerned with both the spiritual and material development of self would be one mainly "...of personal impulses and preferences."[39]

Not only does this self-developing individuality, because it is already sufficiently channelled, serve the interests of society, but it does so unintentionally. That is, such a self-regarding individual cannot help but contribute to the well-being of society simply because he is following his 'good' impulses in an energetic yet highly personalized manner. Such behaviour, Mill believed, by its very diversification, would greatly hinder the formation of a society whereby "...human life would become a stagnant pool."[40]

The 'bad' actions of the individual even contribute to his own self-development, because any restraint put upon him is "...restraint put upon the selfish part"[41] of his nature. Therefore, any person who expressed his character in this way by 'encroaching on the rights of others,'[42] would in his peculiar way still benefit himself. For "...even to himself there is a full equivalent in the better development of the social part of his nature."[43] Anyway, it is certain that in the case of misguided individuality, law will assert itself. Coercive measures are justified because ...

> The means of development which the individual loses by being prevented from gratifying his inclinations to the injury of others, are chiefly obtained at the expense of the development of other people.[44]

Restrictive law, in this case, is good for both the individual and society. It is assumed, by Mill, that in the state of advanced civilization in which he found himself,[45] there ought to be general consensus as to the role of law. Under one form of Mill's individuality a person is encouraged to dissent from common opinion and so to work to repeal or change the law; but having accepted this role, the individuality of self-development is bound by the law. The law is mutually self-regarding, in Mill's eyes, both to the society and the individual. It must also be _seen_ as such for, by definition, individuality is only restrained in the face of 'the greater individuality' - that of the general interest.

Mill seems to have absolute faith in the role of law and the lawmakers. In On Liberty a system of law is assumed to be necessary. But one may question this assumption: it is curious that Mill believed that one could only achieve individuality under such circumstances. The libertarians, among others, do not believe this to be the case. They, like Mill, see conflicts between the individual and society, but unlike Mill, the libertarians see even greater conflict and evil arising out of the system of law which Mill so resolutely affirms. Mill, in a sentence, gives us a description of the individual under law, but it is a view that could just as well pertain to the individual who does not live under law.

> He who chooses his plan for himself, employs all his faculties. He must use observation to see, reasoning and judgment to foresee, activity to gather materials for decision, discrimination to decide, and when he has decided, firmness and self-control to hold to his deliberate decision.[46]

Regardless of whether the law is present or not, and we know that it is for Mill, this is in conformity with "...human nature...[which is]...but a tree which requires to grow and develop itself on all sides, according to the tendency of the inward forces which make it a living thing."[47] Mill's individuality, under the weight of legal sanction "...is desirable...in things which do not primarily concern others."[48] Those things ought to be apparent for they are not expressly forbidden by law or worthy of moral disapprobation. For, in the first instance, Mill believed that "...among the works of man...the first of importance is surely man himself."[49]   So too would the libertarians begin their discussion

on individuality.

To Guy Aldred, for example, man 'dominated by the will to be'

must adapt his individualism to living in a society of equals.

> For, self-contained as each individual should be, loyal
> unto the internal canons of thought as opposed to
> external authority, man is, nevertheless, so far as his
> sense impressions and social existence is concerned, a
> part of the social organism; an ethical unit, and an
> intellectual cellular activity acting and reacting upon
> the society of which he is a part, and upon the cellular
> activities to which he is related. Each of these
> activities, or social atoms, is dominated by the will to
> be, adaptation being the order of being.[50]

In this interpretation, man, or the individual, guides his

actions in relation to other men – the rest of society. There is an

overriding individual concern about the rest of society. But the

libertarian society does not always or necessarily mean the whole

amorphous mass of people who live within a state boundary. Their

society is generally seen by them, even in respect of it being the

whole of humanity, to be a smaller unit, a community for instance,

which is seen as being societal only by virtue of the fact that it has

relations with other communities in the broader context.

To the libertarians, communities, or parts of society wherein

one has immersed his time and effort and hence one's interests should

not be made artificially cohesive by the use of law or coercion.

Kropotkin, writing in <u>Anarchism – Its Philosophy and Ideal</u>, said,

> ... if by following the very old advice given by Bentham
> you begin to think of the fatal consequences – direct,
> and especially indirect – of legal coercion; then like
> Tolstoi, like us, you will begin to hate coercion, and
> you will begin to say that society possesses a thousand
> other means of preventing antisocial acts.[51]

Like Mill, Kropotkin firmly believed that one of those other

means was opinion. Such opinions, insofar as they were not necessarily part of a custom, were to be given and received by individuals by virtue of their close proximity to the very persons who engaged in antisocial acts.

Another cohesive force in society would be, according to Kropotkin, the establishment of 'communist customs,' but, he added,

> ...they must be looked to for establishing such relations between men that the interests of each should be the interest of all; and this alone can unite men instead of dividing them.[52]

In reference to individualism Kropotkin, in the same article, went on to say,

> Communism is the best basis for individual development and freedom; not that individualism which drives man to the war of each against all...[53]

We can hear faint echoes of Bentham and Hobbes in these words of Kropotkin's, but a certain vital point is illustrated by this reference to individualism. For like most socialist, and particularly Marxist, critics of the concept, the libertarians tend to attach very derogatory connotations to the idea of individualism. They identify individualism with selfishness, atomization, competition, and small-mindedness - all of which, they believe, constitute the epitome of 'bourgeoise liberalism.' This is, in many instances but crude thinking on their part, but like many other misrepresentations, there is some truth in their feelings about individualism. The libertarian position regarding this rather popular definition or identification of individualism with selfishness, etc., is perhaps best illustrated in an article which appeared in the Communist Anarchist journal, Freedom. Strangely enough, in the context of this discussion, this article was written as a defence of the anarchist notion of individuality, which, so the author thought, had been falsely accused as being individualistic. The author was J. Burns-Gibson, an anarchist of the communistic variety, who was closely associated with members of the Freedom Group, the Fabian Society and the Socialist League. It was entitled Anarchism Kills Individualism. In a statement, with which in isolation, Mill would certainly not disagree, Burns-Gibson gives us his picture of individualism:

> Individualism is this striving, grabbing, over-reaching and self-seeking of atoms, that seek to possess human individuality, but go about their quest in the wrong way.[54]

Mill, especially in his essay On Liberty would consider such a form of individualism to be on the negative side of self-development or, more precisely, to denote the energies of a person who was "...hurtful to others, or wanting in due consideration for their welfare."[55] Even so, Mill would not treat this egotistical form of individualistic behaviour as a violation of 'constituted rights' (i.e., "certain interests, which either by legal provision or tacit understanding ought to be considered as rights").[56] Certainly he would conclude that,

> The offender may then be justly punished by opinion, though not by law.[57]

In other words, for Mill, an expression of individuality which was exemplified by 'striving, grabbing, over-reaching and self-seeking' would be 'bad' only insofar as it hurt others. On the other hand, Mill would never accept such behaviour as being virtuous,[58] but might refer to it as the development of undesirable character traits which ought not to be displayed. Burns-Gibson could not on this evidence alone correctly maintain that Mill's liberalism condoned a selfish form of individualism. But Burns-Gibson went further than this particular criticism of individualism. For he connected it to concepts which, on the whole, were acceptable to Mill and which point out the very great divergence of belief which existed between Mill and some libertarians. Burns-Gibson claimed that 'selfish' individualism gave rise to many forms of behaviour which he, as an anarchist and a communist, would not tolerate. He linked individualism to certain concepts.

> It [individualism] calls itself civilization, fair competition, free trade and many other fine names. It is, in reality, internecine war and suicide.[59]

Such a statement as this helps confirm the thesis that the libertarians are working from an entirely different set of beliefs and values than Mill's. This is made even more apparent in libertarian literature which deals with what Mill accepted as progress and civilization,[60] and continues in their beliefs about the social role of law, custom, and the notion of freedom. A fuller discussion of these points will be found in the critique of Mill towards the end of this chapter. It suffices to mention here that the libertarians and Mill are in many instances working on entirely different assumptions.

Individuality, as opposed to individualism of the kind Burns-Gibson criticized, is, while formed around different beliefs, essentially the self-development concept[61] of Mill. Yet self-development is not necessarily restricted by law, nor in any obvious way does it seem to be restricted by society or by the abstract principles by which Mill has justified limitations upon the expression of individuality. As Burns-Gibson said,

> ...to destroy individuality is to destroy society. For society is only realized and alive in the individual members. Society has no motive that does not issue from its individual members, no end that does not centre in them, no mind that is not theirs. "Spirit of the age," "public opinion," common weal or good," and like phrases have no meaning, if they are thought of as features of something that hovers or floats between man and woman. They name what resides in and proceeds from individuals.

> Individuality and community therefore, are equally constitutive of our idea of human life.[62]

On the surface Mill and the libertarians do not seem to disagree, for the problem of giving the individual the greatest possible amount of freedom within an orderly society is prominent in both doctrines. Yet the divergence is there, and it is twofold. Firstly, their basic assumptions and categories are different. Secondly, Mill accepts limitations on the freedom of the individual, which are in the main, rejected by the libertarians. It is necessary to detail the function and scope of these limitations, and the manner in which they have been justified by Mill. For this, we must look at the role of law and opinion, both of which, for Mill, are, under certain circumstances, legitimate restrictive measures.

Restricting Individual Behaviour - By Law and Opinion

In relation to the individual's ability to live in society, Mill stipulated, as we have seen, that rules of conduct were paramount. These rules of conduct were not to be bound or defined by custom, but were to be established, in one set of situations, by law, in another, by the opinion of others.

Mill assumed that law was necessary for the conduct of happy relations in a free and civilized society. This law tended to be more prohibitive in its effect, according to Mill, upon the minority for the benefit of giving protection to the majority. However, laws which set out established rights, although protecting minorities, also tended to extend privilege to that minority vis a vis the majority, e.g., the owners of capital as opposed to those who worked it. To Mill, law was one of the essential ingredients in the struggle for both the greatest happiness and the greatest amount of freedom and security. Mill viewed law as one of the main methods for setting out what the proper rules of conduct ought to be. Codified law was prescriptive, to a degree, for it anticipated certain forms of intolerable behaviour, and it simply codified the rules which were to be followed as guides to conduct.

Mill believed that people, if they were to conduct themselves in a 'civilized' manner, had to know what was expected of them.

> In the conduct of human beings towards one another it is necessary that general rules should for the most part be observed, in order that people may know what they have to expect.[63]

With respect to the legitimate restraint on liberty, the most general of these rules was to be self-protection. This criterion of self-protection applied, in turn, to both the individual and society at large. The notion was greatly complicated by Mill in his chapter on 'Applications,' for he seemed to suggest that judgment always rested on the merits of individual cases. He reiterated what he considered to be his only two criteria of judgment.

> The maxims are, first, that the individual is not accountable to society for his actions, insofar as these concern no person but himself.
>
> Secondly, that for such actions as are prejudicial to the interests of others, the individual is accountable and may be subjected either to social or to legal punishment, if society is of opinion that the one or the other is requisite for its protection.[64]

In other words, it is ultimately up to society and its institutions to define the parameters of individual freedom in conformance with the interests of each to one another. Liberty, in most instances, was granted by some authority. The principle of freedom, for Mill, revolved around individual behaviour - it was concerned with individuality and self-development. As for letting the individual proceed with his actions at will, Mill stated that one should be forewarned of the consequences of his actions, both to himself and to others. "For liberty consists in doing what one desires...".[65] Society, on the other hand, had an obligation to its members to curb certain forms of desire, except where there are cases of "...purely self-regarding mis conduct [which] cannot be meddled with in the way of prevention or punishment."[66]

Mill continued to assert that the 'principle of liberty' should remain intact in the consideration of the necessity for restrictions. The burden of proof must rest with the restricting authority. Mill gave several instances, by way of example, how certain forms of restriction could be justified, and these instances were notable for the way in which they viewed public behaviour. The examples which dealt with taxation, drunkenness, prostitution, and gambling exemplified to Mill the subtleties inherent in prohibiting certain acts solely on the grounds that, as public displays, they were more likely to be both offensive and harmful. Yet he still maintained that the principle of liberty itself ought not to be violated, for,

> Whenever, in short, there is a definite damage, or risk
> of damage, either to an individual or to the public, the
> case is taken out of the province of liberty, and placed
> in that of morality or law.[68]

The notion of self-protection also included the right of the police or licensed authorities to control public establishments where conspiracy to commit future offences might take place. That is, "...if it becomes a rendezvous for concocting and preparing offences against the law."[69] Such 'concocting' behaviour was wrong because of the ultimate aim of those involved, i.e., to commit an illegal act. It is similar, though not the same as to "...give advice or offer inducements..."[70] to someone to perform an act which could put the public interest in jeopardy. This form of 'conspiring' is only wrong in Mill's eyes if the instigator makes such advice "...his occupation for subsistence or pecuniary gain..."[71] and even this must be shown to be an 'evil' against society.

Society, as represented by the state and its laws, may also legitimately "...take precautions against crime before it has been committed, as well as to detect and punish it afterwards."[72] The state, in other words, must guard against those influences which it regards as detrimental to society or a segment of it.[73] However, the state or the government must justify the ends for which it needs to exercise control over social life. For, as an overseer which holds the monopoly of power, the "...state...is bound to maintain a vigilant control over his [the individual's] exercise of any power which it allows him to possess over others."[74]

Mill's initial discriminating idea of self-protection defines not so much the principle of freedom but the actual survival of the reality of freedom at any particular time. In the realm of law, the first law is that one must not break the law. For, as Mill said, "...everyone who receives the protection of society owes a return for the benefit, and the fact that living in society renders it indispensible that each should be bound to observe a certain line of conduct towards the rest."[75]

This is the moral obligation which Mill assumes every individual ought to concede. The law, as such, is based not only upon utility but has a strong moral base, although it does not include the total range of moral behaviour. Outside of the law it is the weight of opinion or moral disapprobation which is used to encourage proper social behaviour. These moral attitudes are inculcated by the rising generation through education. It is the duty of society to educate its offspring in such a way as to prepare them for the responsibility of freedom, otherwise all will suffer the consequences. Hence, in the liberal world of Mill, the individual can only be coerced by due legal process. The weight of opinion and the appeal to the moral obligations of the individual are the two other means of keeping the individual within the proper bounds of conduct. Thus it is law which is the primary coercive factor in Mill's civilized society; and to have rights and freedoms, one must admit to this primary prerequisite for living in Mill's society. For, without obedience to the state, all other freedoms are in point of fact, abrogated. To Mill law is the guarantor of a progressive and civilized state, if it operates within his stipulated guidelines.

This, I believe, provides the central idea about the role of law and opinion in On Liberty. Mill believes that one's legal obligations subsume certain moral obligations. He believes also, however, that law cannot sufficiently, nor should it, cover all moral obligations to one's fellow man. In other words, there is a limit to what law can do. For what is important is that morality is the basis for all rules of conduct. Law must be concerned with those areas where the action of individuals are viewed as being wholly detrimental to the society at large. Law must control what reason cannot always do, and it is up to the government to pass such laws as will accomplish the least amount of suffering to the greatest number of beings in the society.

In the realm of opinion or moral suasion, Mill had to admit that if the state was able to exert pressure upon the private affairs of the individual, so too should what he called an individual's 'particular public.' In reference to the 'socialistic' opinions of the artisan class, Mill stated that he did not believe,

> ... that any individual's particular public can be blamed for asserting the same authority over his individual conduct which the general public asserts over people in general.[76]

For although he did not agree with it, he could not fault the individual who followed the dictates of a 'moral police' because it related to interests in a narrow sense. This is an admission that the individual, if he so wishes, will probably be persuaded by his peers rather than by the anonymity of a general public.

In the end, the liberal discussion on freedom, which can be epitomized in On Liberty, is true to its own principles. But what we must remember is that many of the basic assumptions made by Mill affect in turn the way in which the principle of liberty is applied. For example, Mill claims that the principle of liberty is not violated by Free Trade[77] because the restraints which could be applied to trade or production "...do not really produce the results which it is desired to produce by them."[78] In other words, the restrictions on liberty are, for Mill, justified by their effects as well as the ability of the legislators to competently benefit society by such actions. Could this same criterion not also be applied to many other types of law? The libertarians believe so. For, to Mill, outside of the principle itself, freedom of action is not an intrinsic good which supercedes the notion of utility. Mill was worried about the results of particular forms of choice or behaviour as he aptly suggested when he asked us to "...suppose a considerable diffusion of Socialist opinions...."[79] This obviously related to what he felt society might become. Some forms of choice may well be wrong, but this only illustrates the central problem which is involved regarding the type of restrictions which can legitimately be placed upon the individual by society. The libertarians were one group of people who concluded that the methods of restriction outlined by Mill were not only unfair, but wrong. In other words, there was considerable disagreement over both methods and priorities. To Mill, freedom without the sanction of law was, in practice, impossible. It is therefore possible to agree with someone like Mabbott, who assumed that liberal freedom (as a good or guiding moral principle) "...seems to be a good which is not great enough to be made the centre of a political theory, nor so great that much else of intrinsic value must be sacrificed to it."[80]

The libertarians felt that Mill certainly put the rule of law before the principle of freedom, but even more adamant were they that Mill's doctrine did not go far enough. They believed this because they felt there was no **prima facie** evidence to suggest a change in the concept regarding the rulers and the ruled.

The Rulers and the Ruled

Mill did not speak directly of the distinction between the rulers and the ruled as two separate self-serving groups. Instead he discussed the role of government within society, and, by way of historical example, showed what effects it had upon individuals.[81] Even the mechanics of government, to which Mill addressed himself somewhat briefly at the end of On Liberty, were largely ignored.

For Mill preferred to deal generally with the function of government under the title of society. It was society which created and maintained government, and Mill believed that government and law were the practical and necessary realities involved in the concept of state. Society operated, in the best way, under the umbrella of a

constitutional and legally regulated state. In this context, Mill
pointed out that both the individual and society were meant to have
their proper shares of influence.

> Each will receive its proper share, if each has that
> which more particularly concerns it. To individuality
> should belong the part of life in which it is chiefly the
> individual that is interested, to society, the part which
> chiefly interests society.[82]

There is a curious use of terms here, for as it has been
explained earlier in this chapter,[83] Mill's individualism proposed
that 'individuality' was but a part of the concept of individualism.
It was the part which went along with 'self-development.' Keeping this
in mind, one is able to see that the above quoted statement is open to
several interpretations. It could be taken to mean that, for only that
part of individual concern which relates to self-development, can there
be any legitimate individual claim. The individual's claim concerns
only the 'individuality' part of his individualism. In other words, to
take a liberty and turn Mill's sentence around "...to the individual
should belong the part of life in which it is chiefly individuality
that is interested..."[84] There is a difference here between the
two words, individuality and individual, but as the sentence continues
"...to society [should belong] the part which chiefly interests
society."[85] But the question now arises: Are we therefore to
assume that the word 'society' is meant to have the same meaning with
each usage?

First, we may assume that 'individuality' and the 'individual's
individualism' are conceptually the same, while accepting at the same
time that the two uses of the term 'society' are similar. This
interpretation makes the whole statement seem quite straightforward, as
the one meaning of 'individual' is balanced against the one meaning of

'society.'

On the other hand, having suggested that 'individuality' was not the same as 'individual,' or the 'individual's individualism,' we might look at the alternative meanings of the term 'society' in this context. If we do this, I believe we can derive some valid and interesting insights regarding the relationship between the notion of society and that of rule.[86]

We must ask first, "Who defines the 'proper share' of liberty which chiefly interests society?" For we know already that, to the individual who wished to find out, it would be made quite plain to him through law, or through the opinion of others. The individual, by developing his individuality within the confines of societal obligations, is to a very personal degree, the <u>author</u> of his own self-development. The 'bad' side of his individuality is curtailed by the dictates of society. Individuality, therefore, is defined by society, for it is the opinion of one against many. Society, of course, ought not to infringe upon certain individual rights (for this was one of the main points Mill had to make) and predispositions, but this does not mean that it <u>cannot</u> or <u>will not.</u> Since it is society who lays down the rules, are we to expect, as Mill does, that the solitary individual can ever rise above what society itself considers to be harmful? And is it 'society' which is making his judgment, or is it a particularized 'public,' a section of the society, which makes the judgment? Is it not the law-makers, the government, the legislature, and the judiciary who pass judgments upon individuality and individualism?

If one were to share this sentiment, as indeed the libertarian writers do, then it should not be denied that there are those who rule in an individual and a collective manner. And there are many more other individuals, who, in spite of initial assumptions or justifications, are in essence, ruled. Mill, in accepting the legal-constitutional system, knew that even the rulers were ruled for they were bound by law and its interpretation. This is of course quite obvious, but the libertarians have argued that this law must be made by someone, and that it is generally made in the interests of those who rule.

Therefore the argument is not so much about the particular form of government or rule although this is obviously very important to the individual. The argument is about whether the ruler-ruled dichotomy is a fact and whether it can be justified. Mill was not particularly worried about this question in On Liberty, for he was wholly in agreement with, although often critical of,[87] institutional rule. He accepted that the world did not begin yesterday for in the nations with which he was concerned "...mankind have attained the capacity of being guided by their own improvement by conviction or persuasion...".[88] Mill was under no illusions about the possible tyranny of a rule-oriented society. Even when he spoke about so-called self-government, he made this point very clear, although it seems he was later to ignore his own misgivings. With reference to a certain democratic republic he said,

> It was now perceived that such phrases as 'self-government' and 'the power of the people over themselves' do not express the true state of the case. The 'people' who exercise the power are not always the same people with those over whom it is exercised; and the 'self-government' spoken of is not the government of each by himself, but of each by all the rest.[89]

This could not have been more aptly expressed by any libertarian, for it referred to a form of rule which was in many ways intangible but somehow all-embracing. The libertarians had exactly the same fears as Mill, and while Mill liked to refer to some of them as 'the tyranny of the majority,' or 'social tyranny,' they were just as prepared to call it 'legal licence' or 'class rule.'

Mill, therefore, cannot be criticized for not addressing himself in more detail to such problems as class rule; but he can, in libertarian terms, be criticized for not developing these ideas in terms of the problem of rule in its relation to the law-makers themselves and the ultimate effects upon the freedom of the individual.

Mill knew that the values of the rulers and the common mores of opinion were, in the larger cultural arena of society, emanations from a class which considered itself superior. What he later referred to as the middle class[90] was influencing society through both law and opinion, in many cases for its own self-interest.

> Whenever there is an ascendant class, a large portion of the morality of a country emanates from its class interests, and its feelings of class superiority.[91]

Recognized by Mill for what this was rather than for the effects it might have on others, Mill still believed that a principled system of law could arise out of the situation. To the libertarians, this ascendant class theory seemed all but a truism and a very pernicious one at that. For they believed that this led to the working class being ruled, in more than law, by the middle or privileged classes.

While speaking for the abolition of government, or the rule of one man by another, Kropotkin attempted to spell out the difference between the communist-anarchist view and the state socialist and liberal views of rule. He claimed that there would be greater freedom without state rule.

> A section of Socialists believe that it is impossible to attain such a result without sacrificing personal liberty on the altar of the State. Another section to which we belong, believes, on the contrary, that it is only by the abolition of the State, by the conquest of perfect liberty by the individual, by free agreement and association, and absolute free federation, that we can reach Communism...[92]

Of course Mill's aim was not the establishment of a communist society, but his aim, like Kropotkin's, did include the greatest amount of personal liberty and happiness. The actual goal of happinesss was not different, but the methods to obtain happiness would have been quite foreign to Mill's mind. Libertarians thought differently than Mill, and while both proposed solutions for the good of mankind, it was the libertarians who believed that the present state of society, because of the role of law, was wholly unacceptable. But since individual liberty was the primary concern of both doctrines, we are able to begin to understand the subtleties of libertarian thought much more fully when they are stood against the liberal assumptions of Mill.

Libertarians, like Kropotkin, saw the laws of the rulers as convenient, 'neutralized' tools made to subjugate the greater part of the populace. The law was sanctified by those in power. With more emotion than Mill might have used, Kropotkin never hesitated to identify law, as well as morality, with class.

> Every liberal law, every radical programme, may be summed up in these words, 'abolition of laws grown irksome to the middle class itself.'[93]

The acceptance of the state idea by Kropotkin meant that man was allowing himself to be governed by a set of relations which were not for the good of all but for the benefit of a few.

> The State idea implies quite another idea than to that of government. It not only includes the existence of a power placed above society, but also a territorial concentration of the life of society in the hands of a

few or even of all. It implies new relations among the members of society.[94]

The new relations which the ideal implied were still, however, founded upon power and coercion. Mill knew that coercion was necessary in many instances, and he hoped that law would control its application and use. But Mill still recognized that power was a great source of individual and moral corruption. For when he spoke about mass as opposed to individual leadership, he reminded the 'strong man of genius' of the pitfalls which faced him if he seized control of the government.

> All he can claim is freedom to point the way. The power of compelling others into it is not only inconsistent with the freedom and development of all the rest, but corrupting to the strong man himself.[95]

Yet on the other hand Mill was fully aware that,

> ...The likings and dislikings of society, or some powerful portion of it...[were]...the main thing which has practically determined the rules laid down for general observance, under the penalties of law or opinion.[96]

Mill did not sanction this, but he still believed that law and opinion, under such circumstances, could be made to serve the cause of freedom.

George W. Reid, a libertarian critic, echoed Mill's fears in a pamphlet entitled, The Natural Basis of Civilization.

> As in the past, so today, we find the foundations of governments are built upon enforced customs, and the bulwark of the government is held in place by the hypocritical manners of the people.[97]

But the main criticisms to arise from libertarian thought regarding the rulers and the ruled centred around the notions of power and coercion. When it came to the practicalities of governmental power, the libertarians claimed, like Mill, that such power was by definition coercive. As Emma Goldman, a communist anarchist, said at the International Anarchist Congress in 1907...

> The State is not a social organization; it is an organization born of despotism and maintained by force, and imposed by force, on the masses...[98]

Somewhat like Mill,[99] Kropotkin believed that the "...best of men is made essentially bad by the exercise of authority."[100] And as Mill himself was for a short while a Member of Parliament, it is safe to assume that he had some reason for believing in the possiblity of a utilitarian legislative programme. Kropotkin (who was never in Parliament) did not seem to have his optimism; nonetheless he suggested that,

> ...the theory of the 'balancing of powers' and 'control of authorities' is a hypocritical formula, invented by those who have seized power, to make the 'sovereign people,' whom they despise, believe that the people themselves are governing.[101]

Mill's views in regarding the wisdom of the masses or the middle classes as 'collective mediocrity'[102] seem to support this claim of Kropotkin's. For, in effect, he was saying that a government of law will not work in the interests of most of the individuals in society simply because they are designated as a 'collective mediocrity' who need certain forms of education, leadership, and guidance. Mill, on the other hand, believed that a government, following the Rule of Law, could work if the legislators had some guiding principle which took into account the interests of both the individual and society. Yet it could only be a 'wise or noble' government if the 'sovereign' force was wise and noble. Democracy, as a method rule, would work, if the 'sovereign people' were inculcated with the proper ethical standards. For this to happen, Mill had to have a system of authority to make law both acceptable and enforceable. This law was ultimately based on coercion; the individual was ruled by the 'representatives' or the legislators who had everyone's interests in mind. The libertarians, on the other hand, believed that the legislators, by virtue of their position and status, would not do this and had never done so. For working, as did Mill, in the belief that 'all restraint qua restraint is an evil,' they did not want to codify restraint and hence organized coercion. Therefore they rejected the concept of rule.

A Libertarian Critique of Liberalism as Expressed in Mill's Essay On Liberty

To a liberal like Mill, the problem of responsibility for one's actions and their consequences is both legal and moral. That is, one who lives in a civil society has legal and moral obligations. One is obliged to obey the law and can be rightfully punished for not doing so. But moral responsibility is ambiguous in the realm of action. The individual is not alone, and in the eyes of the law and the opinion of others he is an integral part of that collectivity called society which, in the nineteenth century, was within the boundaries of a state. Thus, references to different societies presumed the existence of different states and various systems of government.

In his essay, Mill, in particular addressed himself to two sets of forces which can be designated as individualistic and societal. And in terms of the freedoms which they were to enjoy, Mill claimed that "each will receive its proper share."[103] The part which chiefly interests society is, of course, interpreted by both the government (as legislator and administrator) and the independent judiciary. It is enforced by the police. Yet the part which chiefly interests the individual is, as far as the law is concerned, coordinated by the same three forces of state. Opinion also counterbalances that which 'chiefly concerns the individual.' Any portion of interest which is left is given to the individual, although it is never up to him to meddle with that part 'which chiefly interests society.' That would pit the individual against both law and opinion which, on the face of it seems to be able to judge upon the overwhelming art of the individual's 'proper share.'

Mill seems to make the implicit assumption that some particular segment of the society is first, worthy of making a judgment, and secondly, is unbiased in the application or regulation of that judgment. These assumptions are essential to the optimism expressed by the liberal view of law. It seems to suggest that one who has attained a position of power or influence, within certain set constitutional boundaries, is there because of his own abilities and endeavours. This, with little qualification, consequently puts him in the best position to both make and validate, through law, the rules of conduct for the society and invariably the individuals who compose it.

For in the case of a dispute between the individual and society, it is the lawmakers and the judges who were to be the arbitrators of any conflict. Although, for Mill, much conflict depended upon the progress a society had made in settling disputes peacefully, law was still a necessary guarantor. For the libertarians, law was necessary in Mill's schema because it was endemic to a society which accepted the liberal precepts of possessive individualism and competitive commerce. If it was apparent to Mill that the individual and society were at odds precisely because of the views held about the way in which man was to conduct his affairs, why did he not expand upon the implications of the conflicts which law itself would cause? Law, to the libertarians, was as much a source of conflict as were the interests of the individual _vis a vis_ society. Mill's system of 'Free Trade' was based on competition rather than cooperation, and he accepted, albeit unhappily, that men would continue to strive for and value power because of the advantages which would accrue by having it. Once this power is legitimized either by the law, or by what Mill refers to as opinion, it becomes an authority which can only be challenged by the individual at his own peril. The legitimacy of such power of command allows for a situation whereby what is, i.e., set laws and opinions, ought to be. In other words, the system and the society is very resistant to change. Mill, of course, hoped that any rules of conduct and the methods for enforcing them would be rooted in the finest of intentions and most stable of principles. Mill gave some specific examples of behaviour which would be well worth controlling.

> Acts injurious to others requires a totally different treatment. Encroachment on their rights; infliction on them of any loss or damage not justified by his own rights; falsehood or duplicity in dealing with them; unfair or ungenerous use of advantages over them; even selfish abstinence from defending them against injury – these are fit objects of moral reprobation, and in grave cases of moral retribution and punishment. [104]

Essentially, Mill treats the concept of society as if it were the individual 'writ large.' He does this to the extent that both the individual and society are viewed as having basic and distinct interests which can be defined and regulated by a legal set of reactions. In all but a very small part of his life, the individual is dominated by the overriding interests of society.

Society, to the liberal mind of Mill, is effectively that mass of people confined within a national boundary who share a broadly based set of values. This society is assumed to be ruled by law through a set of agents, themselves responsible to that society. These agents comprise what the libertarians would speak of as either the state or the government. For it was believed by Mill that the governmental part of state, although often in apparent opposition to the individual, could play a very positive role in the expansion of his freedom. Society could be made free through law yet, at the same time, it could be defined by this law which was to lay down the rules by which this society functioned. The libertarians disagreed not so much with the idea of regulation but with the way in which the regulation was to take place. They did not see law as a neutral and unbiased source of regulatory power; they saw it as an instrument of oppression by a minority over a majority that either did not give its consent or was misinformed by the agents of the law. The liberal, on the other hand, believed that at least, in quantitative terms, the individual would have more of value to choose from in a society governed by law.

J. D. Mabbott pointed out in his book, The State and the Citizen, that the use of the term society has no single unambiguous meaning.[105] Being an individual, for Mill, only has meaning insofar as one is a component of a larger unit. But one must still protect his individuality in spite of this fact. For it is obvious that choices made are, in most cases, either contributory or detrimental to the common weal. As a compromise, or in a realistic manner, Mill posited that one's choices should be limited by the sanction of law, in the interests of all concerned, i.e., for the sake of other individuals in 'society' with whom one is told one has a common interest in spite of any non-recognition by the individual that this is a fact. The liberalism of Mill, to the libertarian mind, would suggest that society and the individual's place in it are determined by the ruling power whose common interest is the maintenance of its own existence. It is this, the power of the governing body to maintain its own existence, which is to define and limit the choice of individuals on the grounds that they would not be able to function as such without a commonality of individualism, i.e., society.

In the end, the liberal doctrine does not see the notion or action of freedom in itself as being intrinsically good for either the individual or society at large. Mill, even though he attempted to be true to the principles of liberty, worried about the results of particular forms of choice as they related to what he wanted to see society become. In other words, to Mill, some forms of choice may be wrong because of their effect not only upon others but of their possible effect upon what the libertarians deemed to be the abstractions of society and the state. To Mill, liberty without the sanction of law or opinion, may be not only defective but impossible in practice. Mill's liberalism, although centred around the notion of freedom, is itself a sacrifice to its own principles. If liberty is 'doing what one desires,' as Mill said, then under a law-bound society rule the individual can only be free insofar as he agrees with the law and the opinions which are forced upon him. The liberal individual appears to be in On Liberty a legislative creation, defined and held in place by the rule of law which does not, even in the utilitarian sense, hold freedom to be of great intrinsic worth.

In appearance, unlike the liberals, the libertarians seem at once prepared to back the notion which posits the 'intrinsic good' of freedom. For although the whole problem of individual action and the necessity for conformity is debated by the libertarians, they did believe that the individual ought not to be restrained by the force of law. To them, the individual must always have the opportunity to make his own choice, unconstrained by the use or threat of force which they believed to be the result of a system of law. The libertarians agree with those theories which argue that compulsion is immoral. Consequently, they view the art of persuasion, on moral grounds, as preferable to the use of force.

Mill was willing to qualify his claims about the worth of freedom in terms of the effects it might have upon individuals and the society at large. Thus coercive law was better than coercive individuals who were expressing their own peculiar brand of liberty. Mill viewed certain forms of action as preferable to others because past generations had learned certain 'lessons' of conduct, and he saw no need for each generation to repeat the 'mistakes' of the past. As a result, Mill, in interpreting the events of history within his own set of values, uses particular facts to back up his argument as to the necessity for rules of conduct.

Although he argued that "...no one pretends that actions should be as free as opinions,"[106] he did not condone those opinions which would incite certain forms of actions. Mill believed that mob rule or mass opinion was a threat to the role of the genuine individual. He judged the restrictions of freedom mainly as a result of what he believed would be the ensuing circumstances. Thus, speaking to a mob in an instigating manner could cause harm to life and property. Such behaviour Mill thought, obviously ought to be regulated.[107] But as a believer in freedom, was this point really so obvious to him were he following the principles of freedom? It could only be so if the notion of freedom was subsumed under the broader one of utility.

> I regard utility as the ultimate appeal on all ethical
> questions; but it must be utility in the largest sense,
> grounded on the permanent interests of a man as

progressive being. Those interests, I contend authorize the subjugation of individual spontaneity to external control, only in respect to those actions which concern the interest of other people.[108]

Utility is of utmost importance in the framing of laws and in judging the circumstances of their application. Mill makes this apparent when he mentions particular examples or instances for restrictive legislation, as with the case of indirect taxation when he said "...that the state, therefore, cannot help imposing penalties, which to some persons may be prohibitory, on the use of some articles of consumption."[109] Mill thus realized that different segments of society must bear the burden of certain punitive laws, and, in this instance, it was to raise revenue for the State. As the existence of the State and its laws were for the benefit of the larger part of society, the argument against certain freedoms of consumption has a utilitarian base. In the end, the punitive laws were even justified as ultimately helping the individuals who bore the burden of those laws. For although Mill recognized that such laws were in many ways opposed to individuality and the individuals whom they affected, he did not seem to be able to grasp that particular segments of the society were far more overburdened by law than others. Because of this, certain sections of the community like the poor or the dispossessed saw the law as one of the forces of retribution rather than the protective device it was said to be. The laws relating to indirect taxes on certain commodities, and especially those on alcoholic beverages would be one notable example of how the freedom of choice of the working classes was restricted. Laws for the protection of private property were designed, according to the libertarians, to perpetuate certain forms of social relations which conformed to a capitalist economic base which, they claimed, was not in the interests of the great majority of working men.

To the libertarians, law always benefited the possessors of property

and capital, to the detriment of those who actually made the

commodities from whence this wealth was derived.   In a lecture on

Private Property,   given in Edinburgh in 1886, Edward Carpenter made

the point well.

> ... I think we may fairly make the following general
> statement, viz., that legal ownership is essentially a
> negative and anti-social thing; and that, unless
> qualified or antidoted by human relationship, it is
> pretty certain to be absolutely harmful. In fact, when
> a man's chief plea is "The law allows it," you may be
> pretty sure he is up to some mischief![110]

Mill's case for supporting the role of law seems fairly

apparent; he is a member of a society which he himself believes to be

one of the most civilized and progressive on earth. This society

traditionally solved most of its disputes in accordance with the Rule

of Law.   In the nineteenth century this process was becoming more

democratic. English society itself was less egalitarian and more

hierarchical than Mill would have wished, but he saw little chance of

any immediate solutions which he would find palatable. The solution

had to be found which would build upon the collective wisdom of the

past within the context of the English cultural heritage. This could

be done, Mill felt, through the piecemeal expansion of the basic

freedoms in conjunction with a multilevel system of universal education

which would be mandatory up to a certain age.[111] There was no

necessity for the people to "rise against the government and make what

is called a revolution."[112] This need not happen in Mill's schema

because the State would not have so much power (as in a Socialist

State) that the State could be held responsible for all the evil which

befell the populace.   No revolution was necessary, but the

apportionment of authority had to be diverse enough to allow people to grow into responsible individuals.[113]

> In many cases, though individuals may not do the particular thing so well, on the average, as the officers of government, it is nevertheless desirable that it should be done by them rather than by government, as a means to their own mental education — a mode of strengthening their active faculties, exercising their judgment, and giving them a familiar knowledge of the subjects with which they are thus left to deal.[114]

As has already been previously mentioned,[115] it was the duty of the state "to maintain a vigilant control over his exercise of any power which it allows him to possess over others."[116] Social life is therefore to be governed by the authority relations sanctioned ultimately by the state and those who exercise control over it. The libertarians, on the other hand, did not believe that anyone had the right to set himself up as an authority over others, and they certainly objected to the state monopoly over such matters.

Of course, Mill did hope, as in The Subjugation of Women, for radical changes in such things as the relation between a husband and a wife. But he would not suggest that the authority relations of society itself should be as dramatically altered as those within the family. In the end Mill did not seem to be able to make the local progression from the one frame of reference to the other, or attempt to apply his more radical ideas to the more all-pervasive social or political arena. Even though Mill believed that institutional and social change could be affected by the law and other political institutions, he did not take into consideration, to a very great degree, that these self-same institutions were themselves the source of many of the ills of society. At times, however, even Mill recognized that many institutions were ill-founded. As he said, in a rather apologetic manner,

> In many cases an individual, in pursuing a legitimate
> object, necessarily and therefore legitimately causes
> pain or loss to others, or intercepts a good which they
> have a reasonable hope of obtaining. Such oppositions of
> interest between individuals often arise from bad social
> institutions, but are unavoidable while those
> institutions last; and some would be unavoidable under
> any institutions.[117]

In other words, Mill was prepared to accept the types of

conflict of interest as a necessary, if unavoidable, part of his social

viewpoint. Was it possible, for example, that the state which defined

the legal relationship between a man and his wife as being

authoritarian, could by the same methods, i.e., by law which is

authoritarian, redefine it and thereby enforce egalitarianism? Can the

mental attitude that authority is necessary be destroyed by the

authority of the law? The libertarians respond with a definitive, No!

-- because there is a certain contradiction, they believe, in trying to

abolish authority by the use of authoritative methods. With reference

specifically to Mill and his views on the family, R. V. Sampson, in his

book Equality and Power, showed how corrupting the notion of such

power could be, and with particular reference to Mill, stated:

> The institution of contemporary marriage, which is his
> real subject, he dissects admirably up to a point. But
> beyond that point he cannot go because of his emotional
> commitment, the parti pris of a modern Galahad taking up
> the cudgels on behalf of an outraged class of people,
> viz., one half of the human species. No doubt social
> therapy required a militant attempt to break through the
> armoury of male arrogance. But the temptation is to
> overlook the complicity of the sex; and thus to fail to
> see that the real problem is a cultural one in which both
> sexes are corrupted in different but equally crippling
> ways.[118]

To the libertarian the corrupting forces come in the guise of

power and authority which perverts the more humane feeling persons have

towards one another. Edward Carpenter concluded that "...it is evident

that no very great change for the better in marriage-relations can take place except as the accompaniment of deep-lying changes in Society at large; and that alterations in the Law alone will effect but a limited improvement."[119] As this applied to marriage, so did it to other institutions which were bolstered by law and authority. Mill did not seem to appreciate or consider that authority was as corrupting as power, and this was mainly so because he believed that authority was a legitimate form of power.

Although it may be a truism that one can only defeat force with a superior force (be it physical, moral, active or passive), Mill does not seem to be able to come to terms with the idea that the legitimate use of power is itself a value which, when inculcated in a large mass of people, is bound to affect their behaviour towards one another and their government. The relations which this attitude engenders is at the centre of any culture (in this case the English culture) and manifestly dependent upon giving priority to the status of authority and power relations. Mill did not want to stress the inconsistency in an argument which implied that the coercive aspects of an individual's relationship with the state would in the end make him respectful, responsible, and peace loving. It is equally arguable that the coercive nature of the relationship between the rulers and the ruled spawns the exact opposite, - disrespect, mistrust, and a feeling of helplessness in regard to the expression of individuality and one's own sense of responsibility to himself and his fellow man. However, Mill does seem to appreciate this problem at times, for example, when he speaks about the power of the growing bureaucracy.[120]

In the end Mill was consistent in what he regarded as the boundaries of individual freedom as it was to be embodied in the law. The interests of the individual were coterminous with the interests of society. The individual was free insofar as his active relations with the rest of society did not run counter to the laws which were meant to protect the individual himself as well as the society in which he lived. Ideally all individuals would be free to express their individuality "in things which do not primarily concern others."[121] As we have seen in Mill's chapter on 'The Individual and Society,' the possibilities of society interfering with individuality under Mill's system were enormous and could be justified on almost any legal ground. This was obviously not the case in point of morals. But at the same time, law was meant to protect the minority or the 'men of genius' from the dominant opinions and expectations of the majority or the 'ascendent class.' Mill did not favour the rule of the majority or even of all if it meant being forced to accept common opinion. In such a case where the populace was at one with their government, even then, or only then, did he claim that "the power itself is illegitimate."[122] Consequently, under Mill's scheme, it is not surprising to find that the ability of the individual to choose ranks highly in the ordering of his values. Yet these choices must be limited by law and opinion in accordance with some set of values which were broadly grouped under the notion of utility. Mill was very concerned about how the individual would cope with freedom, and his fears even prompted him to suggest that most individuals did not even desire it.[123] When Mill spoke of individuality as self-devlopment it is important to note that his examples of 'good' and 'evil' behaviour reflected a particular set of values. And given that most of the values of his time emanated from the middle class, was it not safe to assume that individuality would take on an aura of middle-class respectability, if it had to be sanctioned by law and opinion? To the degree that this was so, it seems that certain forms of individuality were valued more than the equal freedoms of some other dissenting member of the community. As Mill said, to put it into a broader context, the individual "must not make a nuisance of himself to other people."[124]

Therefore, in terms of men's relations with other men, and as they were set out in law, it was the individualism of specific persons which was protected through the denial of the freedom and hence the unacceptable individuality of others. Thus, the libertarians could fairly claim that the laws were made to protect the interests of the 'ascendant class' who, for the most part, were the possessors of capital. The libertarians would maintain their critique of Mill and liberalism that the liberal obsession with the rights of the individual has blinded the liberals to the extent that the freedom of most is restricted for the freedom of the few. The law, held to be the protector of freedom, was what defines freedom. If, as the libertarians believe, freedom existentially, as Mill said, entails 'doing what one desires,' then ought the definition and limits of man's choices to be put in the hands of a body outside of the individuals involved? Should one be restricted at all even if one does not have knowledge of the choices which are open to him? What the libertarians deny is the right of any body (or authority) to impose its will and values to the extent that it makes meaningful choice impossible for those who are the most affected by the lack of alternatives, i.e, the working classes.

Mill, in the essay On Liberty, is essentially demanding the enlightened self-interest of men in similar circumstances to his own. He is preaching an ethical system which is grounded in a utilitarian scheme where it was up to him to make a judgment on the utility of certain forms of behaviour. Everything he saw wrong with an excess of freedom vis a vis the law could be related to groups outside his own station in life. He perseveres in a 'them and us' attitude, and although he was indeed restricted by the same laws as others, it was less likely that these restrictions would be of such a nature as to narrow his own area of 'meaningful choice.' Mill's desire not to dispense with a system of punitive laws, in effect, discloses his ambiguous feeling about the worth (or to use Mabbott's phrase, 'its intrinsice nature') of freedom.

The reality of being free, especially in the realm of action presented many difficulties for Mill. He believed rather than assumed that individual freedom could only have meaning in a pre-defined context. This context was in nineteenth century England confined to the legal-constitutional system. But freedom was also defined by the type of economic and social system of the time which Mill, for all intents and purposes, considered to be 'civilized.'

It is true that Mill believed wholly in the merits of argument about such things as the freedom of discussion and thought, but the argumentative process itself was very much an intellectual activity.[125] What Mill was hoping for was tolerance, which itself was tied up with the manner in which opinion or action was carried out. For the method of delivery, of putting thought, into opinion, into action, "may be very objectionable and may justly incur severe censure."[126] In the realm of thought and opinion it seems that Mill believed that freedom in itself could engender a set of new and better relations between men. When it came to certain forms of action he showed his lack of faith in the principle of freedom by

falling back on a form of coercion which he respectably referred to as
the law.

Although Mill's restrictions on freedom clearly apply to
himself and his circle, a great many would not directly or personally
affect him. But these restrictions (for example, those defining
vagrancy) are at the same time liable to have a monumental effect on
other groups of persons of less privileged stature. For many of the
laws which might expand both the quality and quantity of one's choices
(as a man of genius would wish) do not necessarily do so for most
people. In other words, specific laws meant to apply to everyone
equally (or unequals equally) simply consolidate privilege.[127] In
terms of quality, these laws tend wholly to reinforce the values of the
dominant and/or ruling group and the strata from which this group is
chosen. Thus, the law is not only a reflection of the men who make it,
but itself reinforces their status as lawmakers. Sebastian de Grazia
argued in a somewhat similar vein in an article entitled Authority and
Rationality.

> Man is a desiring creature with his wants and his sight
> fused; with his wants and his sight moulded and directed
> largely by the authoritative parts of his
> community.[128]

With regard to the law, the authoritative part of the community
therefore lies in the hands of those who make it, pronounce upon it,
and enforce it. These are the values which the individual and society
are forced to share. In the essay On Liberty little consideration is
given to the non-authoritative parts of the community and the values
which they hold or whether they are or are not in conflict with the
law. Yet it is precisely this group upon which legislation will have
the greatest and most far-reaching repercussions. Mill uses their

welfare as a rationalization for the laws which support his own particular ethical system and which is not necessarily to be taken as the one generally held. He more or less admits this in his discussion about the need for rules of conduct, most of which he believes must be embodied within the law and its complementary institutions.[129]

But for some reason Mill does not give wholehearted attention to the dichotomy between the class of lawmakers and those who must suffer the burden of the law. Why, could he not have asked himself, are the poor more often in conflict with the law than the rich? Mill may well wish to see a society which is progressive and respectable, but one must not assume that his underlying, or unconscious, notions of respectability and civilization are commonly shared. Both Edward Carpenter and George W. Reid felt that what Mill would call civilization they would refer to as exploitation.[130] Yet Reid's idea about a civilized society was not unlike that of Mill. He expanded upon this in a pamphlet called The Natural Basis of Civilization.

> The natural basis of civilization is that state of
> society in which man enjoys the opportunity of gratifying
> every desire of life, where his efforts to increase the
> opportunities of doing good, and to add to the comfort
> and happiness of life will not be impeded; where enjoying
> all that man can possibly enjoy, no one will need or care
> to limit the enjoyment of others. This then is my ideal
> state of society, but thousands look upon it likewise as
> their ideal.[131]

If, as Mill said, that he was not "aware that any community has a right to force another to be civilized,"[132] he might have done well to consider that one part of a society ought not to have that right either. This is much of what the libertarians are saying about the role of government. Mill said that "...whatever crushes individuality is despotism."[133] Why would he not concede that law itself was just as despotic? Obviously he had faith in the English system. But if he considered individuality to be an expression of freedom, he was therefore bound to believe that freedom must be preserved wherever possible, for when he conjures up the spectre of rule by the people, he begins to see the role of government as possibly being coercive in an unpalatable manner.

> Let us suppose therefore that the government is entirely at one with the people, and never thinks of exerting any power of coercion unless in agreement with what it conceives to be their voice. But <u>I deny the right of the people to exercise such coercion, either by themselves or by their government.</u> The power itself is illegitimate. The best government has no more title to it than the worst...[134]

The libertarians would agree with this statement of Mill's, for they do not believe that government can make laws for the enhancement of freedom or the protection of individuals in a society where there is not a general consensus as to values. To the libertarian mind there is an outright conflict of interest, and when they state that both law and government are instruments of coercion they too deny the legitimacy of both.

One is able to show more specifically the objections and false impressions to which law, by libertarian standards, succumbs. Mill gives several examples in his chapter on 'Applications' of what he considers are legitimate areas where restrictive legislation may be of some value. These examples show how intricate the problems of law and its content can be, yet they point out, to a degree, that the application and interpretation of law is basically the result of a certain set of values.

Mill usually argued both sides of a question, and although he did not seem to disapprove of gambling, he set up a hypothetical case for certain forms of restriction. He did not believe that people should profit from human weakness or misery, and that they ought to be protected from the unscrupulous. Thus the owner of a gaming-house should not promote his establishment 'for personal objects only.'[135] Whether this is wrong or not, it could be considered legitimate for the state to interfere if it viewed such behaviour to be wrong.[136] Therefore as Mill said

> - though all persons should be free to gamble in their own or each other's houses, or in any place of meeting established by their own subscriptions, and open only to the members and their visitors - yet public gambling houses should not be permitted.[137]

What is first clear is that, for Mill, the state has the right to decide on the permissible limits of gambling in order to prevent harm to others. As it stands, if it was made into a law, it would be a law instituted for the public good and to the detriment of the unscrupulous. It is a form of control exercised for the benefit of passersby, observers, and the clientele of such establishments.

However, if one was to think about the problem and the implications of such a legal solution, certain difficulties arise. It would be relatively safe to assume, for instance, that those persons found in such places were likely to be of a different class and background of either Mill or the legislators. Yet, without full knowledge, Mill could contend that such behaviour, as exists in public gambling houses, may be worthy of suppression. The acceptance of such legislation would be made all the easier by the fact that suppression of these activities would in no way affect someone like Mill himself. It is not one of his interests yet he offers an opinion of judgment. He might say that, as a member of society, he thereby claimed an interest in this case. Nonetheless, there are people, unlike Mill, who would be directly affected by a decision of this sort and they would have no noticeable say in the formation of such a law.

Mill leaves the legislators as well as the gamblers with but one assuredly Victorian way out of the dilemma. For, as gambling 'as a public pastime' would be difficult to eradicate, the persons concerned,

> may be compelled to conduct their operations with a certain degree of secrecy and mystery, so that nobody knows anything about them but those who seek them.[138]

In essence, the problem must be hidden from public view and should only rightfully be practised in private. Thus the inmates of a public gambling house should do it "in their own or each others house." The libertarians might well remark that this assumes that everyone has equal access to a house, or indeed even to their own room. For, grossly unequal living conditions, they say, are the reality of the capitalist economic system. In the end, the type of persons who frequent public gambling houses would be forced either to break the law or else forgo the pleasure of gambling because they would probably not be able to rely upon any of Mill's alternatives. Such a law would hurt the dispossessed more than the owners of property or capital.

Mill deemed such laws to be necessary because he believed that certain forms of behaviour could be readily designated as a 'social nuisance.' Yet, in the instance of public gambling houses, it must be added that they are never likely to bother the majority of the populace, and it is this majority upon whose shoulders the claim of the legitimacy of law has been placed. Mill believed that law could make people good and productive members of society. The use of legislative programmes would divide the force of this law more or less equally between the different segments of society to produce, as Mill wanted, the greatest possible amount of happiness.

Mill's use of the term 'public' often refers to little more than that class of people whose habits and common interests he did not share. Mill wanted a cohesive and orderly society which at the same time attempted to maximize individual liberty. Yet the division between public and private behaviour, as set out by Mill, does not take into account the economic and social aspects of obtaining privacy. Individuality and privacy are consequently very closely connected to one another, for the infringement of another's rights is more often than not a public act. To be part of this public, then, meant that the force of law had a very different meaning. To the libertarians it meant oppression.

By looking at most restrictive legislation in this light one can see that the division between the public and the private is quite distinct. For example, what segment of the population is most affected by the law governing the consumption of alcohol? Is it those with a lot of money who can afford the luxury of a private club, or is it those who linger in the 'public' bar of the local?

As Mill notes in reference to the payment of taxes on commodities thought to be unhealthy to the individual consumer: — once the pleasure has been _paid_ for this satisfies "...their _legal_ and _moral_ obligations to the State."[139] No mention is made of the obligations to other individuals or to the society at large except as their interests are meant to be epitomized by the proclamations of the state.

It becomes more apparent at this point that the liberal solutions of Mill must have far more ramifications in their effects than Mill admits. For the effects of accepting the protections afforded by law and received opinion leaves the dissenting individual in a very defensive position in relation to society at large. He has to fight the weight of society or a section of it just because certain forms of activity are restricted by the law. The belief about the 'goodness' of individuality is itself suppressed by the idea that it must in some ways be defined by the law. Mill believed that the individual was free under such restraint. The libertarians did not. Mill felt that law was the most effective way to reconcile the interests of the individual and the interests of society. Restrictive law was necessary to enforce compatibility in spite of the reason for which any incompatibility might arise. The libertarians thought that forced compatibility was a sign of the artificiality of conflicting interests, and most of these conflicts arose precisely because of the nature and content of the law. They saw that, as a rule, compatibility was forced, through the legislative process and the government, by the minority, upon the 'public' majority. The important and authoritative parts of society became those identified with the state and the influential sectors of society which supported its continual incursion into the lives of the greater mass of the people.

Mill's solutions in On Liberty could, if implemented from the beginning, radically alter the foundations of society and the state. But by placing final authority in the lawmakers it, in the end, is bound to reinforce the values of those who play a dominant role in the social and economic power structure. It is because of this that the libertarians sought to remove power from central agencies to allow decision-making a broader base. This, in effect, would greatly diminish the whole system of hierarchical control, or control of one segment of the populace by another. In such a manner, freedom would be more meaningful to the common person for it would allow him an enhanced area of choice on matters which affected and defined his own life-style.

The question is really about where the authority to make decisions ought to lie. Liberalism, although taking into account the individual as an entity, does little to compensate those individuals who do not consent to the plethora of restrictions put upon them. Mill believed that the compensation for restrictions on freedom would be an even greater freedom in the whole range of human activity. That is, certain restrictions were necessary for the better interests of all. The libertarians did not see it this way because they did not believe that the restrictions themselves were fairly or evenly applied. To them, the individual was bound by the laws and standards propagated in his name at the pleasure of the legislators and those who influenced them.

Unlike the liberalism of Mill, the libertarians were concerned with both freedom and the individual in a manner which suggested that individualism, of all kinds, and freedom were almost wholly complementary. Their optimism regarding individual behaviour within society was based on the belief that man was possessed of a 'reason' which, under conditions of freedom, would lead him to a self-imposed morality. As Carpenter said in his paper 'The New Morality' this would not be an easy task.

> Of course the New Morality – to look within, to feel and refer to the needs of others almost as instinctively as to one's own, to refuse to regard any thing as in itself good or bad, and to look upon all beings, oneself included, as an end in themselves and not as a means of personal self-advancement and glorification – while it is the more natural, is also the more difficult in a sense, as providing no set pattern or rule.[140]

The relations of man in society could not be strictly defined except in terms of the widest possible amount of freedom which was itself seen as being wholly conducive to most forms of 'right action.' Men, if left together, so the libertarians believed, would have a cooperative sociability if they commonly believed that coercion could only very exceptionally be justified. As Sebastian de Grazia has put it in his paper on <u>Authority and Rationality</u>,

> Men were born either with a Reason that would lead them to see eye-to-eye on the issues of right and wrong, or with good motives that would move them together toward the Reason of righteousness. By either theory no authority was necessary for men to achieve agreement or concensus and thus to lead the good life in community.[141]

The libertarians did not often concern themselves with the more abstract aspects of such notions as 'rights' and 'society,' but they were concerned with both the idea and the actuality of the state. They did not believe, as Mill did, that the individual had to rely upon the state to safeguard his well-being or his happiness. On the whole they tended to stress the desirability of personal contact within the framework of one or more particular communities. For, as Mill did not seek an excessive use of law and felt that much of what was valuable in life came from individual interaction, so too did the libertarians. Unlike Mill, they wanted much less or no law, much less or no government; they wanted cooperation and voluntary association to be the 'institutional' expressions of individuality.

The libertarians did not propose to plan for others or the future. They wanted the individuals or groups concerned to discover for themselves how to direct their lives even if they did not discover all the things they sought. To the libertarian mind this way of life would give people the opportunity to make meaningful choices about the direction of their lives in concert with the interests involved in pursuing their individuality. It would preclude their being forced by some 'superior' source to accept a course of action which could run counter to their own inclinations. Thus it could be said that many of their ideals would shape their own reality.[142] Pursuing one's own life, in concert with others was, in effect, 'being master of one's own fate.'

Because they held these beliefs, the libertarians have often been criticised as being 'idealistic' or 'unscientific' in their methods and goals. Furthermore, while other doctrines such as Marxism sought libertarian ends, they were prepared to use methods which the libertarians claimed were destructive of the ends sought.[143] The libertarians were calling for a transvaluation within society. That is, they hoped for a shift of emphasis in the dominant mores of society such as would happen if competitive commerce were replaced by cooperative enterprise. The value shift would, in this instance, be away from individual competitiveness towards individual cooperation. As a result of this 'transvaluation of values,' they believed that man would progress towards more harmonious association in his everyday life.

Libertarians did not accept the argument that they were proposing a return to the 'state of nature' or to the medieval period although they admired many facets of pre-Renaissance life.[144] They proposed instead a massive devolution of power and a restructuring of hierarchical organization. The past was looked upon as evidence of the need for change. Even Mill in his most pessimistic moments would not have said that the past must determine the future because the future is most greatly influenced by the description and interpretation of events in the past. We must also not forget, as Mill rightly reminded us, that this is not the only 'society.' Libertarians would hold that we are limited only by our own mental capacities and the way in which we use them. This does not mean that there are not environmental and other physical limitations upon action, but libertarians emphasized a basic optimism. Emerson, the American transcendentalist and essayist, put it succinctly, - "What inhibits us we call Fate: Intellect annuls Fate."[145]

Thus, as did Mill, the libertarians put much store in man's power of reason even though they would not say he was a wholly rational animal, i.e, since emotional drive played a considerable role. In agreement with Erich Fromm, the libertarians thought that certain forms of power did not contradict the sort of life engendered by a cooperative community. However, the form of power to which they did not object could not be associated with either political life or coercive behaviour. It had nothing to do with rule or law. Generally speaking, they essentially viewed power as a form of influence relation between two or more individuals. Fromm makes one distinction well:

> Productiveness is man's realization of the potentialities
> characteristic of him, the use of his powers. But what
> is 'power'? It is rather ironical that this word denotes
> two contradictory concepts: power of = capacity and
> power over = domination. This contradiction, however, is
> of a particular kind. Power = domination results from
> the paralysis of power = capacity. "Power over" is
> the preservation of "power to." The ability of man
> to make productive use of his powers is his potency: the
> inability is his impotence. With his power of reason he
> can penetrate the surface of phenomena and understand
> their essence. With his power of love he can break
> through the wall which separates one person from another.
> With his power of imagination he can visualize things not
> yet existing; he can plan and thus begin to create.
> Where potency is lacking, man's desire is to dominate, to
> exert power over others as though they were things.
> Domination is coupled with death, potency with life.
> Domination springs from impotence and in turn reinforces
> it, or if an individual can force somebody to serve him,
> his own need to be productive is increasingly

paralyzed.[146]

This capacity, 'the power of,' refers in the main to a form of potential which the liberalism of Mill has characterized as individuality. In the context of On Liberty, the individual is restricted in his freedom by both law and opinion. In this respect it seems that, as far as acceptable forms of individuality are concerned, the liberal prefers legally constituted authority. Its extension is a pervasive system of political authority where institutions and people, in the libertarian view, have 'power over' or domination over the rest of society. It is the liberal acceptance of the concept of rule. Rule is necessary to enforce compliance which in turn is meant to ensure 'liberal' freedom. The libertarians reject this mode of thinking. As a result they tend to speak about power and authority in a critical manner. They seek a new form of society where 'capacity' overrides 'domination' and the individual becomes a potent force in shaping his own future.

Beyond this, libertarians will admit often to the primacy of the emotions, –– of those feelings and desires which lead to actions which cannot be readily explained. They do not demand that rationality should dominate, only that reason ought to play a mitigating role in the life choices which persons have to stand up and make. They believe that reason will come to the fore because man, unlike any other species, has a history and the apparently unique faculty of mind. It seemed obvious to them that the world was not a wholly rational place.

Likewise the libertarians refused to separate part of any issue from the whole. They believed in the unity of ends and means, e.g., violent methods would lead to violent ends. The liberals, it seemed to them, sought partial solutions in their search for free development and individuality. The libertarians believed that partial solutions such as the apportionment of freedom would allow for very little change in the structure of what they considered to be a corrupt society. Mill, they thought, had failed to see the basic contradictions inherent in his doctrine. Essentially, the libertarians believed that the solutions, as proposed by Mill, for dealing with the conflicts between the individual and society created more problems than they solved. Mill, for example, wanted to enforce social behaviour through the use of law and opinion. This was one method of getting individuals to change their relations with other individuals. It civilized them and made them social beings. Mill did not seem to consider that antisocial behaviour was an indirect result of the whole capitalist legal system or that the principle of 'protection' itself was quite inadequate in such a context. Because of this, Mill had in the end to sanction the use of coercion through the law.

To the libertarians it seemed that the liberals envisaged a cetain type of relationship between the rulers and the ruled which presumed that there would always be rulers and ruled. Law would ensure that this was so.

Mill offered his solutions in lieu of due consideration regarding the legitimate use of coercion. Since he was concerned with the framing and application of law, this is not at all surprising. Nonetheless, he can be criticized for accepting legalized coercion even though he found coercion itself quite repugnant. For as he said,

> ...compulsion, either in the direct form in that of pains and penalties for non-compliance, is no longer admissible as a means to their own good, and justifiable only for the security of others.[147]

Yet he still claimed that some of the rights and duties of the individual would be defined by the power of the state even though it was imperative that the state give acceptable 'reasons' for its decrees.[148] As a result, Mill, although loathe to place too much faith in the state, implied that it was the only body with enough power to coerce all segments of society into obedience. In general, it could be said that the rule of law was the first method of coercion, and given that the English constitutional system was amongst the oldest in the world, it did not seem 'unreasonable' to make use of existing institutional structures in order to achieve an acceptable balance of order and liberty. On Liberty is certainly an excellent and relatively non-passionate discussion about the proper scope and boundaries for restricting the action of both the individual and society. But in point of practice, it is the state and the so-called legitimate representatives of society whose de facto power is virtually without limit. Although, for Mill, certain moral questions may well arise in the application of state power, it is all too apparent that he does not protest enough. He pays scant attention to those who are, or believe themselves to be, oppressed by the authority of the law and the economic and social conditions which, if the law does not give rise to, at least it tolerates. The power of the legislator to speak through law to the society allows him to protect equally the unequal, for by its very nature, law is meant to be a neutrally applicable instrument. To the libertarians, the individuals who are restricted by law are in many instances unrepresentative of the image of society in whose name such restrictions are enacted. The last words Errico Malatesta ever wrote serve to put this very problem into perspective.

> He who throws a bomb and kills a pedestrian, declares
> that as a victim of society he has rebelled against
> society. But could not the poor victim object: 'Am I

society?'[149]

Likewise, the libertarians object to the liberal solution of Mill which stipulates that his actions must be curtailed in the name of society when, in fact, they are usually being curtailed in the interests of some powerful or vocal portion of that society. Consent or compliance is in the end sought through the coercive force of law which, depending upon the time and circumstances, may be lenient or harsh, well-founded, or misguided. The libertarians, on the other hand, viewed the question of liberty in a manner which eschewed the use of legal-constitutional or coercive methods.

Libertarians, generally speaking, are prone to seeing the state, be it social-democratic, communist, or capitalist, as the ultimate rationalization for, and most all-pervasive form of, coercion. They would accuse most liberals of tolerating the concept of state because it could be put to the service of consolidating privilege and maintaining the status quo. In the liberal system the legislators have exceptional powers to make decisions which affect the lives of everyone. Because of this rule-oriented outlook, the liberal allies himself with the centralization of the legislative process, and in Mill's case with a 'central organ.'

> This central organ should have a right to know all that
> is done, and its special duty should be that of making
> the knowledge acquired in one place available to
> another.[150]

The rules which would make centralized administration viable would relate to personal mores and forms of societal control as well as to the 'administration of things.'

> ... the rules themselves should be laid down by the
> legislature; the central administrative authority only
> watching over execution.[151]

Mill believed that there ought to be "...the greatest possible dissemination of power consistent with efficiency."[152] But the power given to the legislature and his proposal for a centralization of information gathering allows for sinister possibilities. The libertarians argued that the state and its supportive institutions were the final weapon to be used by the liberal in the pursuit of his values; and a weapon which, although it disturbed Mill, powerful groups could use in the furtherance of their own interests. Mill's proposals in On Liberty ultimately fail to deal with the economic and social probems as well as the powerful interests at work in an already existing society whose very structure rested on force and privilege.

Identifying Libertarian Thought

Libertarian thought is, on the surface, a form of nineteenth century liberalism which has been infused with some of the more humanistic and revolutionary aspects of socialist theory. Man is seen as one who not only aspires to an expansion of freedom and equality but actually requires it in order that he may accomplish the task of building the world he would wish for himself. Libertarians argue that man should be allowed to prove, for the first time in history, that he is capable of achieving the greatest possible amount of happiness when unimpeded by coercive forces. Progress is thus defined in terms of the expansion of meaningful choice (or freedom) in respect to the equal claims of others to behave likewise. As egalitarians, most libertarians believe that society ought to be organized, economically and socially, on communistic principles. Theoretically, this is the main way in which they posit their notions of equality while, in fact, they are far more concerned about freedom without which, they believe, equality can remain only a legal pronouncement. Institutional authority becomes the greatest barrier to freedom because it delineates and effectively supports forms of behaviour of the persons and groups which have attained positions of influence. The cudgels are therefore taken up on behalf of those who are not in positions of legitimate power and are less free because of it. They, in short, propose to substitute cooperation for competition, and freedom for authority. In fact what they desire is a change of emphasis to what they consider to be more cohesive forces already present in society.

It could be claimed that libertarian thought, like anarchism, engenders conservative attitudes because of its apparent dependence upon the moral rectitude of the individual and his so-called right to act by whatever 'governs' him. To the extent that libertarians could be said to be those who 'advocate liberty with special regard to thought and action,' this may well be true in some instances. Socialists and Marxists were most persistent on this point.[153] However, we will not be dealing in any depth with those theorists who, although concerned with freedom, interpret this freedom as a form of extreme individualism.[154] Most of those whom we shall designate as libertarians were either socialists, communists, or anarchists. Many of the criticisms levelled against these libertarians showed not so much the ignorance of those who wrote in this manner, but their concern to propagate a myth in aid of their own cause, be it Fabianism, Marxism, or social democracy. For although protagonists may have criticised without understanding the libertarian message, it is just as possible that they understood it too well, for libertarianism was always on the side of revolution.

Libertarians did not accept or reject systems or ideas in their entirety and were consequently far less dogmatic in their views on matters of a theoretical nature. Hence they were attracted to the views of Herbert Spencer because he was so obviously anti-State or to Proudhon as a result of his comments about the relation between labour and property. I would consider neither of these to be a libertarian although both have often been referred to as anarchists.[155] This is where anarchism and libertarianism part company. Anarchism insists first and foremost, and with unique results, that the total abolition of government is a prerequisite to the formation of any new free 'order.' However this is only anarchism in its crudest form and this doctrine is _not_ a necessary part of libertarian thought. Libertarian thought, unlike anarchism, has by our definition no conservative adherents. In its scope and method it was a revolutionary life-style as much as it was a social doctrine.

Once the fundamental anti-State distinction has been made between libertarianism and anarchism, one has great difficulty in theoretically discerning the boundaries of the two. There are men who have called themselves anarchists, and even libertarians,[156] who could not properly be considered to be libertarian, because they held certain forms of authority relations to be not only legitimate but 'good.' A good example is the book The Ego and His Own by Max Stirner. Stirner would not even consider a personal promise freely made to be binding on his future actions and would even accept that might or guile was right.[157] For even if a libertarian would not consent to predetermined authority relations as a matter of duty, he would without doubt be obligated in the moral sense to fulfil contracts or promises freely made.

In the Greek sense of the term, 'anarchos' meant simply 'without rule.' In the broader context, which takes in any form of rule by one man over another, it might be suggested that all libertarians could be classified as anarchists because they would be anti-rule. This would indeed be the case if the libertarians believed that all government by its nature must 'rule,' but they do not, for they envisage organizational bodies, one of which could be called a government, who were not ruling but were responding to the wishes of their membership. The notion of state could in this way be made tolerable.

The anarchists, however, were not only anti-state but primarily anti-government because they believed that no such overall organization of interests could exist, which was not in the end detrimental to the wishes of those who were subject to it. They accepted that all government must rule and therefore had to be either destroyed or abolished. In other words, they began from different premises than the libertarians and were anti-state for a greater variety of reasons beyond their dislike of authority. Whereas most anarchists were concerned with coercion as it related to freedom and the individual, most libertarians were concerned with the nature of authority relations in society and their implications.

Even before Proudhon accepted the term 'anarchist' as applying to his views,[158] the popular view of anarchy had in some ways quite logically been envisioned as chaos. Since the nineteenth century, through both word and deed, the anarchists have cultivated this image by presenting what, in the simple sense, seemed to be a wholly negativistic doctrine. The anarchists, in fact, were very optimistic about the role of man in society although few critics were prepared to concede that this was so. Furthermore, although they were not nihilists (a typically Russian phenomenon with Chinese roots) the majority of people would often equate the two words.

As a result, anarchism has been condemned for preaching negativism and violence, and few have considered the ethics behind it. On the other hand, libertarian ideas have been criticized not so much because they are socially or politically threatening (although they may well be), but because they are seen to be either impossible or immoral. This is so because they propose an alternate set of ethics which are self-imposed rather than externally 'guided' by groups of people who are essentially (so it is said) acting in their own self-interest. Anarchism and libertarian thought overlap, and, to the extent that they do, anarchist ideas form an important part of the explanation of libertarianism. There is, however, no recognized tradition of libertarian thought.

CHAPTER TWO

THE WRITINGS OF WILLIAM MORRIS AS AN EXPRESSION OF LIBERTARIAN THOUGHT

Strands of Libertarian Thought

It has already been suggested in the last chapter that libertarianism, unlike anarchism, does not have any conservative adherents. This could be somewhat misleading for there are many ideas and sentiments held by conservatives which are quite compatible with both anarchism and libertarian thought. One must, however, be wary of the reasons why such ideas are held. For even though the ideas themselves may be similar, the reasons for one's adhesion to them can only become clear in the context of one's particular doctrine. There are many individualist anarchists who take a conservative view of equality, private property, and competition. For example, in relation to equality, they would agree with the conservative view that because people are unequally endowed, inequality of condition, opportunity and treatment can be justified. These individualists, like Benjamin Tucker and the American, Josiah Warren, were defenders of the right to hold private property under conditions of unequal competition which they believed would achieve the most 'just' distribution of wealth, following the maxim -- 'each according to his deeds.'

Such views are endemic to conservative doctrine as expressed, for example, by Edmund Burke, but not to the libertarians with whom we are concerned. However, it might be added that these same individualist anarchists could, in most other cases, be labelled libertarian in their outlook especially with regard to their revolutionary aspirations for a change in the whole basis of society.

Nonetheless, it must be made clear that the libertarians were generally in complete opposition to a conservative doctrine which denies the natural goodness of man, believes in the continuity of history and tradition to quell men's passions, and sanctions hierarchy and private property as a part of 'noblesse oblige.' The conservatives tended to view themselves as 'realists' who have few 'a priori' assumptions which lead them to abstract principles and ideas. Instead their view of history rested on facts, feelings, and judgments, and their 'realism' was a matter of emotional loyalty and religious sentiment as well as abstract reasoning.

As a result, many persons who could be classified as conservative expressed sentiments which were not in the least antithetical to libertarian thought, although we must remember that the reasons for the sentiments and the assumptions were often entirely at odds with libertarianism. As writers are not always consistent in their thinking, it is possible to trace strands of humanist thought through such diverse sources as Godwin, Burke, Paine, Stirner, Carlyle, Ruskin, Spencer, and William Morris. Some of these strands are wholly compatible with libertarian ideas. And since we are dealing with what could be designated as the non-individualistic 'libertarians;' most conservative ideas will of course play little part in the discussions to follow. That is, their compatibility will not be dwelt upon if only because their implications within their own philosophies are too intricate to discuss within the framework of this book. The libertarians with whom we will deal put freedom before individualism but still believe in the right of the individual to pursue his own course in concert with the rest of a free and cooperative society.

The notion of freedom is central to any discussion of libertarian thought or ethics. Libertarians speak of it in both traditional and abstract terms and link the two together with a view of morality which could best be described as humanistic. This ought to become apparent as we proceed through the chapters to our final conclusions regarding the notion of freedom in libertarian thought. Unlike the liberals, and specifically Mill, the libertarians viewed authority, law, and the state as restrictions generating an immoral state of society which needed to be totally transformed. But non-libertarians also expressed some of these libertarian sentiments.

In **First Principles**, Herbert Spencer, who enjoyed some vogue in the latter half of the nineteenth century and was often mistaken for an anarchist, said,

> Freedom being the pre-requisite to normal life in the individual, equal freedom becomes the pre-requisite to normal life in society. And if this law of equal freedom is the primary law of right relationship between man and man, then no desire to get fulfilled a secondary law can warrant us in breaking it.[1]

Freedom was most often viewed mechanistically as an absence of restraint to the extent that, as Spencer said, "the liberty of each can be limited alone by the liberty of all."[2] But for many non-libertarians, freedom was tied to a sense of morality, and this belief led to some very different ideas about the nature and necessity of freedom.

One person who seemed to claim some affinity to both Spencer's and Mill's ideas on freedom was Auberon Herbert.[3] Herbert, an aristocrat who was described by a fellow individualist as "an individualist of the absolutist school,"[4] founded the Party of

Individual Liberty in 1885.[5] In a similar manner to the libertarians, he connected freedom with choice although he did not see them as being synonymous.[6]

> ...without freedom of choice, without freedom of action, there are not such things as true moral qualities...[7]

It seems that freedom was 'good' in moral terms because for Herbert, "force, coercion and power" were 'immoral.'[8] And this indeed is the same conclusion which the libertarians were to arrive at by different methods. The major distinction was that non-libertarians stressed the need for some form of authority to protect private property and uphold laws which the libertarians rejected in their present forms. For as Wordsworth Donisthorpe, leading light of the Liberty and Property Defense League tried to point out in a paper read before the Fabian Conference of 1886,

> ...we must discover some method of inducing people to work. The best method I could think of myself...would be the system of private property. To every man the fruits of his labour.[9]

Authority, for the non-libertarians, was needed mainly to protect private property and to uphold the few laws which were deemed necessary for the protection of individuals in society. This was particularly apparent in the stated aims of the Liberty and Property Defense League who were formed to resist 'over-legislation' by replacing state interference with a policy of 'let be.'[10]

The libertarians did not endorse the general notions of private property and law, while the necessity for authority was held to be a sure sign of an unjust society. Most conservative anti-statists wanted less state rather than no state. Their views on the subject of the state and law were, however, often in accord with the libertarian criticisms.

Distaste of power and violence seemed to be a common denominator in this form of thinking. Even Burke, who respected and recognized the need for authority, was quite aware of the corrupting potentialities of any authority, i.e., power which was used for its own sake.

> Power gradually extirpates from the mind every human and gentle virtue. Pity, benevolence, friendship, are things almost unknown in high stations.[11]

Such beliefs about the 'corrupting' tendencies of holding power were usually based upon some firm moral objections. With respect to the libertarians, it meant that the use of power could not be, as a form of action, separated from the ends sought. In their case, for example, the use of coercion could not in the end engender a resultant coooperative society. For, as Mill said in a seeming reference to socialism, there are certain difficulties in separating the means from the ends or one situation in the hope of a better future situation. Consequently, "...it is difficult to see how, by making a central power controlling everything, we can be making a step towards the abolition of that power."[12] Such was the position of the libertarians and nowhere, they believed, were such tendencies towards coercion and the misuse of power more apparent than in the institution which holds the monopoly of power -- the state.

Thomas Paine, another non-libertarian with libertarian tendencies recognized that government as such was not enough to hold men together in society.

> A great deal of that order which reigns among mankind is not the effect of government. It had its origin in the principles of society, and the natural constitution of man. It existed prior to government, and would exist if the formality of government was abolished... In fine, society performs for itself almost everything which is ascribed to government.[13]

John Stuart Mill, who believed that government and law formed part of the necessary burdens of a civilized existence, would not really disagree with Paine, but Mill did make a very important distinction.

> So long as organizations are held together only by a
> common purpose they will automatically do their work
> smoothly. But when, in spite of conflicting interests,
> you have people held together in a common organization,
> internal conflict results, and some outside force becomes
> necessary to preserve order, you have, in fact,
> governmental society.[14]

The libertarians would reply that freedom breeds its own form of order, and that order coercively enforced by government was bound to lead to injustices against the many. Paine expressed this sentiment well and, while he described government at best as a necessary evil, he was more positively concerned with the society over which the government ruled. He came to this conclusion:

> So far is it from being true, as has been pretended, that
> the abolition of any formal government is the dissolution
> of society, it acts by contrary impulse, and brings the
> latter closer together.[15]

Such libertarian sentiments are not difficult to find if one is prepared to accept and look for strands of thought which play a contributory and complementary role to the tradition which later became explicitly libertarian.

William Godwin, writing at the same time as Paine and thought by many to be the forefather of English anarchism, came to many of the same conclusions. Godwin believed that force grew out of monopoly and that government was the worst of all monopolies because it had the monopoly on force itself.

> We should not forget that government is, abstractly
> taken, an evil, an usurption upon the private judgment
> and individual conscience of mankind.[16]

Given such a stand, Godwin substituted for government the notion of justice which was to be the deciding factor in social relationships, for justice was the 'sum of all moral duty.' Essentially man had to guide himself according to such principles as reason could devise. For Godwin, these reasons were decidedly utilitarian in nature.

> Every community of men, as well as every individual, must govern itself according to its ideas of justice. What I should desire is, not by violence to change its institutions, but by reason to change its ideas.[17]

Herbert Spencer, like his students, Herbert and Donisthorpe, having already connected freedom with morality, was also able to justify disobedience to the state.

> If every man has freedom to do all that he wills, provided he infringes not the equal freedom of any other man, then he is free to drop connection with the state - to relinquish its protection and to refuse paying towards its support.[18]

Evidently these persons express libertarian views. But although these views fit within the context of their own philosophies or doctrines, it must be understood that their reasons for holding them are often very un-libertarian. For example, even though most individualist anti-statists despised government, they did so because they believed in individualism and competitive practices, not because they believed in individuality and cooperation in a society of egalitarians. Yet, the non-libertarians held on to certain strands of thought which, taken even out of context, contribute to a tradition wherein they are not to be admitted. For many ideas which are strongly held by various individuals re-emerge through the ages, like the 'truths' of which Mill speaks,[19] to be taken up by other individuals who are in most other instances quite unlike.

It will be one of the concerns of this book to sift out the strands of thought which come from these diverse sources and show how they came to be linked together by other ideas and assumptions to produce what could be classified as libertarian thought. In the first instance, the ethical foundations of the libertarian view must be examined if one is to understand the solutions and intellectual positions that the libertarians often uphold. Many of the initial and shallower criticisms of libertarian thought are focussed on ethical standards. These criticisms are concerned with whether or not libertarian solutions to problems are possible or even desirable. Consequently, any discussion of the libertarian position should begin with a clarification not only of their ethical ideas, but also of the manner in which they arrived at them.

Furthermore, libertarian thought becomes distinctly political, if only because the conclusions drawn from the moral principles put it at odds with society and the state. Thus, theory inevitably comes into the realm of practice and into the critical gaze of all who are affected or threatened by the revolutionary message contained within libertarian thought. It is by revealing conceptual as well as practical issues that an overall perspective may be gained, and many who wrote for the libertarian cause attempted to do just this. In such a manner one should be able to find out about and describe the essential elements of what we will generally designate as libertarian thought.

Using the Associations of One Individual

We can begin to characterize libertarian thought by looking at a few representative individuals in a schematic fashion. This will include what they wrote and said, what they did, and what was written

and said about them. However, in more depth, and as an individual
case, we could gain an overall initial coherence by looking at the work
of one man. This man, characteristic of the interregnum,[20] is
William Morris. We shall consider him not so much as a designer and
poet (although we cannot of necessity ignore his artistic talents) but
as a social critic and a political activist. For, in many ways, Morris
was a man of his times, but one who has not been recognised generally
for the contributions which he has made to nineteenth century political
thought.[21]

Morris does not easily fit into preconceived notions about the
political life, the movements, and the critics of Victorian England.
This is even more true about the persons who surrounded him and with
whom he worked in his opposition to capitalism, anarchism, state
socialism, and even Fabianism. And although he did not fully believe
in the merit of any of these 'isms,' he attempted until the end of his
life to bring all those who were working for a more egalitarian society
closer together.[22] Therefore, generally speaking, it will not
suffice to dismiss the associates of Morris as being mere anarchists,
utopian socialists, and troublemakers, as has been done then and
since.[23] We must separate the man from the myth and show that his
contemporaries of like disposition were far more active, though not
necessarily influential, than has usually been asserted. What has not
been appreciated is that the anti-state socialists were a formidable
foe, in terms of ideas, to the more orthodox followers of Marx or the
circle which (as the anarchists called him) George Bernard 'Czar'
frequented.[24]

Whether the libertarians, as a group of 'political dissidents,'
can be said to adhere to a particular theoretical position is more

difficult to ascertain than is the more obvious observation that they shared a common ethical stance in the face of both orthodox and radical opponents. As for their being part of a tradition, all one can say at this juncture is that they were a particular nineteenth-century phenomenon. We could of course speak of them in terms of certain 'radical' traditions of a sort which encompassed the 'enrages' of the French Revolution as well as the Benthamites and the Chartists. To the extent that such movements formed a tradition, the libertarians and the anti-statist socialists certainly played their part.

The ideas of men like William Morris cannot easily be categorized although the Marxists, Fabians, Anarchists, and Distributionists have at one time or another considered him to be closest to their sentiments.[25] However, as libertarianism is as much an attitude of mind and the adaptation of certain fundamental assumptions as it is a 'plan' for action, I shall argue that Morris was one of the central and best known progenitors of libertarian ideas.

Morris's criticism of society began with the assumption that the artistic side of man's nature was being offended by the architecture, art, and commodities being produced in his time. This criticism developed into a theoretical and political stance which culminated in his own peculiar brand of action and response. Action meant to Morris, as it did to the rest of his comrades in the Socialist League - education, agitation, and organization. Society had to be changed from the roots up.[26] Morris's ethical viewpoint was quite uncommon for a man who was an 'established' poet and craftsman. And because of his position within the community, he was constantly being attacked for his lack of responsibility in lending his stature to a revolutionary cause. His private life, too, seemed as eventful as his public one.[27] He was an anti-authoritarian yet still accepted the need for certain forms of authority relations;[28] he fought for enhanced political, social, and artistic freedom but remained at odds and in conflict with the liberal notion of freedom; he was himself a revolutionary rather than a mere street corner radical; and he realized that equality of condition was only possible in a society which turned its back on the idea that profit and monopoly were the necessary basis of a 'civilized' society. Morris viewed, albeit prematurely, future society as a harmonious association of individuals grouped in communities and joined by common interest and cooperation. Consequently he totally rejected, in Carlyle's terminology, the 'cash nexus' society based on usury and profit, class war, and competition. It was this society which he saw around him in the latter years of the nineteenth century.

By his own admission,[29] Morris was greatly influenced by the writings (and very specific parts of these writings) of Carlyle and Ruskin. From Carlyle's Signs of the Times Morris gained an insight into what he believed to be the basic follies of English society with respect to commerce and industry. From the chapter entitled 'The Nature of Gothic,' in Ruskin's book The Stones of Venice, he gleaned certain ideas on the relation between art and labour which were to transform him from the role of William Morris - 'Author of the Earthly Paradise' to William Morris - 'Socialist.'[30] However, he was not in agreement with most of the other ideas of Carlyle or Ruskin but, like most libertarians, he focused on a particular line of thought which he then incorporated into his own critical framework.

In a more direct way Morris was also influenced by his colleagues in the early socialist movement. Aside from numerous minor (or rather unknown) anarchists who surrounded him in the latter part of his life, Morris was early on confirmed in his anti-authoritarian views.[31] His remarks concerning authoritarian behaviour were particularly poignant when directed at H. M. Hyndman, one of the founders of the Marxist-oriented Democratic Federation (later known as the Social Democratic Federation). Writing to a comrade about the reasons for his having left the S.D.F. at the end of 1884 Morris stated:

> ... I am sure that the split was unavoidable: Hyndman can accept only one position in such a body as the S.D.F., that of master: some may think that position on his part desirable; I don't, and I cannot stand it. You must not suppose that this is a matter of mere personal likes and dislikes: the cause lies much deeper than that. H. has been acting throughout (to my mind) as a politician determined to push his own advantage...[32]

> I saw that the dispute must come off, and it must be fought out on the true grounds, namely resistance to H's absolutism.[33]

As a result of this dispute within the ranks of the S.D.F., Morris and a majority of the executive left to form the Socialist League on a 'new basis of mutual trust among ourselves.'

Morris was fairly familiar with the teachings of Marx, having read Das Kapital in French, although he did admit to a relative ignorance of the economic side of Marx's arguments.[34] Most of what he gleaned of Marxism came initially from his associates in the S.D.F. and his close personal and academic friendship with E. Balfort Bax with whom he co-authored the book Socialism - Its Growth and Outcome. In commenting on their first joint venture, Morris wrote in his diary of 1887,

> Tuesday to Bax at Croydon where we did our first article on Marx: or rather he did: I don't think I should ever make an economist, even of the most elementary

kind.[35]

But at the very time he was leaving the S.D.F., Morris could not help showing some of his anger at those who accepted Marx as the new prophet. In reply to a particularly dogmatic member of the S.D.F., he made it clear that there was more to life than ideology and economics.

> To speak quite frankly, I do not know what Marx's theory of value is, and I'm damned if I want to know! It's enough political economy for me to know that the idle class is rich and the working class is poor. And it doesn't matter a rap whether the robbery is accomplished by what is termed 'surplus value' or by means of serfage or open brigandage.[36]

Yet Morris's respect for Bax led him to take a more serious approach and attempt to master at least the rudiments of Marx's ideas. Bax, "the learned and distinguished philosopher" with "his fine regular features and busy moustache" proved invaluable to Morris in his literary and editorial chores on behalf of the Socialist League.[37] For Morris, in most ways, was not inclined towards leaving what he had begun in less than capable hands although he always seemed to be doing the majority of the editorial work.

Morris debated with, and associated with, the Fabians from the inception of the Society in 1884 right up until his death although he roundly rejected their ideas regarding the 'mechanism' of social change. Shaw, who first met Morris in the early 1880s, claimed that "Morris heartily disliked the Fabians, not because they undervalued him, but as a species."[38] Nonetheless there was always an ongoing debate between Morris, as a member of the Socialist League, and the Fabian lecturers. They often helped each other with propaganda efforts or by lending one another venues and giving one another access to printing facilities. By the time Morris had formed the Hammersmith

Socialist Society in 1890 he was well on his way towards a conciliatory attitude, and by 1893 there was even an attempt to issue a <u>Joint Manifesto of British Socialists</u>.[39]   Although the S.D.F., the Fabians, and the Hammersmith Socialist Society came together for the occasion, the statement which emerged only served to point out the impossibility of an alliance. But the hopes were there with Morris at the forefront. As was said of these final years,

> This attitude of conciliation on his part also accounts for the frequency with which Fabians, Anarchists and other types of social reformers were invited to lecture at Hammersmith.[40]

For by this time Morris had left the Socialist League in the hands of a seemingly less than capable group of radicals who were eventually to make its journal <u>The Commonweal</u> into 'A Revolutionary Journal of Anarchist Communism.'[41]   To remove himself from the 'politics' of the 'anarchists' in the League, who had been increasing in influence since 1887, Morris withdrew the Hammersmith Branch of the Socialist League from affiliation with the Socialist League in 1890 and formed what was to be known as the Hammersmith Socialist Society.[42]

Although Morris's dispute with the 'anarchists' in the Socialist League has been discussed on many occasions,[43] there are scarcely any two accounts of the proceedings which agree. Morris was ousted from the editorship of the journal in late 1889, but he remained a member of the League and contributed to the pages of <u>Commonweal</u> up until November 1890. What occurred during this year has usually been glossed over although we know that Morris was waging constant battle with the more anarchistic members of the League for at least the previous three years. The whole issue is extremely important for it shows above all that Morris was a man of principle who always sought out common ground, but who would not tolerate continuous infightng when there was serious work to be done. Just as he has split with the S.D.F. because of their 'politicking' and the authoritarian stance of Hyndman, so on the other side he was distressed by the disorganization and lack of leadership which crept into the League in the late 1880s. Although too much has been made of the violent stance of some of the members at this time, it is much more likely that Morris left because he felt he had nothing constructive to offer the majority of his comrades in the League. Morris, as well as being one of the founders of the League, had contributed at least 250 articles and other material to Commonweal, edited it for four years, and continually subsidized both it and the League from his own personal sources. He was not a particularly rich man at this time, and he came to the point where he did not feel that his role within the League was either important or necessary. He had been dissatisfied with proceedings for too long.

> During the last two years of Morris's association with the Socialist League (1888-90) the formal meetings frequently degenerated into arguments among Anarchist Socialists, Anarchists and Anarchist Communists. Tochatti, the Anarchist tailor, would discourse on the superiority of...Anarchy over State Socialism; Mordborst, a Danish Socialist, would insist that "not less but more law" was needed; Munsey, a postal telegraph official, would then complain that the lectures and discourses were becoming too technical and too far-fetched.[44]

More than the opinions it was the atmosphere of contention, as opposed to fellowship, that Morris could not bear. He had in many ways become accustomed to being the leader amongst a group of people who renounced the necessity of leadership. And although his thinking was ambiguous on the subject of the role of violence, he was sure that it was through organization and not violence that the struggle must be carried on. People, he believed, were not ready for socialism and revolution, and could only be made so through mass propaganda and education. For as he said, "our job is to make socialists."[45]

In March 1887, Morris who was strongly anti-parliamentarian himself, still viewed his role as conciliator with some importance:

> I may as well say here that my intention is if possible
> to prevent the quarrel coming to a head between the two
> sections, parliamentary and anti-parliamentary, which are
> pretty much commensurate with the Collectivists and the
> Anarchists...[47]

In the end he failed, but not without being able to distinguish between the various factional elements that existed even within the anarchist camp itself. It was the constant bickering amongst themselves rather than the ideas expressed which upset him most. He did not believe that some of the anarchists were so far away from his own ideas, such as those on communism. He had known and liked Kropotkin since meeting him in 1886.[48]

> [What]...is often the case with 'Communist Anarchists':
> they cannot differentiate themselves from the Communists.
> Their Anarchism consists in a somewhat exaggerated fear
> of a possible re-growth of some of the tyrannical methods
> of the destroyed Society, and a consequent distrust of
> the new Society having any definite form.[49]

But he did separate these Communist Anarchists from the Individualists, to whom he was totally opposed.

> On the other hand, I have met with Anarchists who were
> not at all vague, and who definitely opposed Communism.
> They had, indeed, this in common with militant Socialism,
> that they wished to abolish organized monopoly; but they
> supported unorganized monopoly, or the rule of the
> strongest individual, taking for their motto 'To each
> according to his deeds,' which means the upholding of
> private property with the association to uphold it, a
> position impossible and inconceivable.[50]

It is important that we realize Morris's recognition of the different forms of anarchist thought, for he was latér to make statements which suggested that he was not. It is not correct to blame the 'anarchist elements' within the League for Morris's departure although their espousal of the use of violence in some situations did give him cause to cast aspersions upon their role within the League.

However, it is imperative that we begin with Morris's radicalization back in the 1870s to determine the reasons for his subsequent behaviour, and in doing this it will become apparent that Morris was a pivotal figure in the heyday of libertarian thought in the nineteenth century.

As a tireless campaigner and fund-raiser, Morris lent great weight (by virtue of his reputation) to the socialist struggles of the period. In the collation of ideas derived from his unique surroundings, Morris was able to make an equally unique contribution as an artist and poet, and also as a communist thinker whose beliefs were fundamentally different from those who believed in socialist 'doctrine.' His thoughts were intimately and simply expressed in support of particular artistic and ethical convictions. Morris was more of a doer than a thinker, and it was the things that he did, and wanted to do, which made him realize the incompatibility of the social system with those who laboured to support it. Whenever he saw oppression he fought against it.

The Foundation of Morris's Social Criticism

In Signs of the Times, Thomas Carlyle (as Morris did later in his essays entitled Signs of Change) attempted to explain and criticize the causes and effects of seemingly uncontrolled industrial and commercial expansion. The main cause, according to Carlyle, was mechanization which was changing the traditional relationship between a man and his work. The result was that "...not the external and physical alone is now managed by machinery, but the internal and spiritual also...."[51]

> On every hand, the living artisan is driven from his
> workshop to make room for a speedier inanimate one. The
> shuttle drops from the fingers of the weaver and falls
> into the iron fingers that ply it faster..[52]

Morris was in complete agreement with this appraisal of the
situation. As an artisan himself, he found this same state of affairs
in a more advanced stage some sixty years later. He initially deplored
it for cultural and aesthetic reasons rather than for the more
fundamental political and economic reasons. Yet ultimately he was to
turn to these political and economic dimensions of the problem. He did
not join those who simply favoured reverting to the hierarchical and
structured life of the medieval countryside. Indeed, he believed that
machines were of great benefit to mankind.

> It is not this or that tangible steel and brass machine
> which we want to get rid of, but the great intangible
> machine of commercial tyranny which oppresses the lives
> of all of us.[53]

Carlyle, having insisted that the new 'Religion' "...was
Profit, a working for wages,"[54] anticipated the problems which
Morris would consider, and he was amongst the first to recognize the
upheaval experienced at this time by English society. Since the repeal
of the Corn Laws in 1848 the competitive commerce of the ever more
dominant middle class, along with their ethical standards, had
seemingly reached all sections of society. Even during the recessions
of the 1870s and late 1880s industralism continued to influence not
only the type of work which was being done but also the way in which it
was being done. The conditions of labour, although often appalling,
were, nonetheless, exacerbated by continued industrial expansion. This
drew people into the towns in the hope of escaping the very real
possibility of rural starvation.

Comparing the past with his present, Morris was quick to point out some of the essential differences in the relationship between a man and his work. For, as he saw it, in the Middle Ages,

...the unit of labour was an intelligent man.

...under this system of handiwork no great pressure of speed was put on a man's work...it developed the workman's whole intelligence according to his capacity...[allowing]...them freedom for human development.[55]

But the competitiveness of commercial life brought with it the necessity for and also the worship of profit. Profit became synonymous with 'just reward,' and the common practices of monopoly interests were classified as 'business acumen.' Machinery was introduced for the sake of market efficiency and not 'rationally' to increase the standard of living of the wokers who were tending the machines.

The phrase "labour saving machinery," is elliptical, and means machinery which saves the <u>cost</u> of labour, not the labour itself, which will be expended when 'saved' on tending other machines.[56]

In this limited but important respect, Morris is indeed indebted to the ideas of Carlyle. Carlyle also grasped a point which Morris was to develop vigorously and make into one of the cornerstones of his political and social criticism. In application to himself, Morris heeded Carlyle's warning that,

Undue cultivation of the inward or Dynamical province leads to ideal, visionary, impracticable courses.[57]

Thus, later, Morris was to assert, much to the distaste and incomprehension of his apolitical artistic friends (from his Pre-Raphaelite days), and his wife, that action was imperative to him.

To do nothing but grumble, and not to act, that is throwing away one's life.[58]

Yet Morris also heeded Carlyle's words about the 'undue

cultivation of the outward.'

> Again, though less immediately prejudicial, and even for
> the time productive of many palpable benefits, it must in
> the long run, end, by destroying Moral Force, which is
> the parent of all other force, prove not less certainly,
> and perhaps still more hopelessly, pernicious.[59]

Unlike Carlyle, who in his later life, was concerned with 'undue cultivation of the outward' in his insistence on the necessity for strong leadership,[60] Morris was able to identify completely with what could be conceived of as a Moral Force; Morris believed that a man's character and the better part of his behaviour were directly related to the degree to which he was a happy person. He found this to be true of himself and those who worked with him as artisans, so he thought that it was probably the case with the vast majority of other people. He was convinced, albeit from a privileged position, that there was joy and happiness to be gained in the performance of what he termed 'useful work.'[61] And as man had to work to live, it was essential that his work be pleasant.

> What we want to do is to add to our wealth without
> diminishing our pleasure. Nature will not be finally
> conquered till our work becomes a part of the pleasure of
> our lives.[62]

It was this position which he used as a basis for striking out against those who were living off the labour of others. He did not, like Carlyle, come to the conclusion that the Moral Force was a necessary factor in assuring aristocratic and strong leadership in society. In fact, Morris believed quite the opposite, that society should be organized from the bottom upwards, even if it at times was 'guided' by some form of administrative authority.[63]

Morris himself had inherited a great deal of money from his father as a direct result of the 'competitive' system which he was to

criticise so vehemently.[64] He had, therefore, personally benefited
from the capitalist system to a degree which allowed him to criticise
it from the inside out. He observed the conditions and external
manifestations of life which seemed to him to evolve from the
destructive and competitive elements of society. These manifestations
were the destruction of the country's architectural heritage for the
sake of speculation and profit,[65] as well as the production of
articles of 'folly and luxury' which contributed to the 'shoddy of the
times.' He also observed the degradation of a mass of human beings,
namely the working classes,[66] who were being forced off the land
into the sweatshops of the large industrial cities and herded into the
centre of fetid slums from where they were expected to compete in an
exploitative labour market. These external relationships were the
empirical evidence upon which Morris built his argument, even though he
spoke from the standpoint of a gifted middle-class intellectual and
practising craftsman. Yet throughout his life he was in total sympathy
with the plight of the working classes although he did not venerate
them to the exclusion of all other classes, as was the case with some
more dogmatic socialists.

As an artist, and not a revolutionary, Morris thus came to the
conclusion that man is both creator and creature of his surroundings.
But he also observed that those who created the hideous environs of
nineteenth century industrial England were not forced to live in
them.[67] The capitalist entrepreneurs could retreat into a
comfortable life-style, while the working classes, as virtual
wage-slaves, were locked into a system of competitive exploitation and
degradation.

As E. P. Thompson has written,

The utilitarian competitive ethic he now saw as the ethic of Cain; he had always known that it murdered art, but he had now come to understand that it murdered man's dignity as a creator in his daily labour and he now discovered that it murdered mankind.[68]

As a result, Morris was to come back to Carlyle's Moral Force largely through the writing of John Ruskin and claimed him as "my master toward the ideal."[69] In fact, Ruskin had desired an ordered, hierarchical, and functional society ruled by a trained aristocracy; he rejected both socialism and democracy, and much of his invective was poured out against the liberals. Ruskin was Morris's mentor in a very specialized if important way. He was most obviously influential for his views on the general connection between art, labour, and ethics. Ruskin was often echoed by Morris as when, for example, he said,

> The art of any country is the exponent of its social and political virtues. The art, or general productive and formative energy, of any country, is an exact exponent of its ethical life. You can have noble art only from noble persons, associated under laws fitted to their time and circumstances.[70]

This interest in the connection between art, labour, and ethics is essential to any understanding of the later thought of William Morris. Ruskin, as an art critic and, as a social critic, made Morris aware of these particular ideas, and he was quick to grasp their applicability to his own 'time and circumstances.' The conclusions reached by the two men were, however, greatly at variance with one another, for while Morris was to challenge the notions of hierarchy and authority, Ruskin, like his predecessor Carlyle, desired a restructuring of society in conformance with his own ideas of Truth and Beauty.[71]

The crucial difference between Morris's solutions and those of

Ruskin and Carlyle was that, by Morris's time, the foundations for the society they had sought to establish had disappeared. The Reform Bill of 1832 and the repeal of the Corn Laws helped to destroy that very aristocratic leadership that they wanted to build up -- to the benefit of the prosperous middle classes. The society Morris lived in was not conducive to procuring the type of leadership or 'heroes' which were necessary for the restructuring. Even so, Morris was able to identify forces within existing society which could serve as an essential part of any change which was to take place in the near or distant future.[72] Morris looked at the mechanics of the society in which he lived -- the role of institutional power and economic competition, political power and the conflict of class interests. He saw a system where the 'non-producing class' (the owners of capital) dominated the 'producing classes' (the workers). But beyond the mechanics of constitutionalism and capitalism was a set of ethics which he detested. To counteract the flood of utilitarian thinking and liberal individualism, Morris developed a system of ideas which he believed that persons of revolutionary intentions might use as a guide to thought and action. He presented his case in conjunction with that of the budding socialist movement and outlined an ethical position which could be applied in both making and maintaining a revolution.

As E. P. Thompson, one of Morris's more recent and extensive biographers, has suggested in his <u>William Morris: Romantic to Revolutionary</u>, his greatness,

> ...is to be found...in his discovery that there existed within the corrupt society of the present the forces which could revolutionize the future, and in the moral courage which enabled him to identify his cause with those revolutionary forces.[73]

Thus Morris, in an eclectic manner, was to use some of the

ideas of Carlyle and Ruskin, but he carried them further by attempting to bring together a set of ideas which had some resemblance to a marriage between Marxism and utopian socialism.

It was undoubtedly true that Morris was influenced by his reading of Kapital, but it would be misleading to suggest that he of necessity assimilated much of Marx to his own theories. He was neither a Marxist nor a state socialist; even less was he a Fabian or a mere utopian thinker. Rather it could be said that he held a unique combination of at least three different intellectual positions: anti-authoritarian, communist, and revolutionary. Morris certainly did not call himself a libertarian (nor indeed did Kropotkin use the term himself until two years after Morris's death);[74] he referred to himself either as a socialist or a communist. Even so he did not like such labels. Morris was very much affected by what could be called the 'Romantic Tradition,' not because he considered emotions and imagination more valid than reasoned deliberation, but because, as an artist, his whole life was deeply affected by and through the things he created. He enjoyed simplicity and beauty, but, above all, he placed great emphasis on the act of creation and the conditions which would make 'useful work' an end in itself - an end which would promote happiness. As a result of his own artistic endeavours and his beliefs about the 'production' of commodities, the scope of his thought expanded into a social viewpoint which, of necessity, became highly controversial and political in the revolutionary milieu of the late nineteenth century.

A Man and His Art: A Labour of Happiness

Morris did not accept Ruskin's view that art was meant to bring out and reveal aspects of universal 'Truth or Beauty.'[75] But the pragmatic side of his nature led him to some important and original observations about the reasons for the lack of 'good' art in the 1880's. Here, Morris was influenced by Ruskin's suggestion that a nation's art was 'an exact exponent of its ethical life.' Ruskin meant more than that 'we get the art we deserve,' for the phrase links the act of creation not only to the values held in common by members of a society, but also to the frame of mind and circumstances of the producer. In effect, what is produced, be it art, or, as Morris would have it, any other commodity, is contingent upon the relationships between a man and his product.[76]

Yet if the artist or producer is one of the major exponents of social and political virtues, what was the result of living in a less than virtuous society? Morris had no doubts about this.

> Now the chief accusation I have to bring against the modern state of society is that it is founded on the art-lacking or unhappy labour of the greater part of man...[This]...is hateful to me not only because it is a cause of unhappiness to some few of us who still love art, but also and chiefly because it is a token of the unhappy life forced on the great many of the population by the system of competitive commerce.[77]

Morris argued that if happiness was not present then 'good' art was impossible, and since he did believe that he lived in a society of wage-slaves, revolutionary change became one of his primary concerns. Because 'bad' art and intolerable working conditions were the result of living in a less than virtuous society, his proposed solution was social revolution.

For as "art is man's expression of his joy in labour,"[78] Morris felt that he must act, first by propaganda, in opposing the dominant values of Victorian society. He, unlike Ruskin, was more concerned with happiness than 'Beauty.'[79] Morris's ideas were

hopes for a future which he believed to be realizable and were in no
way the result of more aesthetic preference.

Furthermore, art needed the life force of free creation in the
fullest sense of the term. Fully aware of the hardship and brutality
of the Middle Ages, he did nevertheless make a claim for one aspect of
medieval life.

> ...The art of the Middle Ages, wherein the harmonious
> cooperation of free intelligence was carried to the
> furthest point which has yet been attained...alone, of
> all art, can claim to be called Free.[80]

Upon close examination of the political and social system,
Morris came to the conclusion that the 'ideals' associated with
'liberal freedom' were but a means of subjugating art to the interest
of those who, by reason of their social position or wealth, could best
afford their own 'individuality,' one form of Mill's liberty. Most
workmen, however, could not produce what they wanted and the result,
according to Morris, was quite plain to see.

> This system...has therefore produced the opposite of what
> the old craft-system produced, the death of art and not
> its birth, in other words the degradation of the external
> surroundings of life - or simply and plainly,
> unhappiness...[81]

In the capitalistic system of the time it thus seemed that only
the rich (like Morris himself) and leisured classes could produce art
if they did not have other people to act as agents for them, which of
course, they did. Morris found such a situation to be intolerable
because he believed that all men were not only capable of producing
art, but ought to do so. But the mass of so-called art which was being
produced at the time was nothing less than shoddy mechanical
reproductions of the tastes and desires of those who were only
interested in its manufacture and consumption for the sake of profit.

Many modern products were just copies of skilled craftsmanship which had produced artifacts under free working conditions. To Morris, art and labour were inseparable from the moral codes which gave rise to the conditions and outcome of production. He wanted a society based on certain ethical principles which would guarantee the production of good art and the happiness of its members.

Morris was quite adamant in his opinion that "...all art, even the highest, is influenced by the <u>conditions</u> of labour."[82] The conditions of labour made for a happy or unhappy workman; they influenced not only his day-to-day life but his productive capacity, which, in turn, was reflected in the products of his labour. Morris viewed a good product as being 'popular art.'

> ...art will be used to determine what things are useful and what useless to be made; and since nothing should be made which does not give pleasure to the maker and the user...that pleasure of making must produce art in the hands of the workman; so will art be used to discriminate between the wastefulness and the usefulness of labour;...[83]

Art was not made solely by the conditions of labour but was valued for itself in the pleasure it gave the producer and the usefulness it gave to the consumer or beholder. What Morris wanted to see was a personal bond between the man and his product. Everything depended on whether the reasons for the production of a work of 'art' were valid, i.e, either personal or commercial, and whether the circumstances of production were acceptable, i.e., coercive or free. It was necessary that the art produced be an expression of man's 'joy in labour.' And in the competitive and commercial atmosphere of the late nineteenth century art, for Morris, it was next to impossible for the average workingman to produce art because ever more production was founded on the 'art-lacking or unhappy labour of the greater part of man.'

The pleasure of creating and making art was "...chiefly of three elements - variety, hope of creation, and the self-respect which comes of a sense of usefulness."[84] All of these fundamental elements, Morris maintained, were lacking in the England of his time, and it was due to their general absence that art (or good commodities) was not being created. There was not the proper ethical climate to engender social relationships such as would enable man to produce in a fashion either amenable or beneficial to himself or to the community of which he was a part. Man as both worker and consumer, Morris claimed, was forced to rely upon a wholly artificial economic system which exploited his labour in the name of national welfare. The worker was forced by economic conditions to produce frivolous commodities for those whose major motive seemed to be profit or speculation. This resulted in forms of aggravation which made explicit the deep division of class interests within society. Society was controlled by forces which continually ignored the internal and external needs of the producing classes.

Morris at first looked to the past for evidence of different kinds of ethical and physical relationships. He attempted to explain these relationships in terms of the conditions of labour and the sense of community which was prevalent in the Middle Ages.

> It was this system, which had not learned the lesson that man was made for commerce, but supposed in its simplicity that commerce was made for man, which produced the art of the Middle Ages... The effect of this freedom...and the universal sense of beauty to which it gave birth became obvious enough in the outburst...which marks the Italian Renaissance.[85]

However, it is quite clear that Morris did not want a return to the circumstances of medieval life.

> We cannot turn our people back into Catholic English
> peasants and Guild Craftsmen, or into heathen Norse
> bonders, much as may be said for such conditions of
> life.[86]

Nor did he despise the machinery of his time which was being

used to save labour-time and effort although he did believe that most

machinery was being used to gain more profit rather than alleviate the

harsh conditions of labour.[87] He maintained, however, that the

advantages of machine production must accrue to all of society and not

just that part of it which profited by its use. What his writings on

art made patently obvious to his readers was that 'good' art, beauty,

happiness, and truthfulness of individual expression could not arise

out of a system of competitive commercialism. The values and

sentiments engendered by the constant attention paid to profit and loss

statements did not really take man into account as a human being but

merely as a monetary device. Morris believed that the division of

labour tended to destroy the peculiar and necessary expressions of

individuality which were potentially in the hands which ran the

machines and in the minds of those who were becoming ever more

alienated from their 'functional' positions within the capitalist

hierarchy. He referred to such a situation as the "...present

anarchical tyranny which is misnamed Society."[88]

But seeing in this society the seeds of its own destruction,

Morris observed that the misuse of machine production was leading to

the creation of factional groups. One of these, the producing yet

exploited class, had a hope of changing the basis of society.

> For the fuller development of industrialism...while it
> has taken from the workmen all pleasure in their labour
> or hope of distinction or excellence in it, has welded
> them into a great class, and has by its very oppression
> and compulsion of the monotony of life driven them into
> feeling the solidarity of their interests and the

antagonism of those interests to those of the capitalist
class: they are all through civilization feeling the
necessity of their rising as a class.[89]

For his own part Morris, from this time onwards (1884), was
thus committed to using education, propaganda, and socialist
organization to foster discontent, not only amongst this class but
throughout all ranks and classes. He would not concede the usefulness
of the parliamentary process.

In relation to work, Morris gives certain criteria necessary
for the production of art and useful commodities. These are closely
linked to the notion that labour is the essence of human survival and
development. In one's work there must first of all be hope, -
"...Hope of rest, hope of product and hope of pleasure in the work
itself."[90] This work must give pleasure or a sense of usefulness
to both the producer and the person who receives the fruits of his
labour. Man's work in the community must also be a two-way
relationship with one's fellow man and also with the forces of nature.
'Nature gives nothing for nothing' and man ought to make use of his
individual skills by working in concert with the rest of the community.
If a man wants to produce something useless as a form of pleasure
(which then makes it personally useful) he should be free to do so in
his own time with his own effort so as not to interfere with the
reciprocal relations necessary for the continued existence of any happy
and well-organized community. Thus, "...art will be used to
discriminate between the wastefulness and usefulness of labour."[91]

> Art is man's expression of interest in the life of the
> man; it springs from man's pleasure in his life; pleasure
> we must call it, taking all human life together, however
> much it may be broken by the grief and trouble of
> individuals; and as it is the expression of pleasure in
> life generally, in the memory of the deeds of the past,
> and the hope of those of the future, so it is especially

the expression of man's pleasure in the deeds of the present; in his work.[92]

Man would work to satisfy the needs of himself and his community, and he would produce art, the result of useful work,

> This, I say, is how a reasonable man would act if he were free from man's compulsion; not being free he acts very differently.[93]

The difference between 'useful work and useless toil' rests on the hope of the individual who is labouring in a free and cooperative community rather than a coercive and competitive capitalist economy.

> What is the difference between them, then? This: one has hope in it, the other has not. It is manly to do the one kind of work, and manly to refuse to do the other.[94]

Useful work related to pleasure and happiness is, in its product, synonymous with the creation of art, commodities of value, and beauty.

> Thus worthy work carries with it the hope of pleasure in rest, the hope of pleasure in our using what it makes, and the hope of pleasure in our daily creative skill.
>
> All other work but this is worthless; it is slave's work - mere toiling to live, that we may live to toil.[95]

These thoughts are brought into the social context as soon as Morris compares the sordid surroundings of his time with the people who have to live and work in them.

> Terrible as this is to endure in the present, there is hope in it for the future; for surely it is but just that outward ugliness and disgrace should be the result of the slavery and misery of the people; and that slavery and misery once changed, it is but reasonable to expect that external ugliness will give place to beauty, and the sign of free and happy work.[96]

Essentially the aim of art is to give happiness and self-fulfilment to all concerned in its production, for, as labour, it is but a means of restraining restlessness and instilling self-respect;

and it makes one responsible, as "...art cannot be the result of external compulsion."[97] Freedom therefore becomes an important ingredient in the whole production process. The distinction between art, labour, and leisure becomes increasingly blurred, as long as overt external compulsion is not present. Thus the absence of compulsion is a primary prerequisite, and one of the major influencing factors in the production of art. This is central to a system supposedly founded on communal mores and a shared value system. Because of the amount of freedom required in such a society the problem of authority is one not easily dealt with when the desired ends are cooperation and association in the place of competition and atomization. In a quite different manner than liberalism and particularly the liberalism of Mill, Morris's libertarian methods inexorably linked the individual with the community as a whole rather than to particular interests in that community. By association without compulsion, man was to become, through the production of art, the full expression of his better self and master of his own individuality -- an individuality which was to be conducive to the peace, pleasure, and productiveness of the entire community.

As an optimist, in respect of cooperative association, Morris was convinced that whatever the results of such a form of association, it would indeed be preferable to the 'civilized' society of his time.

> For my part I believe, that if we try to realize the aims
> of art without much troubling ourselves what the aspect
> of the art itself shall be, we shall find we shall have
> what we want at last; whether it is to be called art or
> not, it will at least be life.[98]

This is not the type of statement one would expect from a man who committed his life to the study and production of art. During his 62 years, Morris tried his hand at painting and architectural design, fabric and wall covering design, stained glass design, and book illumination; he also designed and wove tapestries and was a poet of considerable renown in England and Europe; he wrote prose and chants as well as political tracts and ended his life as a publisher of illuminated books produced by his own company, the Kelmscott Press. In other words, Morris knew how to produce useful work, his 'share of art.' But the fact that he. was able to devote so much time to his political activities, showed beyond a doubt that Morris was not content to stand above or outside what he believed to be his duty. His charismatic eccentricities tended to make him a leader in other fields than the arts although being thrust in such a position was not wholly to his satisfaction.[99] Morris was concrete in his outlook, for his primary interests lay in the alleviation of suffering and hardship by pursuing free and useful work. He was not seeking a mere revolution in the concept of art (although to some extent he did) but he did believe that the application of his artistic views would, in conjunction with organized propaganda, involve man in revolutionary change. The artistic revolution would lead to a social revolution, for the two concepts were inseparable.

> No one can tell now what form that art will take; but as it is certain that it will not depend on the whim of a few persons, but on the will of all, so it may be hoped that it will at least not lag behind that of past ages, but will outdo the art of the past in the degree that life will be more pleasurable from the absence of bygone violence and tyranny, in spite and not because of which our forefathers produced the wonders of popular art, some few of which time has left us.[100]

Morris used the concept of art to describe and explain the relation of a man to his work, regardless of what that work was. This in turn forced him to look beyond ethical and aesthetic principles in the first instance towards a vision of the future of society.

> In such a state of society laws of repression would be
> minimized, and the whole body of law which now deals with
> things and their domination over persons would cease to
> exist.[101]

Such beliefs led Morris towards a commitment which he felt
could only be realized upon the overthrow of the capitalist system. He
chose to replace it with a form of socialism which "...does not
recognize the finality in the progress and aspirations of
humanity."[102] This could be achieved if one sought the <u>aims</u> of art
which could in themselves guarantee art, beauty, and happiness. These
aims, as we have seen, were staunchly linked to the workman in the
performance of his labour, under conditions of 'liberty, equality, and
fraternity,' or, as Morris would have put it, 'freedom, equality, and
brotherhood.' In the end, Morris wanted to see 'fellowship' win over
'mastership.'

The Critique of Labour: Those Who Must Perform It

According to Morris, labour is able to function within two
various forms of constraint, both which have their own peculiar
problems and obligations. First of all, he likened the normal
condition of work in the nineteenth century to a form of modern slavery
in which the worker was under some form of 'mastership' either of a
person, in the form of a boss, or a thing, in the form of a machine.
This presumes some form of authority-structure for the work being done
is the result of economic compulsion, or a 'working to live so that one
may live to work.' This, as we have seen, has been designated as
'useless toil' by Morris for it puts men in a position where they do
not even recognize the baseness of their own condition or that the
ugliness of their lives could be transformed.

> Men living amongst such ugliness cannot conceive of
> beauty, and therefore cannot express it.[103]

With this form of 'compulsory' labour, externally maintained by some authority structure, the worker is forced into a position of working only at those things he is allowed to work at. Aside from the rather dubious distinction of being allowed to work at all, the worker is given little choice in determining either the method, mode, or outcome of his own production. These are the limitations imposed upon him by a competitive system which operates somewhat like a meritocracy or has a relatively high surplus of labour determined by forces and conditions beyond the control of the worker and, at times, even the employer. Workers were, in as much as they were a capital investment, mainly thought of as functional units operating within the integrated structure of the factory or workshop. It was for this reason that art could not be produced, for the conditions of labour did not facilitate it. One of the aims of art was therefore,

> ...to destroy the curse of labour by making work in the pleasurable satisfaction of our impulse towards energy, and giving to that energy hope of producing something worth its exercise.[104]

The second sense in which there can be constraints operating upon the worker relates to what is in fact the absence of compulsion. The individual can be constrained by his own perception of his situation, or the ethics of his community. That is, the individual has consciousness as well as conscience. As Morris said in his article, Communism and Anarchism,

> The time may come, and I hope it will, when the social conscience will be so highly developed that coercion will be impossible, even on the part of the community.[105]

In this sense, man is restrained somewhat by his own physical and mental limitations as well as by the moral obligations which he may assume towards the rest of the community. Ostensibly the worker is not then producing in a coercive society based on what Morris termed 'a system of artificial authority.' If such a condition of society were possible, then man could work in order to overcome the perils of nature in concert with his fellows for the betterment of all, rather than work to increase his own bondage to a master or a capitalist economic system. Until that time, Morris felt that a 'collective authority' "...which is prepared to coerce [individuals] not to coerce"[106] might be necessary in some instances.[107] Nonetheless, Morris believed that socialism was the most preferable method of carrying out the task at hand, i.e., changing the foundations of society.

> Socialism is a theory of life, taking for its starting point the evolution of society; or let us say, of man as a social being.

> Since man has certain material necessities as an animal, Society is founded on man's attempts to satisfy those necessities; and Socialism, or social consciousness, points out to him the way of doing so which will interfere least with the development of his specially human capacities, and the satisfaction of what, for lack of better words, I will call his spiritual and mental necessities.

> Socialism is to substitute the relation of persons to persons, for the relation of things to persons.[108]

Morris had already observed that the general condition of labour was intertwined with the authority of market competition and the will of the master. The market to which socialism economically addressed itself[109] was an artificial competitive system reinforced by laws which were to a large degree made for and by those who had an interest in the means of production mainly for the sake of profit. The power of the employer over the worker was due to the private and monopolistic ownership of capital and not to any vindictive or conscious attitude held by the 'non-producing' classes.[110] Morris believed that the wealthy were as much slaves to the situations which they engendered and the system in which they worked as were the workers themselves. In reference to the middle-class (which included the trading, manufacturing, and professional people in society) he said,

> For their work itself, in spite of the sham dignity with which they surround it, they care nothing: save a few enthusiasts, men of science, art and letters, who, if they are not the salt of the earth, are at least...the salt of the miserable system of which they are the slaves, which hinders and thwarts them at every turn, and even sometimes corrupts them.[111]

Morris came to believe that power and authority relations were the manifestations of certain economic relationships which were brought about by monopolist practice. And it was for this reason that he accepted the Marxist view that labour was in a position of war vis a vis capital as long as the two were forcefully kept apart by the authority of the state through its laws. The workmen, who formed the useful class of producers even though they did not always produce art, were valued because they made that which was consumed by all. To Morris, the seeds of revolution and dissatisfaction with the system were to be found amongst such producers even though they could not be considered a homogeneous or conscious group. And it was this group with whom he was not to identify, but rather to support in the struggle for socialism. Essentially Morris demanded that labour be set free, while at the same time he realised that his demand could not be adequately served unless there was a social revolution.

This revolutiion had to come from the bottom upwards[112] by changing the relationship between a man and his work in a conscious and deliberate manner. Revolution "...means a change in the basis of society."[113] Fundamentally this meant a change in the moral foundations of society, a society wherein even Carlyle recognized that - "...in all senses, we worship after power...."[114] The desire or power was usually exemplified by political success and ambition. Success itself was often measured by the accumulation of material possessions which, in many ways, epitomized social and economic inequality and the evils which it brought about.

According to Morris the revolution could not succeed unless there was a change in the values of the workers who would be the main force behind any permanent change. Morris believed that violent upheaval was virtually inevitable, and he accepted this as ultimately beneficial as long as the workers had been properly educated to cope with the outcome.[115] Morris was prepared to ferment discontent amongst all classes through the use of propaganda and education. But he stressed the uselessness of a purely 'mechanical revolution' whereby there was merely a transfer of power from one group of rulers to another.

He maintained that the revolution, once inspired, was not a struggle between the democrats and the autocrats but between those who supported 'Fellowship' as opposed to 'Mastership' regardless of their class origins.

> [Men]...individually grow into being the master of others by the development of certain qualities under a system of authority which artifically protects the wealth of every man, if he has acquired it in accordance with the artificial system, from the interference of every other or from all the others combined.
>
> The new order of things says, on the contrary, why have masters at all? Let us be fellows working in the harmony of association for the common good, that is for the greatest happiness and completest development of every human being in the community.[116]

Mastership and fellowship essentially connote the present and the future -- two systems of opposing thought -- embodied either by class war and competition on the one hand or the abolition of class

distinctions through mutual cooperation and the common ownership of the
means of production on the other.

> Society will thus be recast, and labour will be free from
> all compulsion, except the compulsion of Nature, which
> gives us nothing for nothing... The very essence of it
> is freedom and the abolition of all arbitrary or
> artificial authority.[117]

Morris's contempt for the so-called cultural achievements of
his own time, led him, through art, to expound the problem of the
conditions of labour and attempt to provide a new theoretical
foundation for these problems. As a logical extension of his beliefs,
he concluded that a system of communism was the only reliable way of
attaining the goals which he sought. If the community is to have a
social conscience which is highly developed enough to do without
coercion, revolutionary change will have been accomplished.

> [The]...community will be composed of men who so
> thoroughly realize Communism that there will be no chance
> of any of them attacking his neighbour in any way. All
> reasonable men, whatever they may call themselves, would
> rejoice at such a change; and it is because I know that
> this cannot be brought about as long as private property
> exists, that I desire the abolition of private property,
> and am a Communist.[118]

To Morris, communism was the 'necessary development of
socialism' and was the only doctrine which could guarantee man a just
return for his own labours without being beholden to any man or
institution. For, as he stressed in his article, Monopoly: or How
Labour is Robbed, the,

> ...means of production...must be used by those who can
> use them,...according to fair and natural regulations
> agreed upon by the whole community in its same
> mind...[and]...since they are to be used by all, they
> must not be exclusively possessed, i.e., owned by any;
> because, if any private person or groups of such, held
> the exclusive possession or ownership of them, they could
> withhold the use of them, except on terms which would
> place the useful persons in a position of inferiority to
> the useless; in other words, they would be their masters,

and would impose such a life on them as they chose.[119]

Morris also tried to translate his theories into practice. For example, as an owner of capital and an entrepreneur (Morris and Co. - The Merton Abbey Works) he was aware that it was possible to construct a factory or other labouring premises in such a manner as to make them both happy and efficient production centres.

> ...[O]rganization of such a factory, that is to say a group of people working in harmonious cooperation towards a useful end, would of itself afford opportunities for increasing the pleasure of life.[120]

Whether it was due to the organization, or the nature of the artwork produced at Morris's Merton Abbey Works, there is abundant evidence that his ventures, incorporating his ideas, met with overwhelming success.[121] Morris was able to prove, at least to his own satisfaction, that virtually any normal person, regardless of background or education, was able to learn and practise a skill which demanded a high degree of initiative and craftsmanship.

Though, perhaps as a justification for not distributing his own wealth to the workers, Morris believed that any rise in the material standards would have to be accompanied by a change in the culture and habits of the working class as a whole. He did not want to "...see a few individuals more creep out of their class into the middle class..."[122] thereby multiplying the capitalist class. Nor did he see the value in redistributing the wealth of the propertied to those who had none because "...the greatest number of the men kept down by years of slavery would not know how to spend their newly gained wealth but would let it slip through their fingers to swell the gains of the exploiting tradesmen who are on the look-out for such soft-heads."[123]

The first step, therefore, towards the new birth of art
must be a definite rise in the condition of the workers;
...But again, this change for the better can only be
realized by the efforts of the workers themselves.[124]

Morris believed that the best way to prevent the absorption of
middle class values by the workers was to fight for a change in the
conditions of the entire working class; "...the really desirable thing
that being still workmen they should rise in culture and refinement
which they can only attain to by their whole class rising."[125]

On the face of it Morris seems to have a paternalistic and
patronizing attitude towards the working class. But Morris's main
concern here is with the social mores involved and not just with
material change.

> ...social morality, the responsibility of man towards
> the life of man, will, in the new order of things, take
> the place of theological morality, or the responsibility
> of man to some abstract idea.[126]

One of the ideas Morris was most keen to dispel was the very
Victorian notion of 'self help.'[127] Furthermore, in his own
actions, he did not live the life of a dilettante on his annuity but
constantly gave his time, effort, and money to the causes of art and
socialism. His justification for taking the course he did was
described as a 'matter of religion.'

> ...In looking into matters social and political I have
> but one rule, that in thinking of the condition of any
> body of men I should ask myself, 'How would you bear it
> yourself? What would you feel if you were poor against
> the system under which you live?' I have always been
> uneasy when I had to ask myself that question... If I
> had not been born rich or well-to-do I should have found
> my position un endurable, and should have been a mere
> rebel against what would have seemed to me a system of
> robbery and injustice. Nothing can argue me out of this
> feeling, which I say plainly, is a matter of religion to
> me:.... I am bound to act for the destruction of the
> system which seems to me mere oppression and
> obstruction;...the antagonism of classes, which the
> system has bred, is the natural and necessary instrument

of its destruction...[128]

In spite of his detractors, which to some extent included even his official biographer J. W. MacKail who despised Morris's political activities, Morris followed a revolutionary path. By the late 1870s Morris had come to the important conclusion that being a mere critic of society was not enough. He decided that total revolution was not only possible but also the necessary prerequisite to the formation of a better society and that he must act towards that end. He began his agitation by lecturing and writing.[129]

Although Morris joined the Democratic Federation in January 1883, it was not a wholly socialist body at the time, and Morris was not himself identified as a socialist until he gave his lecure at Manchester in March 1883 which attracted much publicity.[130] As the years went by Morris became more and more a libertarian socialist, one who would not compromise with the trappings of democracy even in its parliamentary form. Morris was a libertarian in the sense that he saw no dominating authorities or forces which would direct the energies of man in a socialist society. He was against the idea of compulsion as a technique for organizing human endeavour. When he fully realized the opposition against which he was working (and which was profoundly embedded within the socialist movement itself), he became even more libertarian in his outlook and more acutely opposed to what he called 'parliamentary palliatives.'

> Those who think they can deal with our present system in
> this piecemeal way very much underrate the strength of
> the tremendous organization under which we live, and
> which appoints to each of us his place, and if we do not
> change to fit it, grinds us down until we do. Nothing
> but a tremendous force can deal with this force.[131]

The main counterforce was, of course, organization. As an

activist, Morris continued for the last fifteen years of his life to build up an organization which propagated such ideas as the 'usefulness' of labour, the fruitlessness of parliamentary or political legitimacy, and the necessity of social revolution. Yet he did so mainly as a forceful and labouring intellectual who, in the main, lived the life he so cherished. He wanted to pass his knowledge on to the workers who were far less fortunate than he.

"Whenever he was aware of the existence of a problem he had a quite remarkable persistence in worrying at it until he was satisfied that he had reached a solution."[132] Morris could not, nor would he, disassociate art from labour, morality, socialism, or revolution.

> Truth in these great matters of principle is of one, and it is only in formal treatises that it can be split up diversely.[133]

Morris's Revolutionary Progression

Even during his socialistic activities Morris was still widely associated with many aspects of the arts, as a writer of sagas and poems, a designer, a craftsman, and a leading light in the Society for the Protection of Ancient Buildings.[134] Although one might think that these activities would have been increasingly less important from the time he joined the Democratic Federation in 1883 until his death, in fact, Morris seems to have led an almost 'occupational double life.' Morris's output in the two roles was prodigious by any standard. From 1884 until 1896 he wrote 31 major articles and pamphlets, two books, and numerous poems and chants in the service of the Socialist cause. Above and beyond this he contributed to _Justice_ continually for the first year of its life and wrote at least 250 articles and notes in the pages of _Commonweal_. But running parallel to this, he continued his artistic endeavours, which included 35 articles, 5 books, and 16 poems

on things as varied as <u>Gothic Architecture</u> and <u>Of Dyeing as an Art</u>.
Add to this the many hundreds of lectures which he gave, and we can see
that there is no doubt as to Morris's passion for work.[135]

Consequently, although the 'Cause' as he called it, was the
main driving force of Morris's life from the 1880s, it was not the only
one. During these years he also experienced great personal turmoil, as
he became alienated from his wife and, except for Edward Burne-Jones,
those with whom he had grown up in the Pre-Raphaelite circle. His
artistic interests became important only insofar as they afforded him
relief of work in the form of the variation of energetic activities.

At the same time Morris began to associate with people like
Edward Carpenter, H. M. Hyndman, Shaw, Engels, and Kropotkin, and
although he often acted as a thorn in their sides, his opinions were
respected and his work valued as a contribution to socialism. He
formed the Socialist League to aid this same cause.

Shortly after Morris's death, MacKail, in the role of
biographer, did his best to play down Morris's active role in the
socialist movement by suggesting that he was just going through a phase
of 'journalistic writing' about social and political problems with
which he had superficially identified. MacKail's opinions were
accepted for a long time afterwards, at least until the publication of
Bruce Glasier's book, <u>William Morris and the Early Days of the</u>
<u>Socialist Movement</u>, in 1921. This dispelled some of the illusions,
but it took the publication of May Morris's two volume Supplement to
the <u>Collected Works</u> [136] to confirm the fact that Morris's
political commitments were more than a mere fad with him. Even Aymer
Vallance, who had Morris's consent to write a biography, seems to have
been ignored by MacKail in his initial judgments even though Vallance

reported on Morris's commitment to the 'Cause' in print within a year after Morris's death.[137] Nonetheless, shortly after the Trafalgar Square riots of 1886, MacKail was to express an opinion which he held, in the reporting of the events in his book, to be the tenor of Morris's commitment to socialism. MacKail set the tone which subsequently showed his attitude to this side of Morris.

> It was a time when the vices of that debased journalism with which he had deliberately associated himself, infected Morris most deeply.[138]

This attitude is not wholly surprising, however, as Morris's messages were rarely accepted by those who were in principle opposed to socialist activities. After Morris had been writing and lecturing on social change for nearly two years, The London Echo (unlike the Daily News[139]) had still not seen fit to appreciate the message or meaning of Morris's agitation. The London Echo made a strong editorial comment on Morris's more public activities.

> Mr. Morris...is not content to be heard merely as a voice crying in the wilderness. He will be content with nothing less than the propagation of his ideas by means which must result in social revolution... Judging him by the company he keeps, he would disturb the foundations of society in order that a higher artistic value be given to our carpets.[140]

But Morris was intent on propagating his message, and, while he was in the Socialist League, he was convinced of its efficacy. "Education towards Revolution," he said, "seems to me to express in three words what our policy should be, ... and to do this...we must take part in all really popular movements where we can make our views on them unmistakingly clear."[141] Morris's emphasis on education towards mass organization was no palliative; he also favoured agitation towards class solidarity, which was a primary aim of both the Socialist League and the Hammersmith Socialist Society, which he founded and funded in sequence.

Unlike most other socialists of his day, Morris was, as we have seen, a strong opponent of the use of parliamentary democracy as a means of changing society. It was his view which eventually split the Socialist League and led Morris into closer contact with the anarchist anti-parliamentarians who eventually took it over. In this Morris put principle over judgment; nonetheless he always remained at odds with those in the movement who wanted to make use of the electoral process as a means of gaining a governing position.

> If our own people are forming part of parliament, the
> instruments of the enemy, they are helping to make the
> very laws we will not obey. Where is the enemy then?
> What are we to do to attack him?[142]

He did not accept the practicability of State Socialism and opposed all moves which would lead to an increase in the centralization of power.

> I do not believe in the world being saved by any system –
> I only assert the necessity of attacking systems grown
> corrupt...[143]

Given the various sources of influence acting upon him, the pressure constantly put upon his loyalties to associate with one group over another, it is indeed surprising that Morris managed to develop, as he did, a relatively coherent method and logical approach. He would not accept the 'gradualist' position of the Fabians for two fundamental reasons. First, gradualism meant a tacit acceptance of parliamentary democracy, its methods, and its laws, which were evolutionary rather than revolutionary. Secondly, Fabianism wanted more governmental and institutional control and not less. He regarded the Fabian doctrine as a norm of 'intellectual social planning' or, as Hyndman described it, 'gas and water socialism,' which was supportive not only of state power, but also of State Socialism, which he identified with authoritarianism and incomplete reform. Morris was in disagreement with this 'piecemeal and elitist' solution, which he felt would serve little purpose except to divert the attention of the working class from the important issues regarding the role of capital and labour. In Morris's eyes Fabianism was a form of intellectual radicalism and not a revolutionary factor in the fight against oppression, and he detested it.

> Radicalism will never develop into anything more than
> Radicalism...It is made for and by the middle classes,
> and will always be under the control of rich capitalists:
> they will have no objection to its political
> developments, if they think they can stop it there; but
> as to real social changes, they will not allow
> them...[144]

Radicalism, by calling for legal and administrative reform within a society changed in its mechanisms of rule only, was to Morris in no way revolutionary; indeed, he feared it would be actually harmful in its effects, especially if, as Mill feared, bureaucratic rule became prevalent. Morris believed that Fabianism, as it was then developing, justified his misgivings about it: he repudiated the Fabian policy of separating practical solutions from the ethical - a policy which was frankly asserted by W. Clarke, a member of the Fabian Society in 1890:

> So long as the Fabian Society confines itself purely to
> politics and economics it is doing admirable work. When
> it trenches on ultimate questions of ethics and
> philosophy, it is not only acting ultra vires (according
> to its own rules), but is precipitating problems in which
> there are vital differences among the members.[145]

Morris would have viewed this divorce between the ethical and the practical as one of the major shortcomings of the Fabian Society, but he had other criticisms as well. He did not feel that the Fabians were committed enough to dramatic change throughout the whole of society; rather, he insisted, they were more interested in the machinery or the 'mechanism' of rule. This he feared could have disastrous repercussions. As early as 1885 he tried to make it clear that 'the mechanics of revolution' (exchanging ruling powers differing only in method) could not be separated from an overall 'social consciousness.'

> The working classes must understand that they are not the appendages of capital. When the change comes it will embrace the whole of society... This is what I meant...by saying that I did not want a mechanical revolution - such as would happen if only a small minority were to overthrow the established government...[146]

Morris considered that the Fabians were too concerned with the mechanisms of change to be a revolutionary force. While reviewing the publication of the first set of Fabian Essays in 1890, Morris declared that "Webb's mistake [was] to over-estimate the importance of the mechanism of a system of society apart from the end towards which it may be used."[147] As Shaw later commented in the 1930s, twenty years after the Russian revolution, Morris was one of the few to foresee that a change in mechanism was not all that was needed.[148] The Fabians, humane and intelligent as they were, tended to avoid debates about the character of future society, and even though they were fairly agreed as to the ends sought, these ends did not appear to Morris to be inbuilt in their economic and political programme. But Morris was equally disturbed by the political ambition and parliamentary aspirations of other socialist groups, and he continued to oppose them on the issue.

> I say that our work lies outside parliament and it is to help educate the people...to know their own, to know how to take their own and to know how to use their own.[149]

In terms of propaganda and education, Morris appreciated that the Fabians were probably the most successful of all the socialist groups. But as they gained strength and prominence he noticed that they were looking ever increasingly towards supporting a legitimate and existing power-base mainly in the area of local government. Morris, however, continued to insist that the power-base had to be formed outside of these constitutional institutions and that the most effective weapon was mass organization 'against capitalism and not individual capitalists.'[150]

At the time, as the politicians and journalists of all persuasions were strongly opposed to this apparently disorderly and threatening 'mechanism,' Morris asserted that it would not be effective as long as it was organized to move in a particular direction. For, "neither is it any use claiming our own business unless we are prepared to have some business of our own."[151] Morris also believed that without the understanding that the interests of the producing classes and the Victorian economic system were incompatible, the hope of fostering and advancing social consciousness was doomed to failure.

Morris was no less severe with the anarchists within his own organization where he was most often in dispute with them on tactical grounds. He was sympathetic to the 'scientific anarchists' identified as the followers of Peter Kropotkin, who himself came to live in London in 1887. He understood the reasons for which people became violently anti-state and suspect of authority at all levels. When speaking about Frank Kitz of the Socialist League, he could express sympathy over his comrade's disposition and circumstances.

> Like most of our East-enders, he is certainly somewhat tinged with anarchism or perhaps one might say destructivism; but I like him very much: I called on the

poor chap at the place where he lived, and it fairly gave
me the horrors to see how wretchedly off he was; so it
isn't much to wonder that he takes the lines he
does.[152]

Although several of Morris's comrades were seen as anarchists
(as was Morris himself at times) because they were in disagreement
about the internal structure of the Socialist League, it was not
because there was any anarchist strategy to make the League serve their
own purpose. As Thompson has written,

> ...it would be wrong to think of the Anarchists within
> the League in 1885 and 1886 as the conscious advocates of
> certain theoretical principles.[153]

Even Joseph Lane, who while on the Council of the Socialist
League wrote The Anti-Statist Communist Manifesto (and incidentally
which Morris voted against issuing as a pronouncement of the League
Council in 1887)[154] and who was the leader of the
anti-parliamentarian wing who influenced Morris's political views, did
not identify himself with the violent stance of some anarchists.[155]
Although claiming to be an Anarchist-Communist after 1887 he
"...rejected both the Anarchist 'propaganda by the deed' and all
methods of political and industrial struggle."[156] Like Morris and
many others within the League, he was a staunch opponent of
'palliatives' and political action which would accept the legitimacy of
parliament. Lane, who had been a Socialist agitator since the late
1860s, had only one main fear - that any individual should arise (as
did Hyndman in the S.D.F. with whom Lane had associated) to take
control of the organization. Yet Lane also realized that one must
'educate' people to be prepared for socialism. His respect for Morris
is shown in the fact that he accepted Morris as actual, if not
designated, leader of the Socialist League. He left the League a year

before Morris, in 1889, because of its decision to put emphasis on agitation rather than education.

Frank Kitz, whose career closely parallels that of Lane, was another associate of Morris's in the stormy days when the Socialist League was trying to determine whether to support parliamentary or extra-parliamentary action. He was described by Bruce Glasier in later years as being "a rebel by temperament rather than an Anarchist by philosophy,"[157] but his associations with the notorious individualist anarchist Johann Most (who was successfully prosecuted for incitement) branded him early on as an anarchist of the violent breed. Kitz lived and worked in the East End, and was, as Morris noted, "tinged...with destructivism."

But although Kitz's obsession with the plight of the working class and the question of Land Nationalization were his constant concern, he too as an anarchist was drawn into the bitter struggle in the Socialist League. In the years leading up to his joining the Socialist League he, unlike Lane, put agitation before education, and sought, as an anti-parliamentarian, to help steer the League in this direction. His anarchist views were secondary to the existence of the League as an organized propaganda organ.[158] He respected Morris and was genuinely convinced of Morris's preference for 'tinkers and tailors.'[159] Yet just because of Morris's association with such men he was branded, along with them, as the uncompromising agent who retarded the creation of a genuine socialist party in the 1880s. In fact, as E. P. Thompson has very clearly shown, it was the pro-parliamentarians and their desire to make the Socialist League into a political party which put an effective end to that organization as an active propaganda force.[160]

Because of Morris's prolonged and continued association with men such as Lane and Kitz, his image suffered at the hands of those pro-parliamentarians, who were later to become involved in other organizations such as the S.D.F., the Fabian Society, and the Independent Labour Party. It is apparent that Morris was strongly and indelibly influenced by the libertarian ideas which were so common amongst the anti-parliamentarian and anarchist groups of the 1800s and 1890s. At times Morris strongly opposed the anarchists on two important points, namely their apparent dislike of forced organization and their tacit acceptance of the use of violence to achieve the ends they sought. But such opposition was based on tactical considerations, for most of all he wanted to organize a cohesive propaganda body which was not dominated by the factional infighting over moot points of theory at a time when the actual work of organizing the working class was of paramount importance. He was prepared to compromise, it seems, on virtually all things except parliamentary democracy. Two weeks before the Annual Conference of 1888 Morris wrote in a letter that he felt the parliamentary lobby within the League were determined to bring things to a head, and he expressed his queer form of dogmatism and compromise as follows:

> ...The parliamentary people are looking like driving matters to extremity, which means driving me out of the League if they succeed. I am quite willing to let this matter rest if they will leave it alone...[161]

They did not leave it alone and from this time onward the Socialist League began its long decline as a socialist body representative of an approach which was motivated neither by economics nor politics. The Socialist League with its branches all over the country continued on as a propaganda organizaton. As a self-avowed communist, Morris was committed to the view that only through principled and efficient organization could social revolution be successful. "Without organization the cause is but a vague dream"[162] Morris said in an argument with Lane. He even maintained at times that the anarchists he knew were unwittingly working against the organization of an effective propaganda machine because they did not give the impression of solidarity. This, he thought, was due to their often excessive individualism and irrational fear of authority. As he said towards the end of his association with the Socialist League and The Commonweal,

> ...If freedom from authority means the assertion of the advisability or possibility of an individual man doing what he pleases always and under all circumstances, this is an absolute negation of society, and makes Communism...impossible.[163]

But Morris knew, as we have seen,[164] that this was not really what men like Kitz and Lane meant by anarchism although he genuinely feared that the membership of the League was wide open to such extreme positions. In fact Morris himself was publicly attacked in the pages of Commonweal by two dogmatists within the Socialist League just before he resigned.[165] Nonetheless, Morris's view of the future society was almost wholly compatible with that of the communist-anarchists within the League.

Morris saw the future in terms of the hope of new forms of organization spearheaded by the working classes and the hope of change. He did not want to impose a system but hoped that the mass of people would, through education, realize their own best interests. He did not propose a new morality which he thought could only come about as a result of the changes themselves. Such was the strength of his optimism.

...I say plainly that I shrink from no consequences of that gathering hope: for when it begins to realize itself (as it will) there will be an end of overwork and anxiety - and then people will find out what kind of education and morals they need and will have them: not unlikely that they may be somewhat different from our preconceptions of them. Meantime to try to settle amongst our present corruption what that education, those morals shall be, except in the most general way seems to me a putting of the cart before the horse.[166]

The difference of opinion between Morris and the anarchistic element in the League did not seem to lie in the direction of theory but mainly in the course of organizational tactics. Morris could not tolerate fancy rhetoric delivered for the sake of effect, whether it came from the mouth of someone like that 'disreputable dog' Edward Aveling, who had close associations with Engels,[167] or from the pen of David Nicoll. On matters concerning the internal structure of the League, Morris was constantly mediating between factions. But unlike the disagreements he had with the pro-parliamentary wing of the League, his disagreements with the anarchists seem to have been more personal and emotional than intellectual. In his book on Morris, Thompson suggests that Morris was much more of a Marxist than an anarchist and, indeed, that Morris was exceedingly anti-anarchist.[168] But this argument is not established satisfactorily on the basis of Morris's writings, nor is there evidence that "...he showed in a common-sense manner the impossibility of the anarchist position:...,"[169] as Thompson has claimed. Anarchism was attacked much more effectively and vehemently by Shaw with whom Morris himself greatly differed.[170] Essentially, however, Morris's dispute with the anarchists revolved around the amount of individualism which was permissible and at what times and to what extent violence might be employed in the pursuit of one's ends.[171] Morris was by no means a pacifist although basically he abhorred the use of violence by either the state or those who used 'propaganda by the deed.' But he believed that violence was a probable ingredient in the making of a revolution.

> The means whereby this is to be brought about is first, educating people into desiring it [revolutionary socialism] next organizing them into claiming it effectually. Whatever happens in the course of this education and organization must be accepted coolly and as a necessary incident, and not disclosed as a matter of essential principle, or even if these incidents should mean ruin and war. I mean that we must not say 'We must drop our purpose rather than carry it across this river of violence.' To say that means casting the whole thing into the hands of chance, and we can't do that: we can't say if this is the evolution of history, let it evolve itself, we won't help. The evolution will force us to help: will breed in us passionate desire for action, which will quench the dread of consequences...[172]

Like many anarchists, Morris was prepared to condone the use of violence, particularly as a defensive measure. Morris had few misconceptions about the anarchist movement, but his letters lend weight to the suggestion that his dispute with them has been greatly exaggerated, if Morris himself is to be believed.[173] He always played the conciliator and did not leave the League until it was obvious to him that he could not provide the necessary 'leadership' which he had, by 1890, become accustomed to. At that time he made his last bid for peace within the Socialist League.

> As for me, I can only say that whatever will give us equality, with whatever drawbacks, will content me, and I find that at bottom this is the ideal of all Socialists. So I think the fewer party-names and distinctions we can have the better, leaving plenty of scope for the inevitable differences between persons of different temperaments, so that various opinions may not make serious quarrels.[174]

From this time onward Morris's political contributions to the Commonweal ceased. But it is worth noting that Morris did not want to call himself an anarchist because he did not want to be identified with its more obvious publicity-seeking individualists, yet he was wholly unsure of the future role of the State, i.e., whether it should be abolished entirely or merely devolved of its power. Although he in many ways agreed with the aims of anarchism, he did not entirely see the similarities between his philosophy and the ideas and methods of the communist anarchist - Kropotkin. As a communist, Morris was committed to a form of organization, and he did not believe the anarchists were prepared to accept this discipline even though most of them, like Lane and Kitz, had shown otherwise. Morris believed that it was essential for the socialists and indeed for the anarchists to "...grasp the fact that individualist effort to break the chains of society must fail."[175]

In the end Morris was convinced that the force of the oppressors in society could only be met with counter-force, but he was repelled by the thought of being an actual participant in such measures. Yet he would have participated (as he did in his pet hate -- open-air propaganda) should the occasion arise. He tended, like the communist anarchists, to rationalize the acceptance of certain forms of coercion over others, but he was not happy with this conclusion. The use of coercion is a major dilemma for anyone espousing a belief in libertarian ethics. In general, however, it could be said that the use of violence could be legitimized in the post-revolutionary context only insofar as it was defensive. Yet this in itself raises considerable problems as to the nature of 'defence' and the role of those who would be granted the authority to use coercive methods. What Morris did not want to see was the blatant use of violence as the major method for defeating the capitalist class. It was to be a last resort. He objected to it on both moral and tactical grounds. In reference to what he mistakenly put forth as anarchist theory rather than anarchical action (the state of chaos resulting from extreme individualist violence), he made the following statement:

> For your own sake and for those who honestly think that the principles of anarchy are right, I cannot for the life of me see how such principles, which propose the abolition of compulsion, can admit of promiscuous slaughter as a means of converting people.[176]

In historical terms, according to Thompson, "Anarchism in the late 1880s was no mere parlour philosophy: it shaded down, through various stages, from 'leftism' and 'anti-parliamentarianism' to the advocacy and practice of crime."[177] It was this latter type, along with Nihilism, which had little theoretical structure and whose adherents justified all action as being political that Morris condemned.

Morris and the Libertarian View

Morris could not envisage a society along anarchist lines (as he understood them) as long as he continued to believe that anarchist theory was both individualistic and anti-organizational. But as we shall see shortly, his overall understanding of anarchist theory and opinion was not as limited or as unsympathetic as writers such as Thompson would have us believe.[178] Two letters which he wrote in the *Commonweal* just before his departure from the day-to-day participation in its production give what amounts to his authoritative and final opinions on the subject.[179] It is undoubtedly true, however, that Morris was genuinely disturbed by the factional disputes which occurred in the Socialist League after 1888. This was not so much because of the content of the disputes themselves, but because personal rivalries they engendered and the time spent on them, were destructive of the very organization which he hoped would inspire the socialist cause. Nonetheless he was outspoken about individualist positions for he believed that the individual could only fully develop in concert with a community of equals which had abolished private ownership of the means of production. In economic and organizational terms he was a 'pure' communist,[180] and he expressed his hopes for the future in a like manner.

> Equality as to livelihood, mutual respect, and responsibility, and complete freedom within those limits - which would, it must be remembered, be accepted voluntarily, and indeed habitually - are what Socialism looks forward to.[181]

Morris thought the device known as the 'authority of the majority' was a practical if somewhat pernicious means of settling differences. For he was convinced (although he was not happy about it) that "...all but a very small minority are not prepared to do without masters...";[182] but in the making of a communist society this deficiency would be overcome by the notion of 'Fellowship.' Each man would become his own master since he would labour to please himself and his community, thus being able to reassure himself of his unique and individual position within the community structure. Such a society, Morris claimed, "...is held together and exists by its own inherent right and reason," and not by "...what is usually thought to be the cement of society, arbitrary authority."[183]

Now this latter statement is not altogether clear, especially as Morris was not one to talk in terms of such general abstractions as 'inherent right and reason.' He was the one who always insisted that "...individual men cannot shuttle off the business of life onto the shoulders of an abstraction called the State, but must deal with it in conscious association with each other...."[184]

This "conscious association" is the key to much of his argument regarding the cohesive elements which could be brought out in a society, if that society were composed of happy producers. He considered unhappiness the result of an 'immoral' system which was all the more intolerable because it came from sources outside the control of the individual. Morris blamed unhappiness on 'arbitrary authority' and believed that "We have to do away with the causes that have compelled this unhappy way of living."[185]

> But when revolution has made it 'easy to live' when all
> are working harmoniously together and there is no one to
> rob the worker of his time, that is to say, his life: in
> those coming days there will be no compulsion on us to go
> on producing things we do not want, no compulsion on us
> to labour for nothing; we shall be able calmly and
> thoughtfully to consider what we shall do with our wealth
> of labour-power.[186]

In simple terms, the causes of unhappiness were not only political, economic, and social compulsion but also the relationship of men to one another in a competitive commercial system which encouraged the notion of 'self-help' and carried on monopolistic practices under the guise of free trade. Through the accumulation of wealth it was usually assumed by its possessors that their power over others was increased accordingly. Enhanced social and economic status in many respects allowed the possessing classes a greater freedom of action in comparison with those whom the socialists designated as the 'wage slaves of capital.' Those who actually worked for wages and produced the wealth with their physical labour were, in physical terms, less free, according to Morris, because they were not able to make the choices, if only in quantitative terms, which would allow them to function as responsible and dignified members of the community. Morris wanted the workers to have a share in the wealth which he felt was being wasted and squandered by the owners of the means of production and their political allies. To this end he encouraged discontent among the workers. This organization of discontent, using the vehicle of the Socialist League, was meant to fuse itself with the interests of the non-possessors and act as a counter-force to the power of the commercial class. He believed that the vacuum of power, caused by the defeat of this class in its aspirations, could be filled by persons acting in common rather than in competition.

Although hesitant, Morris suggested "...a revolutionary administration whose definite and conscious aim will be to prepare and further...human life for such a system..."[187] of cooperative enterprise. In attempting to justify such a system he went back to what he considered were first principles. The basis of society would be,

> ...that something, made up of the aspirations of our better selves...the <u>social conscience</u>, without which there can be no true society.[188]

> ...Real society asserts itself in the teeth of authority by forming genuine unions of passion and affection.[189]

Although Morris was no student of the traditions of European philosophy and analytic technique, he had a firm grasp of European history and culture from the Middle Ages. He was an authority on Northern European (Iceland and Scandinavia) cultural history and folklore as is evidenced in his many Norse ballads and translations. It was with great difficulty that he was able to articulate his ideas on the political and economic problems facing the Victorian era. Yet, in the end, what he did write was very straightforward and amenable to quite practical interpretation. He wanted to see the birth of a new society which would replace the one he believed to be so corrupt.

Its ethics will have to be based on the recognition of

natural cause and effect and not on rules derived from ' _a priori_ ' ideas of the relation of man to the universe or some imagined ruler of it; and from these two things, the equality of condition and the recognition of the cause and effect of material nature, will grow all communistic life.[190]

Like most libertarian thinkers Morris concentrated a great deal on the means or kinds of action which would be necessary for the attainment of change as well as the ends which he ultimately sought. For he too believed that man first had to cope with nature in a manner which would not put him into conflict with the rest of men who were trying to overcome the same physical perils. Like Kropotkin, Morris claimed that the most beneficial way for all would be through cooperative effort, a means which would engender ever more social cooperation. To do this, man must work and live in a fashion which is unhampered by 'artificial authority' which creates divisions and inequalities that make free cooperative effort impossible. To Morris 'artificial authority' was founded on coercion because it hampered the free development of the individual who sought merely to contribute to the commonweal. 'Artificial authority' was a system of coercion, edicts, commands, laws, and rules which expressed the interests of one group of persons over another and allowed the former group to accumulate wealth and power by depriving the producers of their just reward, i.e., the product of their labours. Any authority which created social division through competitive practice was, for Morris, 'artificial.' Because of this view, he saw that the social and economic progress of the great majority of the population was being impeded by a system which was bolstered by a parallel constitutional governing-body made up of those who generally accepted progress in terms of Gross National Product and Imperialist economic growth.

Because of this situation Morris felt that one must not fight for piecemeal reform as it gave little more than the percentage spoils of an already corrupt society. Since he viewed the end of labour to be a form of happiness which was only obtainable through cooperative effort in a free society, he rebelled. For happiness can only be attained on a general scale through equal and free association which was not hampered by a history of rules and precedents. This would allow for a new relationship between a man and his labour. For Morris, all products of such labour would, in effect, be art, and the notions of equality and freedom were essential pre-requisites for both happiness and the production of art. Of the effects of a change in the basis of society, he always remained optimistic.

> I am prepared to accept as a consequence of the process
> of that gain the seeming disappearance of what art is now
> left us.[191]

Morris knew the type of society in which he would be happiest, and he believed that it would make the greatest number of people content in their associations. In The Society of the Future, an article written in 1887 three years prior to the publication of News From Nowhere and at a time when he was being pulled towards a more anarchistic and less economical position, he described some of his hopes for the future.

> It is a society which does not know the meaning of the
> words rich and poor, or the rights of property or law, or
> legality or nationality: a society which has no
> consciousness of being governed, in which equality of
> condition is a matter of course...
>
> It is a society conscious of a wish to keep life
> simple... It would be divided into small communities,
> varying much within the limits of due social ethics...
>
> ...Divisions of labour would be habitually limited...the
> social bond would be habitually and instinctively felt,
> so that there would be no need to always be asserting it

by set forms... The pleasures of such a society would be
found on the free exercise of the senses and passions of
a healthy human animal so far as this did not injure
other individuals of the community.

Take this for the last word of my dream of what is to be;
the test of our being fools will be that we shall no
longer have masters.[192]

What is noteworthy here is that there is no mention of any

transcending general principles nor any explicit statement about rules

of conduct. When Morris refers to the fact that his society would have

'no consciousness of being governed' could one take that to mean no

government or no masters of any kind? Indeed, in relation to the above

passage, there is a subtle implication regarding some sort of social

bond, not an 'artificial' authority or controlling group which actually

governs but of an ethic which proliferates throughout the society. In

an attempt to isolate the phenomenon Morris himself, who was never fond

of abstract notions, made reference to it as the 'social conscience.'

This social conscience presumably was to initially emanate from

an organized revolutionary group (such as the Socialist League) which

was to encourage certain beliefs and actions on a mass scale. For

Morris, the transformation of society was dependent upon a change in

social relationships, and this 'change for the better' "...can only be

realized by the workers themselves."[193] Initially what was

required was,

Intelligence enough to conceive, courage enough to will,
power enough to compel... These three qualities must
animate the effective majority of the working people; and
then... the thing [revolution] will be done...[194]

The destruction of the capitalist system, for Morris, would

bring with it the end of 'artificial authority.'

...The present and decaying order of things...has to be
propped up by a system of artificial authority; when that
artificial authority has been swept away, harmonious

association will be felt by all men to be a necessity of
their happy and undegraded existence on the earth, and
Socialism will become the condition under which we shall
all live, and it will develop naturally, and probably
with no violent conflict...[195]

He had already observed that in the system under which he lived
there were authorities which bolstered up the legal monopolistic
practices of the commercial sector of the community. The power of
these authorities was both political and economic. If, as Morris
claimed, they used government to further their own interests, they also
tended to drag down the rest of society to their own ethical level,
i.e., one based on the principle that power and competition were the
necessary ingredients in the structuring of society. So, in essence,
any moral or legal code which sanctioned such behaviour at the expense
of the majority was 'artificial.' The 'artificial authority' of the
laws and institutions of capitalism (especially the respect for private
property) created what Morris referred to as 'false society.'[196]
This society was ruled for and by the 'useless' class.[197] A system
such as this, society being its image, could only function with an
artificial form of authority because authority itself was the most
efficient and arbitrary bond which would weld a society, governed by a
few, into a stable nationalistic conglomerate. It seemed only natural
to Morris to conclude that, as art and society were artificial, the
cohesive forces themselves, as epitomized in the law, must likewise be
designated as artificial. Morris saw the rulers as having authority in
terms of having the legal power to dictate their preferences but
insisted that these dictates were not for the good of the whole
society. Morris expressed antipathy towards the authorities because he
knew that they substituted 'Mastership' for 'Fellowship,' and that they
were in essence not only responsible for most of the ills of society

but were representative of all that was meant by the word
'artificial.'[198] Freedom had to be substituted for compulsion.

> Society will thus be recast, and labour will be free from
> all compulsion except for the compulsion of Nature which
> gives us nothing for nothing. It would be futile to
> attempt to give you details of the way in which this
> would be carried out; since the very essence of it is
> freedom and the abolition of all arbitrary or artificial
> authority;...[199]

However, Morris never claimed that one could do away with the
necessity of all forms of authority (hence his use of the adjective
'artificial'), and this, as we can see, was in many ways at the heart
of his dispute with the more radical and anarchistic elements of the
Socialist League. His idea of acceptable authority was the 'social
conscience,' or if one wanted to put this in numerical terms, it could
in the long term sense be considered as 'will of the effective
majority.'[200] The social conscience was the overall binding force
which would replace 'artificial authority' while the will of the
majority would be the mechanism of the decision-making process. Morris
barely managed to distinguish between power and authority because, in
the sense in which they were generally used, he linked both notions
together as being coercive relationships. He did not believe that
these forms would be necessary in the future mainly because they were
instituted to serve the purposes of a system of private property. In
Morris's own lexicon, authority is little more than the exercise of
legitimate influence of one individual or group of individuals upon
another individual or group of individuals within a communistic social
milieu which had abolished private property as a first economic
principle. Within the context of legitimate influence, Morris does not
suggest that there is any inherent right to seek to establish authority
over another. Nor did he suggest that such authority would have legal

backing because community consensus would be sufficient. He had, as was already mentioned, stated the position of the anarchistic element, and, in doing so, his own, on the point of authority in the future society. He contended that they did not seek freedom from authority in all circumstances nor did they believe in always doing as one pleased. This was how he initially pictured the anarchist position, but in the last two non-fictional contributions he made to Commonweal[201] one can deduce that his comprehension of the anarchist position was far from limited. In referring to a statement about the individual doing 'what he pleases always and under all circumstances,' Morris added,

> ...But when you begin to qualify this assertion of the right to do as you please by adding 'as long as you don't interfere with other people's rights to do the same,' the exercise of some kind of authority becomes necessary. If individuals are not to coerce others, there must somewhere be an authority to coerce them not to coerce...[202]

This passage might be interpreted as allowing for the use of force, and Morris seems to legitimize this use of force when he adds the stipulation "...that authority must clearly be collective."[203] The legitimate use of power as well as influence thus becomes very important for Morris as 'artificial authority' has somehow been replaced by some new form of restrictive relationship. The criteria of legitimacy for the new form of authority related directly to an established communism and the bond of social conscience.

> The bond of Communistic society will be voluntary in the sense that all people will agree in its broad principles when it is fairly established, and will trust to it as affording mankind the best kind of life possible.[204]

Thus Morris's social bond in the society of the future, the new form of authority, is the result of an agreement between people who "...must agree on some common rule of conduct to act as a bond between them, or leave their business undone."[205]

> And what is this common bond but authority – that is, the conscience of the association voluntarily accepted in the first instance.[206]

And this is made up,

> ...of the aspirations of our better selves, and is the <u>social conscience</u> without which there can be no true society.[207]

Morris is in a common dilemma. He abhors the use of force and violence because it is inhumane, uncivilized, and, in many ways, all too unpredictable in its outcome. Nonetheless, common experience of life tells him that even in the future there are bound to be disagreements between persons. This "...experience shows us that wherever a dozen thoughtful men should meet together there will be twelve different opinions on any subject which is not a dry matter of fact (and often on that too);...."[208]

Morris has become a momentary 'realist' and much to his own consternation is seen to have to qualify his views of an ideal of society where power, or the threat of its application, should not be of any advantage to an individual in the settlement of a dispute. Yet, for example, when he discusses the limits to which one individual can interfere with the actions of another if the first individual is engaged in the same actions, Morris asserts the notion of equality as being of overriding concern, i.e., 'that you have a right to do as long as you don't interfere with your neighbour's right to do as he likes.' In reference to this 'right' he said,

> ...I assert it again, and also assert that the social conscience, which being social is common to every man, will forbid such individual interference, and use coercion if other means fail:...[209]

However as to the method of agreement regarding general modes of action, Morris's sense of optimism prevails.

> Where all men are equal, I believe 'the give and take'
> would have such influence over men's minds, that the
> 'authority of compulsory representative institutions,' or
> whatever took their place, would be so completely at one
> with the Social Conscience that there would be no dispute
> about it as to principle, and in detail,...the few would
> have to give way to the many; I should hope without any
> rancour.[210]

However, in an attempt to work out his own ideas about making a

decision within the limitations of some form of authority structure,

Morris continues to qualify his earlier words on the subject. Since

this was an open letter on the subject of anarchism, Morris could be

accused by some of his critics of softening the tenor of his argument

for the sake of compromise. But given Morris's highly principled stand

on other occasions, this seems highly unlikely. As he explained to the

readership of Commonweal, on the subject of authority.

> Now I don't want to be misunderstood. I am not pleading
> for any form of arbitrary or unreasonable authority, but
> for a public conscience as a rule of action: and by all
> means let us have the least possible exercise of
> authority. And with equality of condition assured for
> all men, and our ethics based on reason, I cannot think
> that we need fear the growth of a new authority taking
> the place of the one which we must remember is based on
> the assumption that equality is impossible and that
> slavery is an essential condition of human society. By
> the time it is assumed that all man's needs must be
> satisfied according to the measure of the common wealth,
> what may be called the political side of the question
> would have taken care of itself.[211]

Like most libertarians, Morris felt that responsibilty and

respect would be the mainstay and pith of that collective bond known

through the all but indefinable emanations of the future social

conscience. The exercise of authority is not so much the exercise of

legitimate power but remains a question of acceptable or legitimate

influence which is defined by the 'ethics of reason' in terms of the

interference with one's freedom. It could be put under the general heading of 'reasonableness.'

> ...I am bound to suppose that the realization of
> Socialism will tend to make men happy. What is it then
> makes people happy? Free and full life and the
> consciousness of life. Or, if you will, the pleasurable
> exercise of our energies, and the enjoyment of the rest
> which that exercise or expenditure of energy makes
> necessary to us. I think that is happiness for all, and
> covers all difference of capacity and temperament from
> the most energetic to the laziest.
>
> Now, whatever interferes with that freedom and fulness of
> life, under whatever specious guise it may come, is an
> evil; is something to be got rid of as speedily as
> possible. It ought not to be endured by reasonable men,
> who naturally wish to be happy.[212]

Morris thought that men who were happy who worked for pleasure

under circumstances of free production (receiving the fruits of their

own labours) would be reasonable. They would be quite unlike the men

who inhabited the factories and slums of a competitive capitalistic

industrialized society as it existed in nineteenth century England.

'Doing their own business' they would act with self-respect and

responsibility in their social relations.

> First you must be free; and next you must learn to take
> pleasure in all the details of life: which, indeed, will
> be necessary for you because, since others will be free,
> you will have to do your own work. That is in direct
> opposition to civilization which says, 'Avoid trouble,'
> which you can only do by making other people live your
> life for you. I say, Socialists ought to say, 'Take
> trouble, and turn your trouble into pleasure': that I
> shall always hold is the key to a happy life.[213]

The key to the whole of Morris's social and political doctrines

is contained in the above paragraph which was taken from his article

The Society of the Future which he put forth as a 'practical vision of

one man' to wit, himself. The foremost pre-requisite for Morris was

freedom -- the liberty to do what one desires without artificial

restriction. Man must be free to express his individuality in concert

with the hopes of the rest of the community, and in doing so, create his own environment. "Man must and does create the conditions under which he lives; let him be conscious of that, and create them wisely."[214]

Morris did not believe, as did Mill, that law would extend the quality or range of liberty within a society which he saw as having been corrupted by the very existence of that law. Individuality in general behaviour, work, and leisure could only have meaning if the individual was at liberty to pursue his own best interests, i.e., "the pleasurable exercise of our energies and the enjoyment of necessary rest,"[215] unhampered by such artificial restrictions as were embodied in the laws of the land. Thus to pursue individuality, to use one's freedom in a creative and satisfying manner, one had first to overcome the physical and mental obstacle of 'freedom from.' That is, one must obtain a state of liberty before individuality could be pursued, putting the new found freedom to positive use. Liberty, to Morris, had to be obtained before freedom could be used to better the condition of the whole of society. Liberty is gained through revolution, but what is done with it depends upon the extent to which people freely cultivate the individual will "...shaking off the slavish dependence, not on other men, but on artificial systems made to save men mainly trouble and responsibility."[216] Men would follow a libertarian doctrine wherein the goal of life, whatever it may be, would be sought through the free development and association of man's conscious faculties.

Morris's best and latest description of his personal utopia is to be found in the prose work News From Nowhere, which was published in 1891.[217] It is not a prediction but a highly personal statement of how life would be lived were his principles applied on a large scale, and, in this sense, it brought together many libertarian ideas. Peter Kropotkin called it "...perhaps the most thoroughly and deeply Anarchistic conception of a future society that has ever been written."[218] But throughout his vast contribution to the socialist cause Morris had said, already, virtually everything which was contained in the book. In his conversations as Guest with Old Hammond, who knew almost everything about the past, it is as if one is reading one of Morris's essays in Signs of Change, the language and ideas being so similar. But as Morris himself so wisely pointed out, one must assume that "...the only safe way of reading a Utopia is to consider it as the expression of the temperament of its author."[219]

In summing up Morris's contribution to libertarian thought with reference to his ideas on communism and socialism, I shall draw mainly on the four most consistent and terse statements which he has made on the subject.

During April and May of 1888 Morris wrote to the Reverend George Bainton of Coventry four letters in which he attempted to put forth his views on socialism. They were reprinted privately in 1894 "with Mr. Morris's permission though not upon his initiative."[220] The fact that he let them be reprinted unedited, at that time, leads one to believe that he was still in relative agreement with their contents. This is most obviously so if one looks at three more statements in conjunction with these letters, while remembering that his lecture The Society of the Future, given in 1888, was the real precursor of News From Nowhere. These three are The Socialist Ideal,[221] How I Became a Socialist,[222] and Communism,[223] and are the final political statements made by Morris on the subject of socialism. Many of his ideas, especially those regarding authority and the necessity for a habitual form of morality, were close to those of the communist-anarchist Peter Kropotkin who outlived Morris by twenty-five years. Kropotkin claimed that the only criteria for judging law and its effects under any system, were by its "usefulness and hurtfulness,"[224] to the individuals and groups to whom it is applied. Morris would have concurred, for in spite of his constant appeals to fight for an 'ideal' system and work in the name of the socialist 'cause,' he was above all concerned for the welfare of the ordinary mass of workmen. He hoped that they could be made socially conscious and in this way follow the communistic way to freedom, equality, and prosperity. Although a workman who was not part of the working class as we understand the term, Morris was determined to fight for such a change either with or without the aid of the working classes. Morris's ideal of communism was in essence a call for a system 'of practical equality' as the normal condition for the basis of society – a society which would put people before things. As true as this appears to be, most of Morris's commentators have failed to point out that it was Morris's hope for a better future and its realization which drove him forward -- the hope that man would express his pleasure in life through the labour of production. To desire change meant having an ideal vision and Morris succeeded in partially creating one.

> ...it is the desire to escape from the present failure which forces us into what are called "ideals", in fact, they are mostly attempts by persons of strong hope to embody their discontent with the present.[225]

For Morris, the criterion of judgment for the working man -- he who laboured, who produced art, was the usefulness of the end product, "...because the primary purpose of the goods, their use in fact..."

ought never to be lost sight of.[226] This, and not any system founded on doctrinaire theory, would lift society out of what Morris considered to be the degradation of nineteenth century England.

As we have seen, Morris, although not a state socialist, believed in the necessity of some form of organizing body to deal with the administration of things. He was no anarchist.[227] Nor did he believe in the necessity for hierarchical authority, centralization of authority, or discrimination by function in the division of labour. Regarding the question of forms of authority, it was the freedom of the individual and the emancipation of a class which was at stake -- not the freedom of the liberal individual who relied upon the protection of the law for the furtherance of his own interests, or the protection of privilege. The latter goes contrary to Mill's notion of law nonetheless, but Morris sought a libertarian solution, finding freedom through fellowship and cooperation. The functional discrimination of labour, when it was translated into an economic division of labour, i.e., the payment of different wages for different skills, was anathema to him. Within his proposals he was able to justify the position that no one skill ought to be accorded greater merit or status than any other for a system which condoned this would make 'practical equality' unworkable. For Morris, the pleasure in the work itself would be its own reward (or as he once put forth, the reward was life itself)[228] for this would allow all the basic needs of the individual and his community to be adequately met. There would be no rich, so there could be no poor.[229]

Initially it appears that Morris was more concerned with equality of condition as an end than he was with freedom of thought and action. However, if one looks closely at his work, it is apparent that the end itself cannot be established in any practical way without the absence of coercion, that is, through liberty. Man was to gain his liberty through the struggles with dominating authorities; his freedom would be the result of his maintaining this liberty through reciprocal relationships with other members of society. As he stressed in his article, The Socialist Ideal,

> ...I know that no worthy popular art can grow out of any other soil than this of freedom and mutual respect...[230]

To have 'popular art' ("...a knife, a cup, a steam-engine or what...")[231] one must be free, but in furtherance of this freedom and if liberty from oppression was a fact, the necessity of behaving in a reciprocal fashion was paramount for without it equality would not flourish and continue to spread throughout the whole of man's personal life. The equality of condition is embodied in the spirit of production.

> All this means is that he is making the goods for himself; for his own pleasure in making and using them. But to do this he requires reciprocity, or else he will be ill-found, except in the good that he himself makes. His neighbours must make goods in the same spirit as he does;...[232]

For Morris, equality could only be achieved in a society unfettered by interfering institutions who would not allow a man to work at the tasks he believed would give him the greatest happiness. It was the spirit in which this labour (ultimately the production of art) was done which was important. A spirit which would make people long for equality of condition and would give them faith in the possibility and workableness of socialism.[233] In short, man needed faith in his ability to bring his hopes to fruition.

What is unique about Morris's ideas centres around the

relationships between men who have learned that freedom, work, and equality were wholly interconnected in the business of life. Man must work to live, to provide for himself and others. This was obvious to Morris. But he claimed that only by working in an atmosphere devoid of coercion were men at liberty to pursue their own best interests in the form of useful labour. This allowed them the initiative to freely create a product which Morris believed would be ultimately produced by "...a natural compulsion, which would prevent any man from doing what he was not fitted for, because he could not do it usefully."[234] This is important because man is not made to construct, build, or create out of any obligation which is divorced from the self, the socialist self which plays its part in the community for ethical and not political or ideological reasons. With the absence of authority and coercion, either political or economic,

> ...nothing which is made by man will be ugly, but will have its due form, and its due ornament, will tell the tale of its making and the tale of its use, even where it tells no other tale.[235]

But, one may well ask: Was equality, apart from being the desired end in one instance, necessary for the happiness of mankind? Morris was a communist because he believed communism to be the only theory of life which held equality of paramount importance. To him socialism was a 'theory of life.' The equality he spoke of was for the most part economic insofar as it was a condition of life, but it had to be accompanied by "...an ethical or religious sense of responsiblity of each man to each and all of his fellows."[236] As Morris said in the first of his four Letters on Socialism,

> Socialism aims, therefore, at realizing equality of condition as its economical goal, and habitual love of humanity as its rule of ethics.[237]

Morris did not want to see equality enforced or reinforced by either the state or a central administration but viewed it as a part of a cultural inheritance. He believed equality of condition to be a good in its own right because he thought it would produce the best possible environment for work and hence happiness and pleasure in his working relationships as well as his personal relationships. The artificial authority of the law created inequality of condition and was hence responsible, in Morris's eyes, 'for the suffering of the greater part of mankind.' Mastership, the coercive influence of one over another, created false society; 'Fellowship,' the cooperative effort between man and man in the absence of coercive influence, depended on reciprocity or equality of condition to make it realizable - the one was not possible without the other. Men working together would create enough wealth to satisfy all of their needs, needs which would not be artificially created by a monopolistic system. For as Morris stressed,

> ...and I need not say that in order to arrive at the wealth I have been speaking of we must all work usefully. But if a man does work usefully you can't do without him; and if you can't do without him you can only put him into an inferior position to another useful citizen by means of compulsion; and if you compel him to it, you at once have your privileged classes again.[238]

But if you compel him, you also have a condition of 'Mastership' over 'Fellowship,' founded on inequality rather than equality of condition. This is a libertarian argument which is put to full use by Morris. People cannot be coercively organized no matter how important the final goal. Morris has fused the idea of work as art on top of all the abstractions and ethical considerations which go hand in hand with any discussion about freedom and equality, and he shows that both could be achieved without the use of 'artificial authority'. Because Morris was an eminently practical man who worked physically as much as he contemplated, he could not disassociate himself from the appalling conditions in which many people in nineteenth century England found themselves.

It is beyond doubt that William Morris was unique within the socialist movement of the late nineteenth century. His most original theories related man's work to a happiness both within himself and within the community in which he lived. Yet Morris was in many respects outside of the mainstream and most obviously so because of his libertarian sentiments. The ideas which he expressed and the beliefs which he held about socialism were not wholly original, but the way in which he linked them together places Morris clearly apart from the main body of socialist thought in his day. His refusal to consistently adhere to any particular doctrine or writer at the expense of other possible intellectual influences was perhaps why many thought him to be an anarchist or a utopian socialist. Although he was not an anarchist, he was "...genuinely anxious to discover how [their] appetite for freedom could be reconciled with the positive side of Communism."[239] Much of what Morris said in his prose romance News From Nowhere or the more practically oriented A Factory as It Might Be is certainly contributory to utopian literature, but it does little to label Morris as a utopian thinker despite his socialism. Also, such a scholar as E. P. Thompson shows us in his book on Morris that such notions about Morris are based on an incomplete understanding of the man. Yet Thompson himself often dismisses much of Morris's original contribution to socialist literature. This originality, which rests fundamentally on Morris's appreciation of the relation between art, labour, and happiness to social and economic organization, runs continually through all of Morris's work. In 1936 even Shaw contended that Morris could not be considered a Marxist.

> Going straight to the root of Communism he held that
> people who do not do their fair share of social work are
> 'damned thieves', and that neither a stable society, a
> happy life, nor a healthy art can come from honoring such
> thieving as the mainspring of industrial activity. To
> him the notion that a British workman cannot arrive at
> this very simple fundamental conclusion except through
> the strait gate of the Marxian dialectic, or that the
> dialectic can be anything to such a one but a most
> superfluous botheration, was folly.[240]

In spite of much evidence to the contrary from those who knew
and worked with Morris, Thompson sees fit to regard Morris's
non-Marxist solutions to political, economic, and social problems as
mere logical deviations consistent with the way in which Morris led his
hectic life. Morris, unlike such theorists as Hyndman and Bax, was
truly his own man and in no way attempted to confine his theories or
ideas to any dialectical framework. But Thompson, at first claiming
that Morris "...put himself within the Marxist tradition..."[241] and
was, "...until the end of his life, 'on the side of Karl Marx contra
mundum,'"[242] goes against much of the evidence within Morris's
own writings. The only evidence from Morris himself which Thompson
cites is of a very specific kind. It was work Morris had done in
collaboration with someone else, or else it was an explanation of
Morris's personal interpretation of 'scientific socialism' according to
Marx. Morris and Bax wrote Socialism: Its Growth and Outcome and
although Thompson cites some favourable remarks which do nothing more
than show that Morris was present at the Tuesday night writing sessions
of this work, he does not quote the one positive comment which Morris
made in his Socialist Diary that "...we did our first article on Marx,
or rather he [Bax] did...".[243] Also Morris and Hyndman wrote the
Summary of the Principles of Socialism just months before Morris split

with Hyndman over his 'dictatorial nature' and his dogmatic approach to socialism. What are we to believe was the extent of Morris's contribution when he had been a socialist for only a year in collaboration with a man like Hyndman who had been active several years previously? Indeed Morris may well have been a part of the 'Marxist tradition' insofar as he admired many aspects of Marx's writings and was particularly interested in the historical parts of Kapital. But it is patently absurd to conclude that were Morris alive today "...he would not look far to find the party of his choice."[244] On the contrary, Morris would not look at all, for his belief in 'education towards revolution' precluded any such form of activity, especially in terms of party participation in the legitimate political process. As he said to the Reverend George Bainton, political parties and government were both inexorably linked to the poor condition of society.

> ...our present system is the reflection of our class society. The fact of the antagonism of classes underlies all our government, and causes political parties.[245]

Yet Thompson continues to dismiss much of Morris's original thought by saying that,

> No one familiar with Socialist theory can doubt that Morris stood squarely within the Marxist tradition, despite certain secondary circumstances which have clouded the issue...[246]

The 'secondary circumstances' are in fact the whole range of persons and events which apparently influenced or 'led' Morris away from the more dogmatic aspects of Marxism. Thompson tried to make a case against Morris's so-called 'repudiation' of Marxism. He also implied that Morris must be included in the Marxist fold. He blamed "...Scheu, Hyndman, and Bax, each of whom was closely associated with

Morris in 1883 and 1884,...[as being]...all guilty of errors which influenced his understanding."[247] Scheu was responsible for Morris's 'Leftist' leanings "...and helped to implant the 'anti-parliamentary' error in his mind."[248] Hyndman, on the other hand, "...encouraged opposition to all 'palliatives' ...and his doctrinaire use of Marx's name prompted Morris to be especially careful to avoid this kind of dogmatism,"[249] while Bax was blamed for reducing the Marxist dialectic "...to a kind of mystique."[250] Such were the people, according to Thompson, who drew Morris away from the true path of Marxism. And even though there were people around who could have helped Morris overcome these 'errors', i.e., Aveling and Carruthers, "...neither was capable of giving this guidance."[251] This was so because apparently Aveling "...tended to discard all concrete illustrations and historical exposition, and to abstract from Kapital only the 'pure economics'..."[252] (which Morris hated), while Carruthers had "...a failure in historical understanding."[253] In other words, Thompson would have us believe that all the non-Marxist sentiments of Morris were due to 'bad luck' in his choice of friends or the result of a 'false consciousness.' This form of argument or justification can be used both ways but in the way in which Thompson regrets Morris's deviations from the 'official' interpretation of Marx, we can see that he gives Morris little credit for either originality, insight, or honesty in his beliefs, as well as choosing to ignore much of what Morris actually said.

Morris "...did not like the name...Anarchist...and he never would admit the logical deductions as to government and authority upon which Anarchists insisted."[254] In 1912 his old friend Frank Kitz pointed out that,

>...since death removed this great personality from our
>midst a fictitious Morris has been created by interested
>scribes, who have invented for their own purposes a false
>legend around his memory, and seek to deprive socialism
>of the influence which his adhesion gave to the
>movement.[255]

Morris, far from being a party man as Thompson believes,
despised politics almost as much as he did statesmen, and because he
believed that the social revolution must be brought about by education
and propaganda, he forsook any alternative methods. For this reason,
at the very least, he could be included in the libertarian fold.
Shunning political parties as he did, his notion of political power was
thus altered, and he subtly divested the notion of government
(representative democracy or any other kind) by proposing a system of
direct action. Not sporadic action, or the revolt of an uneducated
populace, but total revolution with direct action as a means and an
end.

>By political power we do not mean the exercise or even
>the fullest development of the representative system, but
>the direct control by the people of the whole
>administration of the community whatever the ultimate
>destiny of that administration is to be.[256]

As political power meant direct control, so political action
meant convincing the working man, through propaganda, that the society
in which he lived was based upon his own 'intolerable burden.'[257]
The libertarian notion of responsibility looms large here for Morris
believed that only when the working man himself recognized his own
unnecessary burdens would social revolution come about. The effective
majority of people had to realize that only they could liberate
themselves and bring about equality of condition. As an individual and
as a member of the Socialist League and the Hammersmith Socialist
Society, Morris intended to help speed along the process which he did

not see as inevitable.[258]

Opposed as he was to politics as the dominating force in life, Morris eschewed the whole theoretical framework of a centralizing state socialism.[259] He demanded, as would the libertarian, 'the least possible amount of authority' and believed that wide scale decentralization was the best method of ensuring this state of affairs. Insofar as he wanted any central administration, whose function "...would be almost entirely the guardianship of the principles of society...,"[260] it had to, along with other bodies or communes, conform to the major principle of 'equality of condition.' The situation could perhaps be compared to that of the law being the guardian of law, i.e., the Rule of Law. For Morris did believe that some law or rules would be necessary, ones which "...would mostly concern the protection of the person."[261]

But Morris was not entirely content with what he termed himself "...our government of the future, which would be rather an administration of things, than a government of persons."[262] He was not comfortable with words such as government or law, not because they were of necessity such bad concepts of operation, but because the words themselves conjured up the evil and degrading circumstances of a society corrupted by private property and capitalist monopoly which worked in conjunction with a certain form of political system. He wanted the society of the future to be as free as possible from coercive influences, so that "...nations as political entities would cease to exist."[263] His libertarian sentiments, so close to those expressed in Kropotkin's Anarchist Morality, took him far beyond all ideas of rule or hierarchy. The aims of socialism were clear to Morris.

> So that we should tend to the abolition of all
> government, and even of all regulations that are not
> really habitual; and voluntary association would become
> a necessary habit and the only bond of society.[264]

This is what William Morris wanted to see, and his expression
of these opinions and hopes are clearly and straightforwardly set out
in his letters to the Reverend George Bainton. They are without doubt
the most compassionate and personal statements made by Morris on the
topic of socialism in the total human context. In spite of his
associations with the S.D.F., the long drawn out disputes with the
factions in the Socialist League, and the failure of his final
initiative towards socialist unity, Morris remained optimistic until
his death. He never lost the hope that there would be a more just
society in a socialistic future. As Shaw remembered, Morris was only
one of many powerful personalities who espoused socialist ideas in the
late nineteenth century, but "...not one of them could propagate his
vision of the life to come on a happy earth and his values that went so
much deeper into eternity than the surplus value of Marx. This vision
only he himself could propagate...."[265] His vision of himself as
'an idle singer of an empty day,' although reflecting a scene which
Morris rarely encountered, serves to remind us of a man who literally
worked himself to death in the cause of 'Fellowship.' Even at his
lowest point, during the breakup of the Socialist League, Morris
refused to give up the struggle.

> ...some of [us]...once believed in the inevitableness of
> a sudden and speedy change. That was no wonder with the
> new enlightenment of Socialism gilding the dullness of
> civilization for us. But if we must now take soberer
> views of our hopes, do not reproach us with that.[266]

CHAPTER THREE

LIBERTARIAN PROPAGANDA AND PERSONALITIES IN ENGLAND

Libertarians in England

In moving from the energetic and passionate devotion of one man
whose expression of libertarian ideas made him both a unique and
influential figure within the wider movement, we do not leave him
behind but expand upon his own milieu. William Morris, along with
other socialists such as H. M. Hyndman, remained in the spotlight most
of his life, but there were many other fascinating revolutionaries
active during the same period, many of whom were still young men when
Morris died in 1896; their contributions to the movement and
literature, however, are not well known, and on many occasions very
difficult to document. Among the more prominent members of this group
were the exiles who came to London to escape persecution in their
native lands. Kropotkin had come to London as an exile in 1885 and
remained for virtually the rest of his life;[1] Errico Malatesta, an
Italian born in 1853, was in London on many occasions before he finally
settled in Islington in 1900 for a stay of 19 years;[2] and Rudolph
Rocker, a German emigre, arrived in the city at the age of twenty-one
in 1895, remaining long enough to be interned during the First World
War.[3] In the native English contingent were such people as Edward
Carpenter,[4] Charlotte M. Wilson,[5] Frank Kitz,[6] and Joseph
Lane,[7] who had familiarized themselves with the state of the
English radical movement at a time when such groups as the Social

Democratic Federation, the Socialist League, the Freedom Group, and the Fabian Society were competing for the intellectual leadership of a movement which had remained essentially dormant since the days of Chartism in 1848.

It is general knowledge that England was the physical and intellectual haven for a considerable number of foreign exiles and unconventional thinkers in the late nineteenth century. Most had wanted to return to their homelands and take up the struggle on more familiar ground, yet although they exported propaganda to other countries, they were significantly active in the political and social issues of the day in what had become their adopted homeland. There is little doubt that when these persons joined forces with the radicals and revolutionaries of 'underground' England, they made a considerable impression on the literature and ideas of the libertarian movement. At the very least they helped to establish international organizational connections which aided in the diffusion of essential propaganda, and they translated works of informational and theoretical importance into English. These publications were meant for the consumption of a native population whom many foreigners regarded as having little in the way of a revolutionary tradition.

The lives and ideas of both English and refugee libertarians have gone largely unnoticed until now, not just because these men failed to become political leaders or influential spokesmen but because they were men whose whole consciousness rebelled against this kind of traditional recognition. They were, above all, men of exceptional principle who did not consider political success as an adequate or necessary contribution to social transformation. Although men like Morris and Shaw are still well known, it is for reasons other than their political views that they became 'famous' in the public mind. But to the countless others who toiled in the propagation of libertarian ideas, time has not been so kind. These people form a part of what Herbert Read has called 'underground history,' a history which applies to many other groups besides the libertarian movement.

> History is of two kinds – a record of events that take place publicly, that make headlines in the newspapers and get embodied in official records – we might call this overground history. [But]...taking place at the same time, preparing for these public events, anticipating them, is another kind of history, that is not embodied in official records, an invisible underground history.[8]

To men with a revolutionary aim the official records and newspapers were seen as allies of the major institutions within the state; the press regurgitated the dominant mores of those in the establishment, those with economic and political power. To those living in and fighting against the English constitutional system, politicians appeared as all too willing pawns within the institutions which aided and condoned the landowners and capitalists, the classes who had a stake in British Imperial Policy abroad and the exploitation of the working classes at home.

Of course there are reports and records of the 'underground' men, collected by the Home Office and the criminal courts.[9] Many are still inaccessible.[10] Invaluable as they are in terms of the operation of criminal proceedings, and the personal descriptions supplied by arresting officers these are hardly of a kind which would enable one to build up an adequate picture of the men and their work.

There were also newspaper articles and stories about the revolutionaries of the day, sometimes linking them to an act of violence abroad as well as subversive behaviour in the streets of London.[11] Many articles and headlines were meant to denigrate personalities and their ethnic origins as well as cast aspersions upon the functions of the social clubs in which they met.[12] Newspapers placed actions such as marching and lecturing in a perspective entirely hostile to the issues to which the libertarians were drawing attention, consequently depicting their activity as being socially harmful. Fleet Street was, on the whole, totally unsympathetic and misinformative as to the driving force of the movement and tended to characterize it as senseless opposition by a group of malcontents and violent troublemakers. The true nature of the men concerned and their major goals in life were not discussed at all. One reason for this was that their social work did not make good copy. But the hostility of Fleet Street was so persistent that it is hard to believe that the editors were not subject to less than covert political pressure from various quarters.[13]

This spirit of dogmatic prejudice infected even the radical press itself: Justice could not refrain from making comments about the Commonweal, nor for that matter could Freedom or The Anarchist.[14] This came about, however, only after these journals had been established for some time and, on the whole, when comrades criticized one another the issue always revolved around some theoretical point or a clash of personalities. But before this time, when the socialist groups and particularly the libertarians and anarchists were officially denigrated, it was an urgent necessity for them to create their own communications network for the sake of propaganda and information. By the mid-1880s such an underground press began to establish itself.

This experience proved that men of minority views, even when conversing with their own kind, are not easily popular. And when these views appear to threaten the moral and political values of a highly developed nation, an effective way of discrediting them is through incessant propaganda and harassment rather than through overt coercion. Many of the emigres who were familiar with the tyranny of the Czar in Russia, the repressive legal system in France, or the government of Bismarck's Germany failed to recognize the subtleness of the English political system. Yet they did not react violently towards it. As a result, the major confrontations in Britain at this time were in the press and in certain celebrated court cases.[15] There were demonstrations and strikes, but never a case of bomb-throwing, assassination, or mass-murder by the revolutionists of London. England, compared to most other countries, was a forum for ideas of all possible shades, but even so, certain ideas and forms of expression were opposed much more than others. The extent to which free speech could and would be tolerated was put to the test in the years 1886-7 which saw mob action by the unemployed, the Dod Street Affair,[16] the arrest 'for obstruction' of numerous outdoor speakers,[17] and the fiasco of November 13, 1887 which took place in Trafalgar Square and was known as 'Bloody Sunday.'[18] Yet because of the preponderance of opposition to the libertarians within the socialist movement itself, many of their ideas never reached an informed or wide audience. And while their strength was sapped by poor organization, their cause was further hindered by the police suppression of the libertarian press, as in the instances of the court orders against Freedom, Arbeter Fraint, and the Commonweal.[19]

But censorship and harassment cannot be accepted as the major excuse or reason for the rapid decline of the libertarian movement up until World War I. We cannot assume, as is often done, that minority opinion (and this was a minority within a minority), when not sanctioned by political forces or mass organized support, is destined to failure. Compromise, as the tool of political concession, was the method of the libertarians. Thus, for example, they were staunch anti-parliamentarians because they firmly believed that the electoral process would not lead to the desired goal; i.e., the emancipation of the working classes. They wanted to be a part of a social and the political movement which would abolish both capitalistic and governmental monopoly. Hence they believed that they ought not to join in the legitimate political process or accept institutional concessions in order to gain their ends.

One reason for the apparent obscurity of the libertarians even to this day is partly due to the fact that they were dismissed as persons opposed to the Marxist creed and later swamped by the growing tide of what Cole called the 'New Unionism.'[20] Little research has been done in the field of libertarian thought because it is generally believed that the libertarians made no lasting contribution to the labour movement except to split it up at crucial times in its history. This belief is not upheld by research into the evidence. True the libertarians would not accept political 'palliatives' but they were amongst the most active members of those groups of men who helped organize and educate the workers so that they could challenge the system from a position of strength. Even though many continued at that time to deny or play down the role and need for a strong trades union movement in the struggle for reform, they did assist in its formation, even though at the same time they insisted that the labour movement should not be affiliated to a single political party. They were seeking revolution and not radical reform. They continued in opposition to piecemeal planning and the struggle for legitimate political power.

The libertarians and communist anarchists who took the stand against political participation in elections, the institutional arrangements of party politics, and the idea of parliamentary representation were not alone in their opposition. But in these respects they differed widely in their views from the Social Democratic Party, the followers of the secularist Charles Bradlaugh, and the Fabian Society. The major groups which were the main core of the libertarian movement were the communist-anarchists of the Freedom Group, the majority of the membership of the Socialist League, including those in its various branches throughout the country, and the more individually minded anarchist group around Henry Seymour and his paper The Anarchist. Surrounding these were other smaller groups, which, when they were made up of a majority of the working class, constituted area radical clubs. These would include such clubs as: the Communist Club, the Tower Hamlets Radical Club, the Scandinavian Workingmen's Clubs of London, the Sheffield Socialists, the Clay Cross Socialists, and the Dublin Labour League which were but a few of the workingmen's clubs active in 1887. On the other hand, there were a lot of clubs of a more academic and middle-class membership who, although they often fought for a prominent single issue, were continually active during the many social campaigns of the latter part of the nineteenth century. Among these were the National Secular Society, the Radical Federation, the Fellowship of New Life, and the Legitimation League, all of whom had libertarians and libertarian sympathizers within their ranks. The latter groups, because of their origins, usually had more financial backing than the working class clubs and were thus able to publish their own journals and pamphlets which provided a platform for the poorer groups. Middle class publications did not rely so heavily upon journal sales to boost their finances. Although important in their own areas of activity, the foreign workingmen's clubs most often tended to their own community ethnic need rather than those of the English working class. The exception to this was the Jewish East End Arbeter Fraint Group, who, in the end, were the most effective of all the British anarchist groups in visibly contributing to social change.[21]

Most of these groups saw their mission in the enlightenment of the mass of people who tended then to see oppression and poverty as the natural condition of the working class. They sought to educate and agitate for revolutionary change, believing that the revolution could only succeed as a complement of mass social consciousness. Aside from the fact that their educational ideas did not reach a majority of the populace, it is also true that all of the radicals at that time were fighting for the ear of the same group of persons, notably the newly enfranchised. Since the Reform Bill of 1884 the Tories and Liberals, appearing to be much the same, had to contend with the radical liberals who had a strong organized following. The state socialists attempted to wean this group but also wanted to gather the working man into the fold. This politicized groups, such as the S.D.F., who were anxious to make an immediate impact. Their predilection for electoral politics and piecemeal reform separated them from the libertarian socialists who followed Morris from the S.D.F. to form the Socialist League. The libertarians attempted to reach to all who would listen. But with all these forces vying for committed membership from the same 'floating' group, splits were inevitable, and it was the group with the best

organization rather than the most popular ideas which was most likely
to succeed. The libertarians, contrary to Morris's hopes, never
attained that position of strength.

Many of the libertarian postulates, especially those pertaining
to worker's control and devolution, women's rights, marriage and
birth-control -- those which are now recognized as being socially and
morally advantageous to society -- were in their time too progressive
for the normal electoral parties whose main aim was to stay in
power.[22] But as the years passed, many of these ideas were
summarily incorporated into various manifestos and white papers by the
very constituency which had rejected them in the non-political sphere.
Yet we must recognize the extent to which socially progressive, though
perhaps politically imprudent, ideas were part of the libertarian
platform long before they were accepted as viable political
propositions. Never in a position of power as the arbiters of moral or
social doctrines, the libertarians were sapped of their strength by
those who incorporated libertarian ideas under a different banner. As
Rudolf Rocker readily admitted in his autobiography The London Years,
-- at the end of almost four decades of struggle it was "...the War and
communism which drew off the great strength of the Syndicalist movement
in Britain,..." as its failure was not wholly due to internal
dissension within the organizational structure itself.[23]

At a time when literacy was one of the most obvious yardsticks
of social mobility in an expanding economy, the cheap use of print
allowed thoughts, ideas, and ideals to become the common property of
all those who cared to take the time to assimilate them. The printed
word became for many a justification, not only of past and present
action, but began to suggest a vision of the future.[24]

It was the underground press and socialist press which were most consistent in their critique of society and government and which were still able to propose solutions for change. These solutions varied from the basest of individualistic anarchy to the most tightly controlled of state administrations which would abolish all private property .[25] People were bombarded on all sides with various 'truths' and 'programmes' which promised to cure all social ills. Merely by reading and joining in the public debate one was able to follow the formula of one's choosing and still have the authority of the written word or an organization to back it up. It was indeed a time of transition and transmission in new ideas. For the thirty years prior to World War I everybody had a story to tell, and the extent to which they could tell it depended upon resources, which in turn depended upon their following. The debate on the need for drastic social change gained momentum in the 1880s, and the libertarians had as much of a start in this race as the rest of the propagandists. The story is one of success and failure.

Libertarian Propaganda

Education through propaganda was one of the main aims of libertarian activism. The motto of the Socialist League - 'Educate - Agitate - Organize' encapsulated what had to be done by the revolutionaries to get their message across to the mass of people. It took, most importantly, organization, to achieve the propaganda objectives of education and agitation.

The propaganda of agitation usually brings to mind lending bodily support to one activity or another whether it be open-air demonstrations and rallies, attending lectures and commemorative celebrations, recruiting members to the cause, or selling literature.

In fact, agitation meant the effectual dedication of a person to the propagation of a certain set of ideas on every occasion possible, whether it be arguing with a friend in a pub or standing with unsympathetic or misinformed comrades on the picket line. To agitate was to be continually on the move, making an occupation out of talking, listening, and arguing. It was a task for the committed for it demanded much more time and devotion, with less tangible reward than writing articles and pamphlets or editing an organizational journal. The thousands of ordinary people who devoted themselves to this form of activity left few records behind but they are an instantly identifiable source of libertarian propaganda.[26]

The propaganda of education, although not wholly unconnected with agitation, was more properly left to those lecturers, journalists, and writers who used their particular skills before a mass audience. Most of those who wrote also lectured, even though in many cases they should have left it to more competent speakers. William Morris, for example, although he wrote fascinating poetry and chants, was still able to write about political and social issues which he then spoke on, usually from notes. But he was not a good speaker and as Frank Kitz reminds us,

> So convinced was he of the utility of open air propaganda that he stood by my side on many a windy inclement night at the corner of the same wretched East End slum whilst I endeavoured to gain him an audience by addressing a few listless stragglers as 'the working class of England...' he was no great orator.[27]

But it is interesting to note that, invaluable as Morris's articles and pamphlets were to the cause of socialist propaganda, his efforts were not appreciated by some of the working class revolutionary elements in the Socialist League. According to the editors of Freedom of October-November 1892, who were commenting on the then recent demise of the Commonweal, Morris was forced from the editorship because "the majority of the League thought that Morris's style was too much over the heads of the people." Could it have been his Oxford education?

It must be remembered that the journalists and pamphleteers were not writing for posterity, for their very raison d'etre was to preach and to expose to others a new way of looking at the world. Success in this mission was reward in itself, for it made them the legitimate forebearers of a set of ideas which could be more generally expressed to the public at large. This was the first object of the propaganda of education. The second was to convert the sympathetic and teach the ignorant. All of this called for organization by those who were active in every form of propaganda, and, being the heart and soul of any movement, are destined to be called the activists.

The Activists

The language of the activist tends to be much more emotive and cliche-ridden than that of his more restrained fellow-travellers. For this reason one may well say that such blatant propaganda has little academic interest. Yet all information imparted in a cause is in essence propaganda, meant to cajole and stimulate its audience. We must look behind the words even of the most vulgar propagandists to learn about the libertarian movement of the time.

We must discover what types of persons were involved in activist endeavours and to what degree they were motivated by things other than those they admitted. In fact, we must attempt to discover what their actual interests were. Were the people involved just foreign malcontents? Were they agents provocateurs, or disgruntled criminals? Were they the unemployed and dispossessed, or just hotheaded students and the 'radical chic' of the day? And finally, did they represent the opinions and beliefs of anyone but themselves or were they the spokesmen of a larger movement?

Although the activists were on the whole men of ideas, they were themselves largely drawn from the class which they sought to help first and foremost; i.e., the working class. As a result, many of their arguments were developed in conjunction with their activities, for rarely did they enter the struggle in any ideologically committed manner. Rather, they seemed to be drawn into it as a result of the times and circumstances of their work, while their links with particular organizations assured that their voices would be heard in one way or another.

Three of the most notorious members of the Socialist League, those who took it into the anarchist fold, were men of indisputable working class origin: Joseph Lane, Frank Kitz, and David Nicoll. Lane, a carter, was seventeen when he first came to London and by the time of the First International in 1871, had already been active in the Manhood Suffrage League, an organization which sought to extend the vote to all males over the age of eighteen. At the age of twenty-eight he founded the Labour Emancipation League whose main platform was the complete nationalization of land. From this time onwards (1878) Lane, who had come into contact with Kitz in the L.E.L., associated with any group who was attempting to get organized socialist propaganda into the public arena. In 1881 he formed the Homerton Social Democratic Club, while remaining Secretary of the L.E.L. In that same year he went as a delegate from the H.S.D.C. to the International Anarchist Congress which was being held in London.[28] Shortly thereafter he concluded that the newly formed S.D.F. was performing a valuable service to the socialist cause, and he became a member of the Executive Committee in 1884, but left with Morris and others six months later to form the Socialist League early in 1885. E. P. Thompson has claimed that Lane "...was for several years to exercise some influence over Morris's political views,"[29] and the extent to which this may be true could be summed up in May Morris's words many years later that "Joe Lane was an uncompromising anarchist, but a dear."[30] Nonetheless, as Lane was one of the major anti-parliamentarians within the Socialist League until he left in the late 1880s, we can well assume that Morris was sympathetic to many of his ideas.[31]

Frank Kitz was brought up by his mother in and around Soho. By trade, he was a dyer, and in his late teens walked the southern counties searching for employment, and when he could not find it, he would enlist at various army recruiting offices under a false name, collect his first week's wages, then desert. He was never caught.[32] He, more than Lane, was obsessed with the question of Land Nationalization and was determined to put his views across at any cost. Describing the first printing shop he ever set up in 1879, while he was still affiliated to the Manhood Suffrage League and the Labour Emancipation League, Kitz says that it was done "...with a view to starting a no rent agitation and an onslaught against landlordism...."[33]

> The furnishing of 'the printery' (Boundary Street, Shoreditch) was a model of economy and simplicity. Our seating accommodation was made of packing cases provided upon the involuntary plan. A paving stone was our making-up stone and ink-slab combined. Candles stuck in the composing cases was our lighting installation; and a roller hand press our machinery.
>
> From this primitive establishment we issued the leaflets 'Fight or Starve', an appeal to the unemployed; the Malthusians; the 'Revenge' leaflet...and many others,

notably the 'Appeal to the Army, Navy and Police'...which found its way into several garrison towns.[34]

For a short time in 1881 Kitz edited the English version of Freiheit while Johann Most was on trial. The two men had been close from the mid-1870s when Kitz had founded the English equivalent of the German oriented Rose Street Club. Most left England in 1883 after serving eighteen months and Kitz, in 1885, joined the Socialist League, became its Secretary in 1889 and acted as co-editor, with David Nicoll, of the Commonweal. After the demise of Commonweal in 1892, Kitz, having adopted the Shaw penchant for wearing Jaegar suits, threw his lot in with the Freedom Group.

Although both Lane and Kitz declared for communist anarchism in the early 1880s, David Nicoll, having passed through the S.D.F., did not declare himself as such until the latter half of the decade. His origins are unclear, but by 1888, at the age of thirty-four, he was a definite fire-brand prominent in Socialist League activities on the anti-parliamentarian side.[35] Nicoll's main claim to notoriety, however, lies in the fact that he was successfully prosecuted (and served 18 months) for 'incitement to murder.' After the harsh sentences handed out to the Walsall Anarchists, he stated in Commonweal (April 1892) that the judge in the case "was not fit to live."[36] His prison experience seems to have deranged him to some extent, for upon his release he discovered that Commonweal had been taken over by his former colleague H. B. Samuels, whom he later denounced as a police spy. He failed to get control of what was left of the paper and moved to Sheffield in 1896 where for a while he edited The Anarchist. But he was unable to hold a steady job and had little, if any, effect on the movement after this time. His vehemence towards the oppressors of the working-class verged on the paranoic. Yet as a result of his trial, at least his description has been left with us. At the time he "was 38 years old, stood five feet seven inches, and had a moustache and dark brown hair cut close."[37] For all his bombast he was not the caricature of the bomb-thrower. He died, half-mad and in poverty, in the St. Pancras infirmary on March 2, 1919.

The activists, whatever their origins, were doers, who intended to influence others to emulate their particular brand of action and approach to life.[38] They believed that the coercive nature of the state would, in the end, force it to use every means at its disposal to eliminate those elements, including themselves, who were bent on its destruction. If the institutions of the state could be made to react violently to activist pressures, then the activists thought that the violent aspects of state control could be made more apparent to the average person. The activists were prepared to use force as a method of self-defence, and to this end they professed that it was justifiable. Disobedience to the law, if necessary, was but a legitimate means for bringing about social change, if and when a great number of people could be convinced to behave in such a manner. Only by acting on his own behalf could the workingman emancipate himself -- but he must do it without the aid of politicians and governmental institutions.[39] Malatesta made this point clearly.

> In our opinion all action which is directed towards the destruction of economic and political oppression, which serves to raise the moral and intellectual level of the people; which gives them an awareness of their individual rights and their power, and persuades them themselves to act on their own behalf;...brings us closer to our ends and is therefore a good thing. On the other hand all activity which tends to preserve the present state of affairs, that tends to sacrifice man against his will for the triumph of a principle, is bad because it is a denial of our ends. We seek the triumph of freedom and

love...[40]

To many of the activists, philosophical debates about evolution, population control, and economic theories were of little consequence unless they affected the immediate situation in which men found themselves.[41] They maintained that specific answers or solutions could not be rigidly proposed until revolutionary change had established a new and peculiar state of affairs, which meant, in essence, the destruction of institutionalized authority in both the economic and political spheres. But what was essential was a desire for change, a swing of conscious action aimed at upsetting the status quo -- a change in the consciousness of the ordinary man who was, in most instances, too busy trying to survive economically to be able to think of ideal futures. The question was -- could the system as it stood, or through institutional evolution, solve the economic and social problems of the working class? The libertarians believed it could not, but they did not underestimate the formidable task of promoting such change. As Alexander Berkman, a communist anarchist who had tried assassination as a means to his ends, reminded everyone in his Prison Memoirs, democratic states were amongst the most difficult in which to take action. Most of the activists had no faith in the political system as it stood in England at this time; Berkman[42] was only one among many who realized the problems involved in fighting for a new idea of freedom within a supposedly democratic regime.

> The real despotism of republican institutions is far deeper, more insidious, because it rests on the popular delusion of self-government and independence. This is the subtle source of democratic tyranny, and as such, it cannot be reached with a bullet.[43]

According to the libertarians, the ordinary man had to be taught that a better system was not only possible, but within his grasp. Allowing for this, the route to success lay in organization and solidarity with one's fellow workers, and the best way to do this was to form non-political unions. These would be tied to no party or outside interest but would enshrine the principle of participatory democracy.[44] A. Roller,[45] in describing the intricacies of a working system of this sort in his pamphlet The Social General Strike, points out, much like Morris, the visualized end of production.

> After the period of transition work will again become art, because it will be executed free from compulsion and restraint and as art it will, as every art does, give pleasure and satisfaction to the worker and so will the mere pleasure to produce be the mightiest impulse and surest guarantee for all working artists, and a splendid inspirer, sufficient for all necessities.[46]

The activists of the libertarian movement gave their time and energy to this ideal as they worked with the working class and unemployed. They lived and worked in the industrial areas of Sheffield, Manchester, Leeds, and Glasgow, sharing the common needs and desires of those to whom they spoke.

Among those activists who engaged in journalism many could in no way be construed as members of the working class as we understand the term. Morris's friend, John Carruthers, was a distinguished consulting engineer and student of economics.[47] J. L. Joynes was a former classics master at Eton,[48] who wrote for the Commonweal and intended to become a doctor to help the poor. Unfortunately, despite his strict vegetarianism, his health broke down and he died without achieving his ambition. Joynes's brother-in-law, Henry H. Salt, gave up his position as master at Eton to write for both Justice and the Commonweal and later became the founder and leader of the Humanitarian League.[49] And of course there was Edward Carpenter, said to be the direct inspiration for much of D. H. Lawrence's best work.[50] Left an inheritance of 7000 pounds by his father who was a Brighton magistrate, Carpenter left his Fellowship at Trinity Hall, Cambridge, for a life of vegetarianism and simplicity at Millthorp, near Sheffield. He wrote several books of prose and poetry and continued to be active in radical circles throughout his life.[51] He is generally acknowledged as having been the first to introduce the sandal to England[52] and is an interesting example of the alienated but militant homosexual.[53]

Thus here we have a very different group of men who worked in conjunction with men like Lane and Kitz who never made it into any political arena, as well as with men like Tom Mann, John Burns, and Jack Williams who were superb working class orators who never hesitated to lend their support to the institutionalized and more political side of any controversy.[54] It was their devotion to the cause of socialism which drove these men on, even though in the end many could not be designated as being libertarian. What was important is that, on the whole, they all worked together for revolutionary change.

With the journalists who were activists there was a constant intermingling and continual debate as to what ideas should go forth and how they should be expressed in relation to the general theories which they were propounding. As a result we get the Fabian Shaw writing in The Anarchist,[55] Engels, just a year after Marx's death, contributing to the Commonweal,[56] and E. Balfort Bax, one of Morris's closest allies, explaining socialist economics in the pages of Justice, which Morris himself was to do again in the 1890s. The network of 'exchange journalism' extended to Europe, America, and even to Australia.[57]

This international connection was boosted by a third category of individuals who made most of their contributions in the form of pamphlets and books. The pamphlets were cheap, usually a penny, could be circulated in bulk, and easily distributed at rallies, meetings, and lectures throughout the world. They were usually sold to groups by the quire to encourage maximum distribution with the minimum of postal expense. These are of primary importance because they were usually presented as the best aspects of the entire journalistic onslaught. Many of the more inferior pamphlets dealt with specific issues and tried to relate certain 'facts' which were not generally acknowledged by the conventional press of the time. This was particularly true of the events surrounding the Paris Commune, the Haymarket Affair, and the Walsall Anarchists. But most were statements of principle of a wider interest and were sold as adjuncts to the more regular and predictable opinions of the journals and newspapers. They were, in the main, exploratory works meant to give the reader a groundwork of information from which he could interpret the sum total of information to which he was subjected.

These pamphlets were published by the many radical societies or else by various 'labour press' groups which dotted the country and who were willing to publish for the sake of propaganda rather than profit. They will be discussed in more detail in the next section; we are here interested in the authors and some of the things they said and did.

Most of the libertarian journalists were not prepared to work within the political system, for they were convinced, almost as much as those who took to the streets, that only through social action could political change be secured. Hence, they did not demand reform but hoped for a complete transformation in social _mores_ emanating from the actions of the working classes. They were promoting their propaganda towards a situation in which the workers could control their own destinies rather than be mere participants, representatives, or followers of a new working class elite who defined their own interests in terms of political expediency and compromise. They demanded industrial democracy whereby those who worked, owned, and controlled the means of production and could contribute first and foremost to the community in which they lived and not to the larger entity - the state. This was not a rebellion against the system, nor a means of seeking concessions. It was a revolutionary attitude meant to serve the positive aspirations of those who produced the wealth of the country but had not received their fair share. The libertarians maintained that the workers must enjoy the fruits of their own labour through their community in order to attain greater personal autonomy and happiness. To be revolutionary was to act thus.

George Barrett, an Edinburgh mathematician, in a pamphlet entitled The Anarchist Revolution, attempted to show how this was possible and how revolutionary action was different from some forms of narrow self-interested rebellion.

> To come out on strike, then, is merely rebellion, and is essentially not the revolution, however thoroughly it is done; to stay in and work, in the condition of equality, free from the dictates of a useless master class, is the real objective of the revolutionist.[58]

Barrett does not mean to suggest that the anarcho-syndicalist concept of the General Strike is useless; it was indeed widely recognized as a method of consolidating working-class interests. But he suggested that the General Strike would not be effective unless the workers took physical possession and occupied the factories. J. Blair Smith, in his pamphlet Direct Action Versus Legislation, made much the same point. He believed that in the face of a prolonged and continued struggle the combination of occupation and the General Strike would be sure to bring down the government of the day. But although serving obvious political ends, the action was essentially meant to destroy centralized power in its economic as well as political form. The social upheaval ought to be a continuing process with the dual aim of eradicating institutionalized authority and inequality. There was no one theoretical scheme for the achievement of these aims since it was the workers who would decide the direction and scope of their actions. Unlike the Marxists, the libertarians did not seek political power but social justice through the devolution of economic control. This meant that the workers, and not a politicized elite who claimed proxy rights, would have to control the means of production. All of this called for coordinated individual direct action.

> Direct action...in this strict revolutionary sense would mean the taking possession of the means of production and the necessities of life by the workers, and the reorganization of industry according to the principles of freedom.[59]

According to most libertarian thinkers, the reorganization of industry could not be achieved satisfactorily with governmental interference (or "help"), since government, in seeking to maintain its own constitutional position and in presumably acting in the interests of all the people, could not satisfy the needs of specific sectors of the population. And, in reality, certain sections of the populace have more political and economic power than is just. This is reflected in the political system. If government is taken to be what it defines itself to be, i.e., representative of the majority but protector of the minority, then governmental interference at the level of the worker's control of industry could only lead to compromise and reformism.

Moreover, according to the libertarians, it is unrealistic to expect the government to arbitrate when it logically pretends to represent the interests of both parties to a dispute. The workers must disassociate themselves from either centralized or governmental control.[60]

Yet, by the use of direct action, it is maintained that such a conflict of interest that is inherent in government interference can be avoided. The confrontation between capital and labour could not be avoided, but since there are no equal parties between capital and labour, this would be inevitable if the principal of equality of condition were to be acted upon. The owners of capital would be treated as equal partners, or in other words, as but one or two amongst many. Governmental interference would only complicate matters and prolong social injustice through the payment of compensation, or else it would tie the workers, through the payment of subsidies, to its own centralist policies. The libertarian propagandists believed that working problems ought to be solved at the local level, between those directly involved, so as to give the highest social advantage to all concerned. In this manner of localized action, major class confrontation could be avoided, and all-out class war would be a less distinct possibility if certain forms of interference ceased to predominate. It was up to the libertarians, in their speeches, journals and pamphlets, to convince the workers that any government presuming to act in their interests would only compromise their position of solidarity. Therefore, it was argued, the workers must seek the disestablishment of government as well as the capitalist system, both of which kept them chained to the economic bonds of a centralized system.

Through this rather circuitous method we reach the more

anarchistic of the libertarian views. One view is that government is but an unnecessary hindrance on the path to economic equity.[61]

> Anarchism is the No Government theory of Socialism: the doctrine which teaches that people can only be truly happy and prosperous when tyrannical authority is abolished and freedom and comradeship prevail.[62]

The anarchists claim that just as it has been shown that society would not collapse without the spiritual leadership of the established church, so it can be shown that the state is an outmoded adjunct in the pursuit of social harmony. The propaganda and common beliefs about the state sustain its own mythical position in the hierarchical scale of social values, aided and abetted by those in positions of political and economic power who use its institutions to protect their own interests. If people overcome the superstition that government is necessary to greater human development, as they have already done with the church, their lives will be enriched to the degree by which freedom of action and expression is enlarged. What must be removed are those vested interests which stagnate the productive force of the ordinary working man. The libertarian is, in the end, fighting against authority in its most all-embracing and coercive forms -- a direct challenge to the power of the state and its institutions and all of those who benefit from the deification of its laws.

On the whole, the activists with whom we are dealing, once initiated into the struggle, became lifelong converts to the cause of social revolution. From the time of their conversion remarkably few forsook their revolutionary activities, or joined in the process of government.[63] Given the limited development of public transportation at the time, their movements throughout the world were

of an impressive nature, for they travelled on three continents
spreading the word and joining up with conferences and congresses in
support of revolutionary action. London, thanks to the liberal
policies of successive English governments, was the freest hub of the
intellectual movement. Virtually all the activists came to London at
one time or another. Many of the activists emigrated;[64] some were
imprisoned in England[65] and abroad;[66] some died in the pursuit
of the millenium;[67] while others disappeared into the hinterlands
to broaden the base of their activities or to retire from the
limelight.[68] For the most part they shunned leadership roles even
within their own movement. Different individuals 'led' for specific
reasons -- Kropotkin because he was a moral and intellectual giant and
the inheritor of the Russian revolutionary tradition; Morris because of
his literary and artistic talents (he was offered - and turned down the
Chair of Poetry at Oxford, and the Poet Laureateship); Rocker, because
of his organizing abilities. Each made his own particular contribution
to the libertarian tradition.

The young French philosopher, Jean Marie Guyau, who greatly
impressed Kropotkin with his book A Sketch of Morality Independent of
Obligation or Sanction, summed up the feelings of many activists and,
in his own way, apologized for those philosophical souls who spread the
word in a more sedate 'intellectual' fashion.

> ...there is no true morality but in action, and if to
> abstain is to act, that is, by this very reason,
> departure from equilibrium.[69]

To Guyau, equilibrium was not a desirable object in itself as
it had been for Proudhon since equilibrium could be interpreted as a
form of societal stagnation. The result of deliberate action was to
encourage a new state of affairs and to change the balance of societal

mores in favour of freedom and equality, but this balance did not in itself preclude continual flux and change. The resultant activity which arose out of 'non-action' was thus a form of action, somewhat in the tradition of Thoreau and Tolstoi.

But violent action was not central to the tradition of the English libertarians whose great strength lay in the relative freedom to present their arguments to as wide an audience as they could muster. They were as much obsessed with organization as they were with agitation and propaganda, but, on the whole, they did not engage in the violent behaviour of their foreign comrades. England was virtually untouched by the violence of the later nineteenth century which was made a cause celebre in America, France, Switzerland, Spain, and Russia. But the libertarians in England often sympathized with the motives of foreign terrorists although they, in most cases, agreed that the same methods were not acceptable in the British context. Since Britain was one of the least repressive countries in the world at the time, the political atmosphere did not demand such stark solutions. Yet those libertarians whose sentiments were vehemently opposed to the use of violence found themselves still condemned under the same general banner of 'anarchists' or 'destructionists' because, it was said, their non-authoritarian views logically gave support to violent methods.

Errico Malatesta, throughout his life, was but one of the men who clearly distinguished between political and criminal acts. According to him, political acts were defensive mechanisms to be used for the protection of one's person against any institutional coercive element. He contended, as an anarchist, that "...the main plank of anarchism is the removal of violence from human relations."[70] But revolutionary violence could be justified, on moral grounds, in a society which proclaimed the necessity for inequality and whose social relations were themselves based on violence. However, as can be seen from the following statement which he made as late as 1921, Malatesta had no hesitation about jumping from the particular to the general.

> Violence is justifiable only when it is necessary to defend oneself and others from violence. It is where necessity ceases that crime begins.
>
> We are therefore enemies of the State which is the coercive, violent, organization of society.[71]

Such statements do not, in effect, support 'propaganda by the deed' although it was rare for libertarians to outrightly condemn the professed motives of those who threw bombs into cafes and assassinated heads of state. Some papers, such as the Belgian Drapeau Noir which circulated in England, encouraged revolutionaries to use individual terror in the propagation of their principles. But like Johann Most's paper Die Freiheit, which came out of Soho for a time, this was in no way representative of anarchist or libertarian teachings. For some time, while David Nicoll was editor of the Commonweal, he allowed what he later claimed to be agents provocateurs to use its pages for their own purposes. He was criticized by other anarchists for this who said,

> It is time to prevent these milk-and-water people from speaking in the name of Anarchy if we do not wish to fall into a greater slumber than we are in already.[72]

With reference to this, Nicoll later explained why Coulon (one supposed agent provocateur) was finally silenced.

> I am an Anarchist and believe in unlimited free speech, even from "milk and water orators." This is why I, in my capacity as editor, endured Coulon's "Dynamite" notes so long in spite of remonstrances from several comrades. At last, however, my patience gave way. At length he sent me in a paragraph celebrating the blowing up of a cow in Belgium as a great and revolutionary act, and as I would not publish it, Coulon has never forgiven me.[73]

This in itself says much for the kind of individuals involved in professedly violent acts or who sought to incite others to carry them out. Such aggressive sentiments were, in the extreme, wholly unlibertarian for they stressed the autonomy of the individual and his acts to such an extent that ideas about man in the community shrank into insignificance.[74]

Although the possibility of violence was accepted by many, including William Morris and Edward Carpenter, Peter Kropotkin, and Charlotte Wilson, it played a small part in their overall doctrines. As a fact it had to be dealt with, but knowing that much of what they said was totally misrepresented to the general public so as to make the public unsympathetic to their major goals, they said as little as possible about the problem. But still the anarchists in particular were made responsible for the acts of others.

George Bernard Shaw, writing in the first issue of The Anarchist in 1885, attempted to resolve the conflict regarding the derogatory connotations surrounding the word 'anarchist' but concluded that the name itself should not be dropped.

> ...from both camps mud is thrown of the name of Anarchist.
>
> Then, it will be asked, why offend people's sensibilities with it? Why not drop it? They will take care to keep it fastened tightly to us; and if we disown it, and yet when challenged home cannot deny it, will it not appear that we are ashamed of it; and will not our shame condemn us justly unheard? No, we must live down calumny as many other men, from primitive Christians to Quakers, and from Quakers to Socialists, have lived it down before us upon less occasion. What Socialists have done in England Anarchists may do;...[75]

In retrospect it might appear that Shaw was being facetious, or ironical, or simply frivolous, and many people would suspect him of this. But it is more likely that Shaw meant what he said, for as Edward Pease stated in The History of the Fabian Society, in reference to Shaw,

> ...he, like the rest of us, was then by no means clear as to the distinction between Anarchism and Socialism.[76]

Nonetheless, it is interesting to note that this particular article, entitled 'What's in a Name? Or How an Anarchist Might Put It,' was the first piece of Shaw's writing ever to appear in the United States, in the pages of the individualist anarchist journal Liberty (of Boston) which was published and edited by Benjamin Tucker.[77] In fact it was Tucker who gave Shaw his first well-paid commission -- a piece of criticism which adequately served its purpose.[78]

Shaw, of course, always attempted to disassociate his name from that of the anarchists although he was always closely associated with them from the beginning. And even though there is obviously nothing unusual about this, in later years he was in the habit of distorting the anarchist philosophy whenever it suited his purposes. Just after Shaw wrote his plea for the word 'anarchist' Joseph Lane made a feeble attempt at disassociation when he produced the pamphlet, The Anti-Statist Communist Manifesto, while still a member of the Socialist League. Although it was later claimed that this was the first English Anarchist Manifesto, at the time Lane was criticized for not calling it what it actually was, 'The Anarchist Communist Manifesto.'[79]

The problems were manifold. Not only was the public misinformed by the capitalist press, but since Bakunin's battle with Marx at the First International, the socialists themselves started denigrating the term 'anarchist.' If William Morris, one of the acknowledged leaders of the libertarian socialists, believed that the anarchists were no more than destructionists, what hope was there for an understanding and alliance between the libertarians and their closest sympathizers? Was it no more than a case of gaining respectability?

Thus the question of what was or was not anarchism was clouded by constant reference to the important but wholly divisive issue of violence: its apparent relationship with the anarchists made for considerable confusion. The anarchists were constantly put on the defensive because of these associations with their label, as were the libertarians when they were often unfairly lumped together with them. The fact that both the libertarians and the anarchists let their communications networks be used by those who put forth all manner of disparate ideas, including those which were not fundamentally connected with their cause, led to a confusion in the minds of many who were looking for more dogmatic intellectual guidance. The libertarian press was a platform for all ideas ranging across the political spectrum, yet it was the issue of violence and its use which condemned them to the lower depths of theoretical debate. They were branded by the press of all hues - capitalist, socialist, anarchist, and mystic - for being what other people assumed they were.

To give but a small sample of the way opinions abounded, we note that upon seeing the first issue of The Anarchist, the Secular Review, based in America, stated,

> We have, in our time, seen several journals, chiefly
> American, which have distinguished themselves by holding
> a candle to light the march of the Devil, but this
> ANARCHIST is the most bare-faced of them all.[79]

A Mr. Foote, editor of The Freethinker who had recommended

Liberty in America, described _The Anarchist_ as "an affliction," while _The Anarchist_, not to be outdone, described _The Alarm_ of Chicago as being "...somewhat illogical in its leanings towards communism."[80]

Given the extent and the variety of criticism from all quarters, one can well imagine the importance of the work done by the agitators who in most instances acted rather than theorized. They continued to propose solutions to society's ills which were far more revolutionary and wide ranging than anything envisioned by the state socialists or the Fabians. The libertarians had to bear the brunt of the journalistic criticism levelled at those who acted under the same organizational auspices and attempted to create havoc through individual or organized violence when the English groups themselves were trying to change the system through the efforts of a cooperative and well-informed mass movement.

These men were the backbone of the libertarian movement and worked amongst the industrial proletariat and the slum-dwellers. Their task was neither glorious nor spectacular, but it was potentially revolutionary and helped to educate and inform the people who came in touch with them, whether they were sympathizers or not. As has already been well documented in at least one book,[81] Rudolf Rocker is one of the best examples of this form of ceaseless work in the East End of London. He was not only one of the founders of the Jewish Labour Movement which virtually put an end to the tailor's sweat-shops, but he was also in the forefront in reconciling the Jewish and English trade unionists at a time when their mutual distrust could have destroyed the movement towards greater revolutionary solidarity.[82]

Rudolf Rocker, the immigrant from Germany, a non-Jew who taught himself the Yiddish tongue and became editor of the anarchist communist organ Arbeiter Fraint, was an activist who succeeded where many theoreticians had failed. Yet he is but one example of that curious zeal which expressed itself through libertarian ideals.

Libertarian Journals and their Organizational Links

The publication of radical journals and pamphlets was prolific in the 1880s and 1890s. Unfortunately it would be too simple just to say that they were products of the particular organization to which they were connected, especially in the case of the journals. Although some were the 'official organs' of a particular organizational body, others were published by a small group of people dedicated to a doctrine which they were determined to propagate in the most effectual manner possible, even though they produced the journal with little public support. Some journals were the product of those people whose publishing interest led them into circulating material which they believed represented the view of a good number, but as yet unorganized section of the public. We shall deal with a representative journal of each type which found itself in one of these positions.

Since we are limiting ourselves to a specific area of political theory, it is necessary to draw together, in terms of ideas, a few of the journals which are of primary interest to the libertarian movement. They all have two main things in common as a matter of policy, as indeed does all libertarian thought; -- they are advocates of decentralization, through the devolution of power on non-hierarchical lines, and they believed that only through social revolution, as opposed to political revolution, could their struggle for freedom be won.[83] For the sake of the continuity of development and historical perspective we will use journals which existed alongside one another in a particular period. All were published in London during the last two decades of the nineteenth century. Each claimed to be the representative organ of some sectional interest in British society although their aspirations were international. But as well as operating as blatant propaganda organs, they existed also as forums for unorthodox critical debate both in England and abroad and could be read with ease by either the converted or the sceptical. These journals were revolutionary in the sense that they were wholly dedicated to the overthrow of the existing social and political order.

As far as it is possible we shall deal specifically with the three journals which seem to fulfil all of the above criteria: the Commonweal (1885-1892), Freedom (1886-1927), and The Anarchist (1885-1888). Both the Commonweal and The Anarchist are chosen because like many other journals they did not survive the turn of the century. But in spite of this, many of their contributors and staff, by the later 1890s, had affiliated themselves to the Freedom Group which published Freedom. This gives the presentation of ideas within a certain context, some form of continuity even though the revolutionary emphasis expressed in the columns changed in relation to specific events and the flow of ideas as a result of the ever-changing flux in personnel. Many of the changes exemplified the obvious turmoil within a movement which sought to give free reign to the full consequences of its doctrines.

Over the years the more orthodox organ of the communist-anarchists, Freedom, established itself (much as Justice did for the state socialists) as a major theoretical organ of a more diverse and international libertarian movement. This was so because it was wholeheartedly supported by figures of international prestige and responsibility. Kropotkin, one of its founders, was closely associated with it up until World War I, and as he had a great following in international circles, many of his connections led directly to the Freedom Press.

Because they were mainly directed at the foreign elements within Britain, little mention will be made of some journals of a libertarian nature which existed throughout these years. These include the German Die Autonomie, which was published by the club of that name located in Soho, The Herald of Anarchy (1890-2), which was produced by the individualist anarchist Albert Tarn, and Johann Most's Die Freiheit, which was more interested in activities in Austria and Germany.[84] The one exception to this list is the Yiddish Der Arbeter Fraint which, although aimed at immigrants in the East End, was, in circulation, one of the most successful communist anarchist journals ever to appear in England. Nonetheless, it was not published in English and directed most of its attention to a non-English cultural minority and its peculiar problems in dealing with a new homeland. Its most important work, in aiding and abetting trade union organization, occurred towards the end of the first decade of the twentieth century and is hence largely outside the scope of this book.

Other journals which we must exclude for reasons of both content and space are Henry Seymour's Revolutionary Review (1889), The Torch (1895-96) from the Rossetti sisters, and Liberty which was published by James Tochatti after he left the Socialist League in the early 1890s.[85] All of these were anarchist publications. Of those which expressed libertarian views there were Seedtime (1889-98) which was the journal of the Fellowship of New Life,[86] and The Adult which arose out of the issue-oriented Legitimation League and lasted from 1892 until 1898 and published much of Edward Carpenter's

work.[87]   It was for a time edited by Henry Seymour. These are all
very interesting journals but to look at their contents would embroil
us in issues ranging from bastardy and homosexuality to bomb-making and
free-love, in a manner which is not pertinent to our present concern.

        Although they were often relatively articulate mouthpieces for
certain organizational activities, the 'underground' journals of
Britain, and especially London, served many useful functions. They
worked well as access points for opinions, judgments, and published
articles on the interpretation of events and ideas which were not
tolerated in the national press of the day. Most of the 'news' they
printed took the form of socially committed interpretations of past and
on-going events which begged explanation from alternative viewpoints.
They informed their readers of the intricacies and intrigues as well as
the hardships surrounding strikes and lock-outs.[88] They exposed
those whom they believed were working in the pay of the police.[89]
They often gave vivid descriptions of the conditions in the factories
and workshops, detailing the plight of the homeless as well as the
unemployed.[90] In short, they printed the facts behind the news
which were of interest to those who believed in revolutionary societal
change.   In this way they formed a valuable source of alternative
information and gave a fairly accurate picture of the working poor in
the Britain of that day, long before it was drawn to the attention of
General Booth.   They also gave news of what was happening in the
various organizations abroad, acting as part of a vast communications
network for those who were interested in viewing the problems of
society from another direction.   This invariably kept the readership
posted on the state of the movement as a whole.

        While the journals were always in close contact with the

various organizations who helped in the mutual circulation of one
another's propaganda, it was the lecturers who travelled the country,
and the speakers who had regular venues who were responsible for much
of the widespread distribution of libertarian propaganda. Their
activities were advertised in the journals, and the results of their
work or any peculiar incidents were, in turn, reported upon.[91]
During the average week in the 1880s there were at least twenty
open-air propaganda sessions which were taken on, in rotation, above
and beyond their lecturing duties, by speakers who usually gave forth
their views at more formalized gatherings. Morris, among others, often
complained of this arduous task, for it was not one which appealed to
him.[92] The venues, usually in open spaces or under railway arches
if not on a street corner, ranged from Harrow to Mile End and from
Merton to Canning Town. Over the years these speakers were tireless in
their efforts throughout London and the industrialized centres of the
North. They travelled to Leeds, Manchester, Sheffield, Edinburgh,
Glasgow, and Birmingham encouraging others to work in their localities.
In turn they brought with them and distributed literature which offered
support from the much stronger London-based organizations which were
willing to help with any local difficulties. Reciprocal arrangements
were made for speakers to come from the provinces and report on the
continuing struggles of the people who were in the areas where most of
the country's working class lived. These activites were also reported
in the journals even though in some cases, as in Sheffield, the local
groups had their own press.[93] The activists and their followers
reported from the field to the London-based press which then fed it
back into the areas from whence it came and where fresh information was
avidly picked up and circulated in support of the struggle. Such

communication, the content of which formed the basis of a growing solidarity between different areas, was essential to the well-being of the whole movement.

On what could perhaps be seen as a typical week in the life of the London propagandists (June 1886), George Bernard Shaw, now a member of the Fabian Society for nearly two years, gave a lecture on 'Socialism and Malthusianism' at the Socialist League Hall in Clerkenwell. Two days later Charlotte M. Wilson, who did so much to smooth out the differences between the Fabians and the libertarian socialists, spoke on 'The Future of Radicalism' at the Educational Club in Berner Street in Whitechapel. On the same day Frank Kitz put forth the anarchist position with a speech entitled 'The Criminal Classes: High and Low' at the Notting Hill Debating Society.[94] And these were but a few of the more formal activities of the speakers involved. Debates were always popular. There was one between John Turner of the Socialist League and Henry Burrows of the S.D.F. on 'Anarchy Versus Social Democracy' in the Britannia Coffee House in Islington on September 25, 1889, in which it was decided that those present were speaking about different forms of anarchy.[95] One of Kropotkin's most popular speeches was the one entitled simply 'Communist Anarchism,' and it was eventually published as a pamphlet.[96] Libertarians gathered to speak and listen to most of the public debates whether they were held in the South Place Institute, the Hall of the Socialist League, or in the rooms of the Fabian Society. At the annual meeting at the Fabian Society in 1886 representatives from the S.D.F., the Socialist League, and the Liberty and Property Defense League were all in attendance. Apparently,

...the most successful paper was by a strange gentleman

whom we had taken on trust as a Socialist, but who turned out to be an enthusiast on the subject of building more harbours.[97]

Both the Socialist League members and the S.D.F. members were very keen on speaking out of doors directly to the people. According to Shaw, the Fabians were not quite as adept in the 1880s as many of their comrades:

> The Fabians were disgracefully backward in open-air speaking. Up to quite a recent date, Graham Wallas, myself and Mrs. Besant were the only representative open-air speakers in the Society, whereas the Federation speakers, Burns, Hyndman, Andrew Hall, Tom Mann, Champion, Burrows and the Socialist Leaguers were at it all the time.[98]

Nonetheless, the journals were very particular in reporting the active propaganda work which was going on. Many strange and wonderful tales must lie behind those lists of regular meeting places, the pubs, and coffee houses, where much of the real contact with the working man was made. At this grass roots level there is little more than conjecture in measuring the impact of the journalistic propaganda. Frank Kitz, in 1912, thinking back over 30 years recalled how things were at the height of libertarian revolutionary activity.

> Mile End waste was our outdoor rallying point, and indoors - let not the temperance reader be shocked - the clubrooms of various public houses, where under the guise of debating societies or similar harmless sounding titles we pursued our propagandist work. The Radical Clubs...have long since been nobbled by the middle class and brewers, and the amateur negro minstrel stands where the lecturer should be.[99]

For it was undoubtedly the speakers, who appeared in person and lent their physical presence to a usually unpopular cause, who initially aroused the attention of the ordinary working man. These activists were often his first contact with a movement which needed his support. As the journals tried to point out, such gatherings allowed people to come out of their isolated circumstances into a movement which had both national and international connections. The activists offered hope as well as alliances and gave the members of their audience a chance not only to read but also to make their voice heard through organized action and the use of an alternative press.

But the way in which information was presented in the journals is of considerable importance; it laid no claim to being objective even though it was meant to be truthful and factual. A small sample drawn from The Anarchist indicates the general pattern of such reporting.

> Commenting on the late dynamite 'outrage' at the House of Commons, our friend the Boston Liberty says: "at any rate the explosions...will cause legislators everywhere to sit much less easily in their seats, for which unquestionable blessing let us be duly thankful."[100]

In this small piece of information which really surrounds one relevant fact, that is, the bombing itself, there is combined the name of a foreign anarchist paper with its opinion. This is, in turn, endorsed by The Anarchist, and it is all done without the serious breast-beating air of the many more ideological papers like Justice. Thus the reader was able to identify the type of news presented very closely with the propaganda line to which the paper subscribed.

On the other hand, types of information which were meant to serve an educative function were usually contained in a list of publications which were made available by the publisher of the paper. These could be bought post free in any quantity. Although some of these pamphlets were in the form of reprints of original articles which appeared in the journal, the great bulk of books and pamphlets advertised came from very diverse sources. Many were very unlibertarian pieces of work.[101] But what was important was that they represented an alternative or unpopular viewpoint, and as such they were distributed by journals which, in several instances, ran counter to their own doctrines.

Besides such anarchist and libertarian classics as God and the State by Bakunin, and What Is Property? by Proudhon, such publications as A Vindication of Natural Society by Burke, The Communist Manifesto by Marx, and Man Versus The State by Spencer were also advertised. Also represented were some highly individualistic works by Auberon Herbert of the Party of Individual Liberty, as well as such titles as Liberty and Law, distributed by the Liberty and Property Defense League. There was a wide range of choice in the fields of individualistic and socialist literature made available to the reader.

This choice can be attributed to the libertarian belief, already expressed previously by David Nicoll, that all forms of dissent were worthy of discussion if not of total sympathy. Yet one does not see such apparently inconsistent literature being advertised in the pages of Justice, or the more orthodox state socialist organs, even though they were accepting advertisements from The Anarchist.[102]

The reasons for this should become apparent in the more detailed discussions of the journals which we shall next consider. As much as possible I will try to steer away from the personality clashes and personal feuds which crop up from time to time in these journals. This is particularly obvious in the pages of The Anarchist which was dominated and largely written by its editor, Henry Seymour, however, the personal feuds are only important insofar as the dispute was on theoretical grounds. What is important is that one sample the flavour as well as the actual content of these journals in order that they may be more constructively appraised in relation to the development of libertarian ideas.

'The Anarchist'

The first issue of The Anarchist appeared, as a monthly, in March 1885, one month after the birth of Commonweal. It was printed and published by the International Publishing Company of 35 Newington Green Road, Islington in London. As far as can be ascertained this company was largely and sometimes wholly owned by Henry Seymour, who edited The Anarchist and who first came to prominence in 1881. At that time, on the advice of Charles Bradlaugh, the Secularist, Seymour had pleaded guilty to posting an obscene libel in Tunbridge Wells.[103]

In the first issue came the first of the editor's many statements of policy for the paper, and, as the paper was almost wholly dominated by the personality and contributions of Seymour, we might note that this has some significance. As to The Anarchist he said,

> It believes, not in the logic of force, but in the force of logic; not in might, but in right. It is tooth and nail opposed to all the nonsense known as 'public morality' as set up by a 'public opinion.' and affirms that there is no morality but liberty.[104]

As to the overall editorial policy of the paper, its content was to be the result of individual, but responsible free expression with, what we may assume to mean, as little editorial interference as possible.

> The present number may be taken as a fair illustration of its general outline. The mysterious editorial 'we' will be abolished to give encouragement to individual and independent expression of opinion.
>
> Each writer must be alone morally responsible for his or her own views, and can only be expected to necessarily endorse such as may appear over his or her own signature, and with the support and assistance of friends favourable to Anarchistic propaganda it is hoped that THE ANARCHIST may prove itself useful and long lived.[105]

The Anarchist, entirely dependent on the work of Seymour and unreliable outside contributions, continued its existence with some difficulty as either a fortnightly or a monthly, up until August 1888.

Because of the lack of any even semi-permanent group of contributors, Seymour relied very heavily on information from the continent and America, and one of his favourite ploys was to reprint articles and opinions from other radical magazines. Thus, from the beginning, although it was the first anarchist paper in Britain since Kitz's English edition of Die Freiheit which had closed down two years earlier, it did not intend to just cater to any particular English movement.

The first issue points out the diversity of both source and material. Elisee Reclus, the French anarchist geographer, sent a message of solidarity from French comrades with a central internationalist message. "Let us learn to love one another the world over. Behind us there are centuries of hatred to redeem."[106] Also from the continent, 'The Lyons Anarchist Manifesto' was reprinted and there was a greeting from 'The French Speaking International Anarchist Circle of London.' In this issue George Bernard Shaw made his only voluntary contribution to the paper with an article we have already described. It was called 'What's In A Name? (Or How An Anarchist Might Put It).' There was a piece entitled 'What is An Anarchist?' by Henry Appleton which is rather confusing for while he attempts to clarify the distinction between government and the state, he seems in the end to be saying that an anarchist can in good conscience support 'government.' However sophistic, this essay was destined to be the first in a series of wrangles about words and definitions. Appleton is worth quoting here if only to illustrate the extent to which words can be twisted in the service of a cause, yet out of all sense of conventional usage. Thus, he speaks about government and the state.

> The thing that they are trying to abolish is the State.
> The State is not Government in the sense of Nature. The
> State stands for usurpation and usurpation makes
> Government impossible. The State hinges on usurpation
> backed by force. Government only begins where usurpation
> ceases and force is superceded by consent.

> To force me is not to govern me.

> True Government is never present where voluntary consent
> is absent. When I say I am governed by reason,
> conscience and love, liberty is always presupposed. I
> can only be governed as liberty is present. Political
> Government is an artificial trick set up to head off
> social Government, which is the only natural Government
> possible. Social Government if not interfered by force
> is always voluntary and flexible.[107]

It is interesting to note that Malatesta made quite the opposite distinction, but this is not surprising when we find out that Appleton was more concerned with the individualist approach to freedom than he was with anarchism.[108] The last written contribution made to this one penny issue of The Anarchist was by Francis Barry on 'The Marriage Contract.' a subject which always interested Seymour as can be seen in his editorship of The Adult in 1898.

As the publishers did not expect the sale of the paper to initially cover their costs, they set up a 'Propagandist Fund' whose first contributor was one E. Pease, Esq., who gave one pound. Was he the same Edward Pease who was prominent in the Fabian Society?

Seymour, who had advertised Commonweal in the first issue, soon began his petty, if not vindictive, behaviour between himself and other members, journals and radical organizations. He seemed to be always either on the defensive or the offensive with regards to other members in the movement, for his egoism and dogmatism stand out in the pages of The Anarchist. In the second issue he claimed that the "Socialist League ought to hide its diminished head, as Mr. Morris has identified himself with the selfish policy of attempting to explain the Socialist view of the cause of the Soudan War..."[109]

The Socialist League was only four months old at this time and did not benefit from this kind of bickering statement from one of its so-called comrades. In the same month the Commonweal carried a note written by Morris which was enthusiastic about the publication of The Anarchist:

> ...we welcome the temperate discussion of differences between various socialist schools, in the hope that the obvious necessity for a revolutionary society will force us all to study the question so diligently that the path may at last become plain to us.[110]

However, a month earlier Morris had written to his daughter, May, a more private comment: "The Anarchist has appeared a poor little sheet with, it seems to me, very little raison d'etre."[111] Seymour was not to know this, and he had other axes to grind. The S.D.F. Justice also came under fire:

> Mutual mistrust makes men Anarchists. Justice says so. It is rather odd that a political paper should have the honesty to make this admission, and it might have added the equally damaging declaration that it doesn't make DUPES.[112]

These attacks on Justice, which incidentally advertised The Anarchist within its pages, were ceaseless. By May 1885 Seymour had another complaint.

> Justice is announced in an advertisement on another page as 'the only major paper in England which is independent of Capitalist support.' This is a lie.[113]

The next advertisement of Justice was accordingly changed,[114] and we know not by whom, so that 'only major paper in England' was deleted from the copy. Seymour did not get the same response from other comrades, however, and like Freedom in later years,[115] The Anarchist was boycotted by Bradlaugh and his group.

The Freethought Publishing Company has refused to supply
its customers with this journal, the reason assigned by
Mrs. Besant for this petty meanness being 'that I
untruthfully slandered Mr. Bradlaugh in an American
paper.'[116]

All this goes to show that, from the very beginning, the level
of discussion and debate within the pages of The Anarchist was
considerably lower in tone as a result of the machinations of Seymour.
He later carried on a running debate in the most slanderous manner with
the Boston editor of Liberty, Benjamin Tucker, who, as an
individualistic anarchist, was troubled by Seymour's sympathy with the
communist anarchist position.[117] Seymour also alienated himself
from the London Freedom Group who sounded out the possibilities of
expanding the International Publishing Company and making it the centre
of the English anarchist movement. More about this later. Seymour,
for all the things he said in the pages of The Anarchist throughout,
remained true to his one central principle, and it is this which
basically prevented him from being an equal partner in a growing
movement. That principle, which he considered to be the fundamental
one of anarchy, was this:

> The fundamental philosophy of Anarchy is that an
> individual has an absolute right to do exactly as he
> pleases just so long as he doesn't invade another's
> right.[118]

The paper itself which began in tabloid size, continued as a
monthly paper until January 1, 1886 when Seymour decided to issue The
Anarchist fortnightly, "...at half its present size, but twice as
often" so that "...interest may be continually awakened and
revived."[119] This experiment lasted for only two months, and the
paper then continued monthly until March 1887. Up until April 1886 it
had been subtitled 'A Revolutionary Review' and significantly, after

that, this subtitle was changed to 'Communist and Revolutionary.' This
lasted until the new series was launched in April 1887, again subtitled
'A Revolutionary Review' in which form it continued until its demise in
August 1888.

The most fascinating debate within the pages of The Anarchist
centres around Seymour's battle with the communist-anarchists who
sought to make it a sounding board for their own doctrines. Up until
April 20, 1886, when Seymour claimed that he accepted the principles of
communism, the range of articles seemed to follow only one coherent
pattern -- they were very anarchistic. From June 1885 there were
several contributions extolling the virtues of communism by one Henry
Glasse who wrote from South Africa. This was offset by contributions
from American individualists led by 'Edgeworth,' the pen name of a Dr.
Lazarus. Glasse wrote articles on: 'Social War.'[120] 'The Evils of
Government.'[121] and 'Anarchism and Communism,'[122] while
'Edgeworth' replied to them in a series of long letters.[123] During
this period, Seymour concerned himself with terse replies to
correspondence, anti-voting propaganda,[124] and with his soon to be
out-dated 'The Anarchist's Catechism' which ran into three lengthy
articles.[125] One of his favourite 'bete noires' was the relation
between capital and labour in a capitalist society, a subject about
which the anarchists were not generally well versed. In an article
entitled, 'Labour and Capital' he even claimed that, "...the root of
the evils of capitalism lies in government itself, not in this or that
particular form of government,"[126] which seems a straightforward
enough statement in itself. However he goes on to link this to the
fact that it is because of the existence of the State that this is so
and hence, like Appleton before him, confuses the issue as to what the

anarchists want from either the state or government and which of the two they wish to abolish. The rest of Seymour's writing consists of two biographical sketches, one of Proudhon and the other of Bakunin which were later published in pamphlet form and sold to subscribers of the paper. During this period there was the very novel edition of September 15, 1885, which has miraculously survived not having been used as intended. The centre two pages, which contained the usual articles, were in fact four pages which had not been cut at the top edge. If this was folded out the reader was presented with a full sized poster; i.e., four times the size of one page of the paper, on the reverse side of the printed pages. The essential message of this poster was 'DO NOT VOTE.' set in the most blatant type possible. In the same issue readers were invited to obtain Morris's pamphlet, issued from the Offices of the Socialist League at 27 Farringdon Road, called 'Why Vote?.' The Socialist League reaffirmed its anti-parliamentary stand the next month in the new Socialist League Manifesto written by Morris and Bax. The other articles in this issue were: 'Anarchist Manifesto'; 'Why Do You Vote?'; 'The People in Subjugation'; 'Labour Representation is a Delusion'; and 'No Need For Any Government At All - DO NOT VOTE.' Amidst all of this revolutionary activity, Seymour seems to have had a major interest in selling the polyopticon, which he distributed from his premises.

Then, in what must have seemed a sudden change in the eyes of the regular readers, on April 20, 1886, The Anarchist took on the subtitle 'Communist and Revolutionary.' In a personal statement Seymour assured his readers of his new position.

> In accepting the economic principles of Communism as
> satisfactorily established, I unhesitatingly and
> fearlessly adopt them. This will necessitate some little

alteration in the literary arrangements of the paper. In
true Communistic fashion, the articles in future will be
purely impersonal, thereby allowing the true force of an
argument to stand entirely upon its intrinsic merit, and
not carry undue preponderance with it because this or
that particular individual has contended for it.[127]

But this was not all. It seems that by this time Seymour was
aware of the sad lack of quality within the pages of The Anarchist.
He recognized that he could not take on all the editorial tasks by
himself. Thus, he announced that,

In our new sphere of work I have succeeded in securing
the editorial assistance of several scholarly and
revolutionary writers, so that the paper will henceforth
be conducted on lines of co-joint editorship.[128]

It is not surprising to learn that Kropotkin had arrived in
London just three months prior to this statement and was looking for a
medium for communist anarchist propaganda. Nonetheless, Kropotkin's
name was not mentioned in this venture. The Anarchist, whose
circulation rarely went into the high thousands, had, besides
Commonweal and Justice, other potential rivals to consider if it
wished to consolidate its position within the radical press movement.
In September 1885 Der Arbeter Fraint (The Worker's Friend), a
communist socialist paper, began publication in the East End, and in
January 1886 The Practical Socialist was launched, with contributions
from Pease as well as Charlotte Wilson. Seymour needed all the help
and sympathy he could get, and he sought it by subjecting his ego to
the torment of becoming a communist.

But the joint editorship did not last long even though it was
shared with Charlotte Wilson and Kropotkin.[129] In June, Seymour
resumed sole editorial responsibility, and under the heading 'Snacks
and Smacks' he explained that,

...the collective editorship is forthwith abolished;

that, while looking very well in theory, it hasn't proved so very well in practice.[130]

Rather than back down, Seymour again, in response from Tucker of _Liberty_, tried to redeem the situation by his usual verbal sophistry. He wrote:

> And just let me make a confession of faith. There exists some sort of misunderstanding. _Liberty_ says I have abandoned liberty in embracing Communism. This is untrue. I have embraced Communistic-Anarchism, but by no means Communism. I am Anarchist at least as entirely as ever. I simply embrace _voluntary_ Communism on ethical and economical grounds.[131]

Even the last sentence in this statement cannot be taken at face value, for Seymour was prepared to ignore one of the basic tenets of communistic ethics, namely, that what is good for the whole ought to be good for the individual as the individual must be prepared to submerge his own selfish interests for the sake of communal harmony.

> For my own part I am not sorry of the circumstances attending the breakdown of the 'con-joint' editorship. They have proved the impracticability of the idea, which is a useful experiment. In all these things, individuality gets extinguished to maintain a 'general tone,' which may for all I know be true communism, but isn't pure Anarchism. Certain advocates of our ideas, who forsake titles and names and responsibilities in the revolutionary press, yet trade on all these when writing for the _bourgeois_ press, may continue to hide behind 'impersonality' if they choose; while they may be severally answerable for the expressions of each other, and maintain a dull and dead level of mediocrity if they will - I for one will adopt a different course. I have nothing to say that I dare not say openly and honestly, and I scorn to conceil [sic] any expression of opinion that the addition of a signature makes me very properly responsible.[132]

Seymour's about face became even more apparent as he lived what appeared to be a double life in his dealings with the newly formed Freedom Group. In July he expressed his doubts as to whether the 'London Anarchist Group of Freedom' even existed,[133] and, in reply to a correspondent, admitted that Kropotkin was one of the members of the defunct joint editorship. In this same reply he dismissed rumours regarding the conception of a new anarchist paper. In answer to the question as to what it would be, Seymour replied:

> ...scarcely another English Anarchist paper. It is to be a bourgeois enterprise, I hear, and initiates from our foreign friends. You need not anticipate its publication as in rivalry with this journal; it is more probably a rival of the 'Liberty and Property Defense League.'[134]

If he was talking about the birth of <u>Freedom</u> here, and in all likelihood he was, it throws light again on Seymour's character. He was one of the founding members of <u>Freedom</u>,[135] yet when it came out in October of 1886, he did not even deign to mention its existence.

From this time onward Seymour led <u>The Anarchist</u> in a direction more appropriate to the individualistic anarchists, although for a time he still tried to justify his communist sentiments. But in spite of his earlier derision of the works of the Liberty and Property Defense League, he began including articles by its founder Wordsworth Donisthorpe, although he did dare to print a rebuttal of Donisthorpe's speech on 'Democracy' (which Seymour had entitled 'Anarchy') by William Morris.[136] But up until the end of this first series of <u>The Anarchist</u>, Seymour relied heavily on reprints from other journals including <u>The Present Day</u>, <u>Le Revolte</u>, and <u>Commonweal</u>. Again he tried to restate his beliefs about anarchism in a series of three articles entitled 'The Philosophy of Anarchism.' He began to take a greater interest in the questions of religion and free love,[137] while some of his claims regarding personal inventions led him into an area which was later to become his <u>forte</u>. In November 1886, he claimed to have invented a steam-propelled torpedo and a type of flying machine which sounds very much like the first helicopter. Being a good anarchist, he refused to patent them; but not being a communist, he also refused to share his secret for fear that someone else might patent them. However, with his characteristic lack of modesty and humour he commented,

> Whatever the world generally may think about these two inventions, I, as a revolutionary anarchist, regard them as two of the most important this century has seen.[138]

By March 1887 Seymour announced 'A New Departure' - the beginning of a new series, together with the admission that,

> At the present time it is a fact that the sale of The Anarchist does not exceed fifteen hundred copies...

He did not blame this on either himself or the content of the paper, but characteristically cited other factors:

> ...I suppose...[it] is to a large extent due to the cessation of the outdoor meetings for the winter session, as well as to the prevailing impecuniosity amongst the working people.[139]

The 'New Series,' The Anarchist - A Revolutionary Review, began in April 1887. It now cost two pence and was notorious, until the end of its days, for being extremely vindictive in all matters, especially regarding personalities in the radical movement. The content continued to favour individualism so that finally, after having disagreed with every communist of note including Morris and Kropotkin, Seymour had to declare his real beliefs:

> Communism is incompatible with Anarchy. It is arbitrarily conventional and tyrannic, however professedly free - I have been behind the scenes. It sets up rights for the community that it denies for the individual, which is absurd, for only individuals have rights, and no community has any rights at all beyond the individual rights voluntarily combined of those composing it.[140]

Doubtless, William Morris would have reached the same conclusion although not beginning with the same premises. The fact is that Seymour was so consistently inconsistent that one could never be really sure of his position or of that taken by his paper. For this reason it lapsed into insignificance although it was presumptuous enough to regard itself towards the end as a serious rival to Freedom.[141] It may well have been if Seymour's intransigent attitude had not been so blatantly displayed for all to see. Towards the end he was advising people to buy two copies of the paper instead of one and give the other to a friend. It is not clear from where Seymour received his money whether from his publishing or inventing. He always seemed to have enough money to continue his own crusades and in the end turned out to be a very successful businessman.[142] It is perhaps significant that the very last entry in the last edition of The Anarchist in August 1888 referred to the power of money.

> Money, in fine, is the universal passport; and all doors are open to it.

But aside from what effect it might have had on public attitudes, The Anarchist is very informative as to the undercurrents of the radical movement of the day. It shows us not only the major topics of concern, such as the fight for free speech and the death of the Chicago anarchists, but gives us some insight into the dead-end issues like vaccination and compulsory schooling which were opposed for reasons other than health or education. Many of the battles which they fought seem strangely incongruous for a group of people who claimed to be lovers of humanity rather than principled eccentrics. The Anarchist was the one paper which, more than any other, epitomized the inherent difficulties of libertarian organization and agreement.

For example, we may consider one of the statements made by Seymour about Kropotkin's essay Anarchy and Communism. Seymour thought he was clarifying things when he tried to explain that,

> All the Communism needed in the relations of life is that
> which may be governed by personal liberty. Beyond this
> Communism becomes a crime. Kropotkin has confused the
> wide and wonderful difference between voluntary and
> compulsory communism and has started at the wrong end.
> Instead of making his pet Communism subject to Anarchy,
> he makes Anarchy subject to Communism. After which we
> must conclude he is an out and out Communist but an
> Anarchist by no means.[143]

This statement illustrates one of the central problems which
beset the libertarian movement, namely the problem of definition. The
whole issue of ideological identification was clouded not only by the
fact that people called themselves different things at different times,
but they were called different names by different people who would
judge their writings for themselves. For example, Kropotkin asserted
that he was a communist-anarchist. Morris, who initially claimed to be
a socialist, modified his position by saying that in the end he was a
simple communist and had no need to append any other adjective or noun
to it.[144] Seymour called himself simply an anarchist, but Tucker,
who also claimed this distinction, called Seymour a 'Collectivist.'

In the main, those who called themselves 'Scientific
Socialists,' were Marxists, while those who called themselves simply
'socialists,' as did Shaw, were in fact 'State Socialists' and partial
followers of Marx who looked to other sources for inspiration. This
eventually forced many anti-state socialists to call themselves
'Communist-Anarchists,' and the anti-paliamentarian socialists to call
themselves 'Communists' rather than 'True Socialists.' Therefore the
people, like Seymour, who simply called themselves 'Anarchists' were
almost always of the individualist type who saw freedom as their
highest value. Such men were intellectually close to another group of
anti-governmentalists, like Herbert and Donisthorpe, who rejected

anarchy but called themselves 'Individualists.'[145] Consequently it was often noted that the anarchists were much more sympathetic to people such as Auberon Herbert who wrote the Anti-Force Papers, and Herbert Spencer who enjoyed a vogue for his book Man Versus the State than they were to their real fellow travellers who they would deride as 'Collectivists' or 'Communists' and not 'Anarchists.'[146] The whole argument was of course centred around the different concepts of freedom rather than that of organization or agitation against the state. Thus it can be said that in ethical terms the libertarians were members of three distinct groups: the 'Communists,' the 'Anarchists,' and the 'Communist-Anarchists,' and it was the latter group in particular who were to eventually refer to themselves as libertarian. The Anarchist, dealing with those problems at the extreme edge of the libertarian movement, serves as a telling example of the difficulties encountered along the way. It was more of a political rather than a social propaganda journal. By this I mean that it reserved much of its vehemence for the concept of state and the idea of anarchism. It was much too introspective, and, by ignoring the interests of its readers, it was abandoned by them.

'The Commonweal'

The Socialist League, which was founded on December 30, 1884, began monthly publication of its 'Official Organ' Commonweal on February 1, 1885. It was printed and published by William Morris, its Editor, and Treasurer of the Socialist League, and Joseph Lane. Edward Aveling, husband of Eleanor Marx, also acted as sub-Editor until 1887. After having at first been published from the Offices of the Socialist League at 27 Farringdon Road, it had moved to more spacious premises at Number 13 by July of 1885.

The first issue, its heading unadorned with Morris's characteristic leaf-work (while all the subsequent ones were), cost one penny. On the title-page was an 'Introductory' by Morris which set out the relationship between the Socialist League, the journal, and its readership. The Editor and sub-Editor of the Commonweal were "...acting as delegates of the Socialist League" and were "under its direct control..." The major aim was "the propagation of Socialism." And as such, Morris claimed,

> It is our duty to attack unsparingly the miserable system
> which would make all civilization end in a society of
> rich and poor, of slaves and slave-owners. In all its
> details we must attack it but in doing so we shall avoid
> mere personalities... The Commonweal will only deal with
> political matters when they directly affect the progress
> of the Cause.

In normal libertarian fashion, he promised that the journal would not shrink from publishing all manner of opinion.

> We invite from all, Socialists or others, free discussion
> of anything we put forward, in the belief that even an
> uninstructed attack may elicit useful information which
> might otherwise have lain dormant.

The articles, although wholly biased towards the Socialist cause, were meant to serve one of the three primary interests of the Socialist League, -- education, whilst the factual and logistical information would serve as a platform for agitation and a basis for organization.

> Our articles will for the most part, be of an educational
> nature; there will be a series on historical revolutions,
> expositions of the scientific basis of Socialism, and
> contributions of men of various nationalities.

The reason that this educational work was so important rested on the fact that Morris was appealing to the workers, "the slaves of society" as he called them. He claimed (and his use of the plural might be somewhat indicative of some notion of superiority) in the following statement that,

> We cannot pretend that they, the workers, as yet know
> much of the principles of the cause that rests upon
> them, of their own cause in fact. We beseech them to
> help us in spreading knowledge of these principles
> amongst their fellows...so that their support may make us
> resolute, patient and hopeful - in a word, successful in
> our efforts for the furtherance of the cause we have at
> heart.[147]

This, "we and they" attitude, on behalf of the Commonweal,
this patronizing didacticism contained within the very first issue, was
to prove disadvantageous. First of all, many of the members of the
Socialist League, viewing themselves as a 'missionary' group spreading
seeds of knowledge amongst the ignorant masses, were from the beginning
somewhat alienated from the more practical needs of their audience.
Most of them were, if not distinctly middle class, both literate and
articulate. Secondly, what went into the pages of Commonweal was very
much the result of decisions taken by the Executive Council which
represented the whole gamut of revolutionary theories emanating from
all manner of sources. The Socialist League, through the Commonweal,
was forced to present a unique socialistic platform largely in response
to the competition from other bodies, like the Fabian Society, or the
S.D.F. And it is for this reason that it presented in full, 'The
Manifesto of the Socialist League' in the first issue. This Manifesto,
the first of several, was to provide the framework not only for the
Branches of the Socialist League[148] but for the journal itself.
Some of the more pertinent declarations are as follows:

> We come before you as a body advocating the principles of
> Revolutionary International Socialism; that is, we seek a
> change in the basis of Society - a change which would
> destroy the distinctions of classes and nationalities.
>
> As the civilised world is at present constituted, there
> are two classes of Society - the one possessing wealth
> and the instruments of its production, the other

producing wealth by means of those instruments but only by the leave and for the use of the possessing classes.

These two classes are necessarily in antagonism with one another...

...change in the method of production and distribution would enable everyone to live decently...

...Men's social and moral relations would be seriously modified by this gain of economical freedom...

...our modern bourgeois property-marriage,...would give place to kindly and human relations between the sexes.

Education freed from the trammels of commercialism...and superstition...would become a reasonable drawing out of men's varied faculties in order to fit them for a life of social intercourse and happiness; for mere work would no longer be proposed as the end of life, but happiness for each and all.

Nationalization of land alone...would be useless...

No better...State Socialism...until the workers are in possession of all political power...

For us neither geographical boundaries, political history, race nor creed makes rivals or enemies; for us there are no nations but only varied masses of workers and friends whose mutual sympathies are checked or perverted by groups of masters...

There shall be no distinctions of rank or dignity amongst us to give opportunities for the selfish ambition of leadership which has so often injured the cause of the workers. We are working _for_ equality and brotherhood for all the world, and it is only _through_ equality and brotherhood that we can make our work effective.

It is well to note here that there is no mention whatsoever of any party political organization or agitation within the institutions of the constitutional government structure. The job at hand was to 'make Socialists.'

The Manifesto was signed by the 21 members of the Provisional Council of the Socialist League, only three of whom came from outside of London.[149] The rest of the first edition, which sold 5000 copies, was typical of the type of format which was to follow for the next four years. E. Balfort Bax, who along with Edward Aveling, was one of the foremost Marxist scholars of the day wrote a piece entitled 'Imperialism Versus Socialism' which essentially blamed the European race for colonial territories on 'capitalist greed' and 'flunkey' patriotism. Imperialism was one of Bax's favourite subjects.[150] Eleanor Marx Aveling gave 'A Record of the International Movement,' while her husband Edward, the sub-Editor, contributed an article called 'English Socialism and The Weekly Dispatch'; Joseph Lane contributed a piece on the 'East-End Workers.' E. T. Craig, an old radical from the Chartist Movement, gave a history of the 'Peterloo Massacre.' There were reports of socialist activities from groups in Charlton, Glasgow, Oxford, Edinburgh, and Southwark, as well as advertisements for the Edinburgh Socialist Society and the Scottish Land and Labour League, both of which affiliated themselves to the Socialist League in due course. The rules for membership of the Socialist League were printed out, and there was a list of lectures which were to take place in the next month. The only actual advertisement was one put in by members of the Commonweal which invited people to attend 'Lessons in Socialism' which were being given in two courses of eight lessons by Edward Aveling at the South Place Institute in Moorgate Street. The intention was to give an analysis of Marx's Das Kapital. The cost was 3 shillings per session or 6 pence per lesson with the proceeds going to Commonweal. Finally, William Morris contributed two more pieces, a chant called 'The March of the workers' and a column called 'Signs of the Times' which dealt with odd titbits of information of current interest. Even from the beginning the Commonweal contained twice the amount of material that The Anarchist did although it was often padded out with rather 'cultured' pieces of prose and poetry. This was largely due to the influence of Morris whose views on art and labour left little room for the suggestion that the one could be divorced from the other in the journal. Morris contributed over 250 pieces to the pages of Commonweal, his last being on November 15, 1890.[151]

There has been much written on the details of the rise and fall of the Socialist League,[152] but one cannot help but notice that little of the disputes involved soiled the pages of the Commonweal. As Morris said in his 'Introductory,' he did not feel that the journal should deal in personalities, a lesson which Henry Seymour could have well taken to heart. Up until 1889 sales of the Commonweal were around 2500 per issue, and by May 1886 it was issued fortnightly due to the considerable effort of Morris and his associates. The membership of the Socialist League reached a maximum of about 1000 by the beginning of 1887 and had no fewer than 28 Branches throughout Great Britain. For the distribution of the Commonweal each Branch was allotted a quota to sell at lectures, demonstrations, and meetings, and when the number of members began to fall, so did the sales of the Commonweal.[153]

But the Commonweal, at least up until 1890, was an immensely readable paper, informative on the whole range of political, economic, and social life. Initially most of the economics writing was done by Aveling and was later continued by Bax whose most notable contribution in this field was done in collaboration with Morris. They called the series of articles, 'Socialism its Growth and Outcome.' The speciality of Thomas Binning, a London compositor, was trade unions, the best examples of which are contained in The Commonweal Supplements for May and September 1885. Binning was one of the first to resign from the Socialist League, claiming that it was too purist even by 1886.[154] Engels, who had originally suggested that Morris ought to bring out a paper like Commonweal to counter the dogmatism of Justice, wrote only two articles, 'England in 1845 and in 1885' (March 1885) and 'How Not to Translate Marx' (November 1885).[155] Frank Kitz, who was a better lecturer than writer, was usually full of bombast in his contributions. A few of his were: 'Our Civilization' (April 1885), 'The Jerry Builder' (May 1885), 'The Unemployed' (November 1886), 'The Criminal Classes of the Future I & II, (February and March 1887), and 'The Blasted Furriners' (April 1888). His contributions, along with those of David Nicoll,[156] were, for the first five years, probably the most emotional ones contained within the journal. Nicoll, when he became editor in 1890, fell under the influence of the more violent and criminal of the anarchists who had infiltrated the League since they gained control of the Council in 1888. This was due to the boycott of the pro-parliamentary body who later left the League in that same year.

Although it is difficult to synchronize the disputes within the League with the rise and fall of the Commonweal, we must try and do so in order to concentrate on its general content, function, and impact. However, the wealth of information contained in this journal over the years precludes dealing with the detail of single issues. Most of the important issues were constantly referred to in its pages, three of the most prevailing being 'The Irish Question' between 1885-1887, the 'Fight for Free Speech' which lasted from the Trafalgar Square Riots in 1886 until the London Dock Strike in 1889, and the 'Haymarket Anarchists' who were arrested in May 1886 and executed in Chicago in November 1887. The repercussions were felt around the world.

Even though Commonweal wanted to educate the workers, its columns did not always suggest any more than an academic understanding of their plight. But from the beginning there were hopes that these problems could be overcome. In a section where East End workers were given space to contribute to its pages, one such writer, celebrating the arrival of the paper, said, before going on to expose the evils of the sweatshop system,

> We workers hail with great rejoicing the appearance of your new paper and hope it will soon come out weekly.[157]

However Frank Kitz, writing in the fourth issue, was under no illusions as to what had to be done if the Commonweal was to succeed in its task. Being from humble origins himself, he felt it necessary to make it plain what the workers were up against.

> In utilizing the space at my disposal for this paper I do not concern myself with advocacy of the abstract principles of Socialism, but prefer to exhibit the foulness, discomfort and filth which capitalism inflicts upon us in our everyday lives and thus negatively to make Socialism understood.[158]

Although this type of point was made very clear in many of the lectures, especially the outdoor propaganda sessions, the same spirit did not often find its way into the pages of Commonweal. For, as was declared as early as March 1885, the Socialist League, and hence the Commonweal, were opposed to political palliatives which included voting at elections, submitting or supporting candidates for election, or even advocating the efficacy of parliamentary government. This was the 'purist' attitude of the Morris group within the League which by 1888 controlled the Council. And it is for this reason that the League, including most of its members, has a due place in the libertarian tradition and, as its propaganda sheet, Commonweal must be considered in the same light. Morris's views on these issues, most of which were published in the Commonweal, were discussed in the previous chapter, and it was because of these views that he always ended up siding with anarchistic elements within the Socialist League. It was unfortunate that the men of 'reasonable' and non-violent anarchist sentiments like Charles,[159] Kitz, Mainwaring,[160] Turner, Nicoll, Lane, and Tochatti[161] were eventually supplanted by less responsible persons such as Mowbray,[162] Dr. Creaghe,[163] Malatesta,[164] and Cantwell.[165]

Morris left the League in November 1890 to form the Hammersmith Socialist Society after having been deposed as editor at the Annual Conference on May 25. Nicoll and Kitz became joint editors of the Commonweal, but Kitz left at the dissolution of the national network of the Socialist League in February 1891. The month after Morris's departure Commonweal reverted to being a monthly. It supported the concept of a General Strike but still rejected trade unionism as a palliative. Since July of that year Nicoll had been calling for a 'No Rent Campaign,' while Kitz was writing his favourite piece 'An Appeal to Soldiers.' The Commonweal of August 16 became much more violent in tenor, and Morris pointed out in a complaining letter to Nicoll that, being the publisher, he was still responsible for its content.[166]

Things rapidly declined, and in February 1891 the Commonweal was declared the property of the London Socialist League. In May it was subtitled 'A Revolutionary Journal of Anarchist Communism,' and Mowbray was the publisher. On April 9, 1892 Nicoll wrote an article called 'Are These Men Fit to Live,' which made reference to the judge and Chief Inspector involved in the case of the Walsall Anarchists. The police raided the Commonweal Offices on April 18, and Nicoll was sent to prison for eighteen months. Mowbray, who was also charged, was acquitted.[167]

The mission of the Commonweal was clear although its impact is much harder to assess. Initially it was meant to reflect the views and policies of the Socialist League, but research into the divisions within that body reveals that this was not the case. It often did not even represent the views of the majority of the Council,[168] and in its last days it merely served as a sounding board for the dispossessed, hostile, and malicious elements within the radical society. As a propaganda organ, it was noticed primarily for two reasons. It was hailed by the capitalist press as a radical socialist journal and for this reason deemed less than respectable. Within radical circles or, as they preferred to call themselves, revolutionary groups, it was both praised and damned, but at least it was acknowledged for taking a dissenting viewpoint even if that viewpoint was unacceptable in relation to particular issues and points of theory.[169] The radical press kept each other's image alive in spite of slandering one another. Commonweal, therefore, was a satisfactory propaganda organ which represented a less dogmatic approach to socialism while still not identifying itself with anarchism.

As its third, and not unimportant function, the journal was to act as a communication bulletin both for League members and interested parties alike. The reports on Branch meetings being held throughout the country enabled other groups to assess their performance, attitudes, and methods in comparison to their comrades. The lectures, social evenings, commemorative meetings, and open-air propaganda sessions served not only to point out what and where activities were taking place, but also enabled readers to assimilate the momentum of the movement as well as the personalities who played a large part in it. They were a source of, if not inspiration, at least a feeling of solidarity. Readers were able to find out what was happening and whether what was happening was effectual. In the later issues of Commonweal, books were reviewed and pamphlets and books were offered for sale, while any 'profits' entailed in these enterprises were immediately reinvested in the journal itself or were used to defray the expenses (usually fines) of some comrade. In short, the Commonweal acted as the primary force in holding the different branches of the League together and when it floundered in 1890, so did the branches. Of course, branch Secretaries kept in touch with one another and with London, but the journal was the major contributing factor in welding together the aspirations of the rank and file of the League whether it was through the content of its articles or the promotion of its services.

'Freedom' and the Freedom Press

> The aims of Freedom Press...consist in the political and social education of the people, the majority of whom have no political ideas beyond those received at school and through a so-called 'National Press' which is in fact the mouth-piece of the ruling class in society. [The Freedom Press]...is chiefly concerned with the publication of anarchist literature...to keep alive the ideas of anarchism.[170]

Keeping this obviously biased statement in mind, one might reasonably enquire whether these very broad based aims were in any way practically achieved either from the anarchist standpoint or from a more objective position.

We may begin by noting that the Freedom Press was initially made up of a group of associates, known as the Freedom Group of London Anarchists,[171] who gathered together early in 1886 shortly after the arrival of Kropotkin in England. They were mainly interested in establishing an anarchist press which would be used as the basis of revolutionary opposition to the capitalist press in general. But they also wanted to put forth a viewpoint which until this time was not represented by any of the radical papers of the day, and they especially wanted to counter the influence of the Marxist orientated Justice.

By October 1886, having failed to link up with the production team involved in producing The Anarchist, they had established a monthly journal which sold for one penny. It was called Freedom: A Journal of Anarchist-Socialism which was edited by Kropotkin and Charlotte M. Wilson, who was also listed as being its publisher. Mrs. Wilson had been on the Executive of the Fabian Society since December of 1884, but whilst remaining a member of the Society itself, devoted herself almost entirely to the anarchist cause. The journal continued regularly (except for a two month gap in January and February 1889 due to the illness of the editor) in its initial form until June 1889 when it was then redesignated as Freedom: A Journal of Anarchist-Communism through the advice of those who held that 'Socialism' had become too ambiguous a term. Charlotte Wilson continued as editor until January 1895 when she left due to the pressure of 'domestic affairs.' By May Freedom had resumed publication under the editorship of Alfred Marsh who had earlier been a member of the S.D.F.[172] By this time both the Commonweal and the Torch had ceased publication and the remains of the plant and type from both papers went to 127 Ossulston Street which was then the Freedom office. The remaining members of the Socialist League in London had by now allied themselves with the Freedom Group. In 1903, T.H. Keell took charge of Freedom,[173] and John Turner published the paper until 1907. During this time Tom Cantwell, who had been active in the Commonweal, acted as compositor. Keell took over the assets of Freedom in 1914 when the Group split over the issue of World War I, and he continued to publish it until 1927. At this time he removed to the anarchist Whiteway Colony in Stroud, Glos. and issued the Freedom Bulletin from 1928 until 1932. Freedom: A Journal of Libertarian Thought, Work and Literature, edited by Ambrose Barker and published by John Turner, began publication again in 1930 and has continued in one form or another, with war-time breaks, ever since.

For the sake of a deeper discussion and avoiding the personal disputes which later occurred, I shall take the second suspension date of January 1895 as a natural breaking point. At this time the manpower of both the Commonweal and the Anarchist were effectively under the umbrella of the Freedom Group and contributed to the wider output of the Freedom Press. From this time forward the whole tenor of the movement was directed towards political and social ends which were different from those presented during the prior ten years.

Freedom, like its counterparts, relied heavily on voluntary labour for its composition and distribution, and donations helped defray its considerable production expenses. A normal run was 2000 copies per month.[174] It depended more upon sales income than did the Commonweal, for at no time did it have any wealthy financial backers (like Morris) who were prepared to pay the debts which were incurred. Freedom, with about the same sales as Commonweal, but more than The Anarchist (which was itself subsidized by Seymour), managed to pay its own way in spite of the tremendous odds against it.

From the beginning this journal had one central message, "Free yourself!"[175] for by doing so you will aid in freeing others and the society in which you live from the oppression of the property-owning class. This theme was constantly reiterated over the years although in various practical, theoretical, and philosophical modes of expression. <u>Freedom</u>, to those involved in the libertarian movement, was the literary embodiment of a coherent set of ideas and a form of organization "...such as is impossible when one hard and fast line is fitted to all conduct."[176] It was not an 'official organ' of any group but an "...advocate of the equal claim of each man and woman to work for the community as seems good to him or her - calling no man master..."[177]

In fact, the publishers of <u>Freedom</u> were determined that the paper should not be closely identified with any one movement and particularly not a political one. For it said, when <u>Commonweal</u> claimed to have become 'A Revolutionary Journal of Communist Anarchism,' in May 1891, that,

> As long as the paper was the "Official Organ of the Socialist League" supposed to express the united connection of a loose organization of branches wherein was represented every shade of Socialistic opinion, from the mildest Parliamentary social reform to the most revolutionary Communist Anarchism, it could not be thoroughly satisfactory to anyone.[178]

Nonetheless, <u>Freedom</u> itself claimed a consistent point of view which it presented as educational propaganda of both positive and negative aspects. Their initial editorial entitled 'Freedom' made this clear, for although anarchism is not here mentioned by name, one is all the more taken by the libertarian approach which they adopt. First, in terms of the individual and society, as it ought to be,

> We <u>believe</u> each sane adult human being to possess an equal and infeasible claim to direct his life from within by the light of his own consciousness, to the sole responsibility of guiding his own action as well as forming his own opinions.
>
> ...we <u>reject</u> every method of enforcing assent, as in

itself a hindrance to effectual cooperation...but we
assert the social duty of each to defend by force if need
be, his dignity as a free human being, and the like
dignity in others, from every form of insult and of
oppression.[179]

In this statement of general belief can be discerned the prime
sentiments of the journal as well as those of the libertarian movement
as a whole -- the twin problems of freedom and authority as they appear
in all social relationships. From this comes the ultimate rejection of
the State and that which is 'merely' political, i.e., legalized
institutional coercion. Yet what can be seen as the 'positive' side of
their propaganda somehow always appeared to be of 'negative' parentage
because criticism of the fundamental institutions in the existing order
of things tended to be viewed by the supporters of the system as a
wholly subversive challenge. This happened because the libertarian
criticisms were grounded in specific moral assumptions and humanitarian
concerns which their opponents believed at times to be correct in
principle but not politically or socially advantageous to a system
thriving on laissez-faire capitalism and imperialism.[180]

As a consequence, the libertarian criticisms expressed in the
pages of _Freedom_ were a logical derivation from first principles. Here
again we have to contend with certain terms. For, at the practical
level, the revolution was to be brought about in alliance with
socialist principles, namely socialism as an economic method of
organization, and not as the Fabians envisioned it, a political formula
by which the state could be run.

In an article entitled 'Act For Yourselves' it was stated that
workingmen must fight against the oppression of the capitalist mode of
production as part of the fight for _economic_ equality.

...nothing short of expropriation on a vast scale

carried out by the workmen themselves, can be the first step towards the reorganization of our production on socialist principles.[181]

Obviously the term 'Socialist' is important here and we must understand fully what is meant by it in economic as well as a political terms, or at least differentiate them. By not doing so we would fall into the quagmire of confusion endemic to many writers of the period. We must remember first that Freedom, in its formative years, professed to be a 'Journal of Anarchist-Socialism.'

In a very lucid article labelled 'Names and Opinions' which was almost certainly written by Charlotte Wilson, it is simply observed that there was "...confusion...as to the real meaning of words."[182]

From the anarchist point of view,

Socialism is an economic term;...Anarchism is the theory of social organization on the basis of equal freedom of all members of the community without the recognition of any rule or authority of one man over the other.[183]

On the other hand socialism, used in the economic sense only, could be subdivided into two different categories - 'Collectivism' and 'Communism.'

Collectivists are agreed that the principle of distribution ought to be, - To each according to his deeds.[184]

But the 'Anarchists' of Freedom claimed to be 'Socialists' in the 'Communist' mould.

Communism...[says that]...all wealth...is a public possession and the principle upon which it must be shared amongst the members of the community is, - To each according to his needs.[185]

So although all 'Socialists' agreed as regards the idea of expropriation, it was upon the method of distribution where most of the disagreement took place. For obvious philosophical and doctrinal reasons all of the anarchists disavowed state expropriation. Instead,

"...they would substitute the principle of unanimity of free consent, for the principle of majority rule."[186] This meant, in effect, that they were bound up in their opposition to parliamentary rule and hence to political participation which could reinforce a system which they did not consider to be democratic or just in the broadest sense.

They were therefore at odds in many ways with the Fabians who, as social democrats, attempted by political means, via their Parliamentary League, to give authority to their opinions by contending for political office[187] and actively supported candidates seeking a seat at Westminster. In anarchist terms they were 'State Socialists of the Collectivist' school. And while the anarchists acknowledged the merits of the Fabian view of democracy, they did not submit to it themselves. For they held that,

> Anarchism like Democracy is a political theory compatible
> with diverse economical opinions. As there are
> Individualist and Socialist Democrats, so there are
> Individualist and Socialist Anarchists.[188]

Freedom considered the really useful work of the Fabian Society to be its public debates and lectures on social questions which were regularly publicized and debated within its own columns.[189] As for the Social Democratic Federation, with whom they greatly disagreed in points of major theoretical importance, they commented that "...Their street demonstrations are capital."[190] Yet, strangely enough, they were at that time less sympathetic with the Socialist League whom they considered to be their closest sympathizers because they continued to "...shirk the question of authority - one of the root questions of our day."[191]

Consequently, by still regarding themselves as socialists, the Freedom Group could legitimately maintain a major theoretical

distinctiveness from all of the other revolutionary groups of the time.
With reference to the whole of the international libertarian movement,
the article on 'Names and Opinions' summed up by saying,

> We...are Socialists, and share with our European comrades
> and the brave men who recently sealed their faith with
> their blood in Chicago, the conviction that Anarchism and
> Communism are political and economic counterparts.[192]

Yet, even after laboriously attempting to make their position
clear, the socialists were not to accept the anarchist stand at its
face value. In the 'Freedom Discussion Meetings' which took place
every month, these problems were constantly regurgitated, and seven
months later there were still signs that all was not going well for the
shaky alliance of radical organizations. For as reported at a meeting
in April 1888,

> ...we Communist-Anarchists are evidently not agreed with
> our Social Democratic comrades as to what is really meant
> by Communism. That must be cleared up.[193]

Two things come out of this. The first being that the various
groups, although often opposed to one another's ideas, did in fact
communicate regularly and support one another on the broader issues in
order to build up the face of solidarity in such campaigns as the Free
Speech Movement and the Irish Question.

But there was in-fighting, and people such as George Bernard
Shaw, who, while criticizing the anarchists could not be said to be
ignorant of their ideas, attempted to 'tar them all with the same
brush.' Admittedly, he disliked all forms of individualism, anarchist
or otherwise, but his conversion to the economical aspects of socialism
made him 'blind' to the more philosophical implications of the
anarchist creed. He leant the power of his pen to what was essentially
a tactical foray to confuse an already complicated situation.

In one instance of attack, while admitting his sympathy with 'Collectivism' by inference, Shaw makes the so-called 'Law of Rent' the focal point of the socialist view. Writing in Today, he dismisses anarchists in one paragraph and certainly suggests that they are not socialists.

> When Anarchism was first heard of in the Socialist movement in England, it was welcomed as a protest against the insane disregard of the lessons of political experience as to personal liberty apparent in some Collectivist ideals. But it has since developed into a doctrine of unmitigated individualism, having for its economic basis, an invincible ignorance of the Law of Rent. As such, it is no longer welcome, or tolerable to Socialists.[194]

Shaw was blatantly trying to disassociate himself and his fellow Fabians from the fairly recently acquired image of anarchists as violent criminals and individual bomb-throwers.[195] There had been a flurry of international awareness regarding anarchism since the trial of the anarchists in Chicago who just that month had been sentenced to death for their part in the so-called Haymarket Affair. Shaw and his friends were even more convinced of their self-righteousness after watching the anarchists drive Morris from the Socialist League and hearing about the exploits of Ravachol in France.[196] However, misrepresentation and libel was true of the whole of the press at this time, and Shaw might be easier to forgive in this context but for his obvious connections with many prominent anarchist-communists.[197]

Surprisingly enough, though, there was a great deal of solidarity on most occasions. One annual event which brought them all together was the celebration or the commemoration of the Paris Commune of 1871. Some even saw the formation of the London County Council as the future London Commune.[198] Another very emotive show of strength was mounted after the Chicago anarchists had been sentenced to death, while the anniversary of their execution was celebrated for many decades as religiously as was May Day.[199] The fact that the 'Chicago Martyrs' were declared anarchists did not inhibit all the groups from uniting behind them to such a degree that for a while the ideas of anarchism were given greater consideration. But in addition to the large London meeting prior to the executions, there were at least nine reported meetings held across the country. On November 11, 1887, these men became martyrs to the whole radical movement and provided it with the supreme example of what could happen in a democratic country which even had a codified Bill of Rights embodied in its constitution.

As well as acting as an agent of communication for the many groups who did not have their own publications,[200] Freedom constantly received reports and stories from corresp dents outside the country. Stepniak kept the readers informed about events in Russia and wrote about the continuing problems of that country in such articles as 'The Russian Peasantry.'[201] Letters came from America which brought the plight of the plains Indians to the attention of English readers.

A letter from Lizzie M. Holmes of the Chicago Freedom, explained how white scouts, like William 'Buffalo Bill' Cody, made sure that there were always 'Indian troubles' in the areas he visited. In reference to the Indians, who had to deal with the hunters and the speculators who were continuing to pour towards the West Coast, she said,

> As to civilization, it is to their credit that they refuse to receive it with all its attendant evils, vices, wrongs, disease, and poverty. They are too brave and free to take upon themselves the bonds that civilization's poor must bear.[202]

It must be added that most socially conscious people of today would subscribe to the opinions expressed by Lizzie Holmes although that was not the case in the 1890s. This was one of the main problems of journals like Freedom, who on the whole expressed views, and advanced solutions, which as we can see today, were far ahead of their time. But this also serves to point out that not all of the people, if even a majority, in the late Victorian era were as prudish and unhumanitarian as the historians would have us believe. It was the colonial policies and the voices of the politicians which obscured these facts. For there were indeed groups within Victorian society who viewed with apprehension and disgust the actions of the political, social, and religious leaders of Britain.

In addition to the articles from international subscribers and correspondents, Freedom also received other radical papers from Australia, France, Holland, Belgium, and the United States, whose articles from time to time were incorporated into the journal.[203]

As exiles, both Malatesta and Kropotkin wrote extensively in Freedom; and it was in its pages that their work was usually first translated into English. Kropotkin's Conquest of Bread and Communism and the Wage System, to name but two works, appeared in serialized form.[204] In the same way Malatesta contributed his well known essay on Anarchy as well as his extensive dialogue entitled A Talk Abut Anarchist Communism Between Two Workers.[205] Of the many of the other names that appeared very few were well known outside the anarchist movement. Many people wrote under pseudonyms or initials, but most of the leading articles remained unsigned and it can be assumed, based on a certain amount of evidence, that they were written by Wilson and Kropotkin.[206]

The names, opinions, and lectures of other notables in the radical movement appeared in almost every issue. Thus we are able to ascertain Morris's views on the relation between the notion of violence and the communist ideal,[207] Shaw's ideas on expropriation and rent, as they pertain to anarchist thought, but seen through the eyes of a Fabian;[208] or ponder Auberon Herbert's individualistic conception of the 'Voluntary State.'[209]

Anarchism was discussed from every conceivable viewpoint. We have the views of a libertarian socialist who wrote for Commonweal, J. M. Brown, who did a series which was simply entitled 'Anarchism.'[210] There was 'Anarchism According to Stepniak' the Russian writer and author of Underground Russia, one of Morris's favourite books.[211] One of Edward Carpenter's most poignant pieces was a long letter wherein he discussed his views and expressed how he thought the whole radical movement ought to be presented to those who were not within its ranks.[212] He was later to lay claim to being an anarchist himself. Kropotkin initiated the first discussion on anarchist morality, and in other issues anarchism was linked to concepts of organization, social democracy, property, the trade union movement, and of course, freedom.

On the whole, the paper rallied around all the conceptions implied by its name but did this in a manner which was to leave no doubt as to the social theory which it supported. For it not only aired the views of other radical organizations but it attempted to put into perspective every aspect of anarchist and libertarian theory in relation to these views. The serious content of these messages delivered by the various organizations did not usually hamper the considerable and continuous dialogue between potentially factionalized elements. A stern demeanour was not always thought to be the best method with which to pursue the personal ramifications of particular social views. The comraderie of those within the movements cannot be better illustrated than to make quick mention of one particular debate. One such discussion -- on anarchism -- took place between the Fabians and representatives of some other groups. It appeared that,

> Mr. Graham Wallas, [was] surprised to hear that Anarchists favoured organization; his belief [was] that there would have to be Acts of Parliament to prevent the people in the galleries of theatres from spitting upon the heads of those in the pits.[213]

Much of the discussions seem to have taken on this somewhat light-hearted vein in the face of some all too serious theoretical disagreements. In an argument about who would 'pull the cord' to hang a man, Mr. Herbert Blands offered to fill the post of Lord Chief Hangman under the rule of Social Democracy.[214] It might be added that this attitude was not peculiar only to members of the Fabian Society although their sense of 'gamesmanship' was more highly developed that that of many of their comrades.

Nonetheless, in spite of its occasional tongue-in-cheek attitude, as a journal campaigning for a revolutionary change in society, Freedom functioned as a major alternative to the state socialists who were everywhere attempting to radicalize and organize the working class into political participation.[215] The state socialists, including the Fabians, believed that revolutionary change could be brought about through campaigns wholly within the legal and political framework of Victorian England. To this extent, the Fabians, as they usually claimed, were a strong radical element bent on evolution rather than revolution, while the S.D.F. took the exactly opposite stand. Along with the members of the Socialist League, and most notably William Morris, the Freedom Group were not prepared to compromise with the parliamentary system. Resting on what they believed to be solid historical evidence, they could have no faith in revolutionary change emanating from a body which was itself inherently reformist. Parliament could not be used as a means to the revolutionary end. In an article entitled 'Parliamentary Rule' they re-affirmed this belief and stated that,

> ...if anything is to be done in a Socialist sense in this country...I[t] will be accomplished outside parliament, by the free initiative of the British workman, who will take possession for themselves of capital, land, houses, and instruments of labour, and then combine in order to start life on the new lines of local independence.[216]

They, as anarchists and libertarians, were fighting for a social and not a political revolution and declared an offensive stand on the economic and political institutions and those who presumably controlled them.

> It is was between the people and their masters, and the hypocritical mockery of judicial calmness and impartiality which those masters would mask their side of the class struggle only serves to make it more ghastly, yet more destructive of all generous and kindly human feeling.[217]

It is indeed the case that there was a considerable body of opinion in the radical movement who felt that the 'palliatives' of parliamentary democracy solved few if any of the problems of the day. However, the anarchists, unlike most of libertarian socialists, were stubborn in their resistance to the demand for some form of government or, as they called it somewhat mistakenly, -- 'State Rule.' The premises on which they held this belief stemmed from two overriding observations they had made on government. First, "...that the centre of political organization lies not in Parliament, as is generally believed, but in the Executive, in the Government backed by the propertied classes; second, that Government secretes power just as Capital secretes wealth. Men called upon to represent other people...use the opportunity for themselves and their supporters. As a result no Government ever has been or will be managed either by the people or for the people."[218]

Although the devolution of power in itself was seen as a good thing, they claimed that it ought not to be done at the will of governmental authority.

> Local governments are obviously as bad, if not worse than central ones. There is only one alternative, abolition of Government, supply its place by free Associations of Workmen, possessing their own means of labour, regulating their own labour, protecting themselves and distributing the products of labour as they like, with no control whatever by a central committee, with no bureaucratic army or any other army; which is precisely the Communist Anarchist position.[219]

Malatesta, in his article 'Anarchy,' dealt with the fundamental problem of government and social control; he was one of the most conceptually clear thinkers when dealing with the problems of state rule. In this essay, in particular, Malatesta displays remarkable insight into one of the reasons as to why the anarchists always seemed to be fighting a rear-guard action despite the fact that most of their criticisms were of a very positive and straightforward nature. In contrast with what Shaw said in the first issue of The Anarchist, Malatesta did not suggest that the cause ought to bear its burdens like Christian soldiers.

> The difficulty which Anarchists meet with in spreading their views does not depend upon the name they have given themselves, but upon the fact that their conceptions strike at all the inveterate prejudices that people have about the function of government, of the STATE as it is

called.[220]

Although this may well be the case, it was around this time that the destructionist side of anarchist action became apparent to the mass of the public. Sensationalist newspaper reports assured that the name 'anarchist' would fall into great disrepute, for people began to identify the idea of 'no state' with the image of chaos and unprecedented violence. It was the major import of the propagandists and the journals to attempt to change this growing opinion which reached its height in the early 1890s. Yet, as Malatesta continued in his article, he felt bound to use the term 'destruction' as a most meaningful and descriptive word if applied in the correct context.

> ...the conceptions which the Anarchists wish to express of the destruction of every political institution based on authority and on the constitution of a free and equal society based upon the harmony of interests, and the voluntary contribution of all to the satisfaction of social needs.[221]

He then went on to make a modest proposal, but one which was of little value unless the 'prejudices' about the name 'anarchist' were wiped out.

> For these reasons we believe it would be better to use the expression ABOLITION OF THE STATE as little as possible, and to substitute for it another clearer and more concrete — ABOLITION OF GOVERNMENT.[222]

However, as we know all too well today, this task was never successfully carried out and it was the 'destruction of the state theory' which gave people grounds for describing the 'state of anarchy' as one of chaos and the anarchist as the enemy of all civilized sentiments. It was thus that the concept of authority and its implications within the philosophical structure of anarchism were pushed into the background.

Yet as early as August 1887 it was realized that in terms of theoretical literature "there was a sad lack of Anarchist pamphlets in England."[223]   From this time forward it came to be the recognized chore of the Freedom Group to reverse the trend of just having sporadic individuals print their personal opinions under the title 'Anarchist.' Lane's Anti-Statist Communist Manifesto was a typical example of a political statement which essentially confused those who read it. For although it did not acknowledge to be an anarchist tract, it did represent anarchist opinion even though it was not easily recognizable in the general British context. It was in fact a statement of anarchist principles in the disguised form of the Socialist League's output of libertarian literature. Another pamphlet, Holy of Holies, Confessions of an Anarchist, written by C. H. Clarke, led Freedom to comment, -- "Lamentations of an egoist would have been more descriptive."[224]   As the result of such occurrences, Freedom gave themselves the task of coordinating, in conjunction with the International Publishing Company, the output of revolutionary and anarchist pamphlets which could be used to raise the general level of discourse and propaganda technique.

The Development of Concepts

As invaluable as the journals and pamphlets were in presenting the issues of concern to the libertarians, one must work very hard indeed to sift out the conceptual ambiguities within what has, until now, been a fringe area of socialist thought. Thus, in dealing with the pertinent concepts I shall draw upon the whole body of literature which I have gathered together in the bibliography.

It is essential to the understanding of libertarian thought, that one familiarize oneself with the concepts involved, but one must also focus upon the way in which they were used in libertarian literature. As has too often been done, a cursory view of the literature is not sufficient for such an understanding, for it invites a form of comment based on entirely misconstrued conceptual formulations. For as we have seen, by using Mill's concept of individuality for instance, one might adequately explain libertarian ideas to some extent. But this would not allow one to assume that libertarian individualism was merely a peculiar form of liberal individualism. To criticize libertarian individualism, on the premise that it is similar to the liberal conception of individualism would be a mistake. Theories or doctrines should not be judged in terms of predefined concepts which are not applicable to them if one expects either a new insight or a clarification of ideas. This is why, in the first chapter on Mill, I did not criticize Mill's ideas on liberty in terms of libertarian concepts, for such notions do not logically apply to what Mill said. The libertarian critique of Mill was meant to show the divergence of ideas and concepts. Similarly, Mill's ideas on custom have little in common with Kropotkin's or Carpenter's, just as Henry Appleton's views on government were not obviously compatible with those of Malatesta on the same subject. For, in fact, people often used the same words to convey different ideas, and, as was the case with Appleton and Malatesta, they even used different words to try and explain the same fundamental ideas. This has been one of the most persistent problems in dealing with libertarian ideas, for the use and abuse of conceptual formulations depends very much on the audience one is addressing.

Having gone through the critical, developmental, and historical aspects I shall now deal with the two central conceptual problems of libertarian thought. These are freedom and authority.

If, as the libertarians claim, they reject all authority as well as oppose it, then we might suppose that their criticisms of the concept itself will be vociferous. What is worthy of note, however, is that they do not want to abolish <u>all</u> authority but only certain manifestations of it. Yet they do not call what remains 'authority,' for the word itself conjures up images which are not only unpalatable to the libertarian, but their use of the word to describe <u>acceptable</u> circumstances would be confusing to the reader. The libertarian rejection of authority is consequently not so straightforward as it first appears. Similarly, the libertarians, in claiming to fight for 'freedom' do not always adequately distinguish between freedom or liberty. But what becomes clear is that they think differently about the two concepts, and the extent to which they do so ties in closely with their ideas on authority. Thus it is imperative that we deal with these concepts in a manner which will subsequently lead not only to a clarification of terms but also to a more thorough and comprehensive insight into libertarian thought.

CHAPTER FOUR

THE NOTION OF AUTHORITY

The term 'authority,' whether preceded by an adjective or not, has had various usages since the Roman conception of <u>auctoritas</u> (as possession of the Senate) and the neater notion of <u>auctor</u>. In conformance with these usages, both past and present, but in particular with reference to libertarian literature, I propose to discuss some of the problems presented by the concept of authority, a necessary step towards an understanding of the libertarian view of the world.

Usage suggests that the term 'authority' connotes a form of power which is often seen, in simplistic terms, as a possession of a particular type of attribute. Further consideration reveals that such power cannot be exercised in isolation; so that authority is usually viewed as a relationship between two or more people. Thomas Hobbes, in <u>The Leviathan</u>, recalled the Latin origins of the word when he attempted to identify authority and its role in a <u>civil</u> society. Hobbesian authority was, therefore, an 'unnatural' phenomenon, and as such meant much more than the straightforward brutal application of power. He stated:

> Of persons artificial, some have their words and actions owned by those whom they represent. And then the person is the actor; and he that owneth his words and actions is the AUTHOR: in which case the actor acteth by authority...and as the right of possession, is called dominion; so the right of doing any action, is called AUTHORITY. So that by authority is always understood a right of doing any act; and <u>done</u> by <u>authority</u>, done by commission or licence, from him whose right it is.[1]

This view of man as authority in a 'civil' as opposed to a 'natural' society is interesting because it incorporates three distinct ideas which have been prevalent in discussions about the concept of authority. First of all, it is the author who bestows authority, by right, upon the actor as a form of possession. To the extent that authority originates from authorship, or is authorized by a person who is not himself the authority, there is, at least at some point, a two-way relationship. So, secondly, Hobbes sees authority as a relationship even though by right some form of possession is involved. Thirdly, once the relationship has been established, this right or legitimizing factor defines the boundaries of the relationship between the author and the actor. Power is involved, or at least implied, insofar as the actor has now dominion over the author in a relationship which is ostensibly beneficial to them both and necessary in the creation of a 'civil' society.

Seen in these terms, authority, without the attachment of qualifications, usually refers to some form of power of one person over another. Yet the extent of this power is limited, for depending upon what is involved in the notion of right, there are either implicitly or explicitly legitimizing factors to be taken into account. This legitimacy, as in the case of Hobbes' 'right' or 'licence', undoubtedly emanates from the author in the relationship, even though it is subsumed within a particular framework through prior agreement. Whether this framework of legitimacy refers to a set of rules, customs, norms, or traditions, it serves to define the 'fitness' of certain forms of social behaviour. The legitimacy is circumscribed by the framework within which it is exercised and with the boundaries set by individuals, groups, or interests in the society, both past and present.

It would seem, then, that both the notions of power and legitimacy are intricately intertwined within the concept of authority. Thus if we think of authority as legitimate power or legitimate influence, we can see more easily many of the libertarian objections to the authority of government and countless other institutions. For the sake of simplicity we might say that to have power is to have the ability to force someone to comply or obey in the knowledge that disobedience could bring sanctions against anyone who disobeyed. Influence, on the other hand, is broadly the ability of one person to effect a change in the behaviour of another without obvious recourse to enforceable sanctions. If such power or influence were legitimized in any form legal or moral, we could say that an authority relation existed. Here we might make two useful distinctions regarding the notion of authority which, for the sake of clarification, will be referred to as command-authority and belief-authority.[2]

Command-authority is exhibited in the type of authority relation where the source of the command, order, or directive issues the command with the expectation that he will be obeyed and the knowledge that he has the resources at his disposal to elicit compliance or else bring sanctions, in the form of unpleasant consequences, to bear. Not only the power, but the necessary coercive forces, are at hand even though it is better that they never be used; for if once force, rather than the threat of force, is used and punitive sanctions actually imposed, then clearly no authority relation can be seen to exist. For in a situation of disobedience like this, where there has been no grant of legitimacy to the source of the command and the consequences, or the price of compliance, mean the use of coercion; we would have, in effect, a _power_ relation. However, if there was no compliance and the right of command from the source was legitimized, then there would be an _authority_ relation and the disobedient person could expect due punishment which, when finally enacted, would be a power relation arising out of the former authority relation. Hence, failure to obey a specific law, for example, would in due course result in the overt use of force either to ensure compliance or as a punishment. In such instances, it is not the legitimacy of the source which is at issue but the content of the command, i.e., the law itself. Thus the law, no matter how much it influences or suggests modes of behaviour, is a definite command at the point of conflict with the individual. Likewise command-authority carries with it the implicit assumption that it must be obeyed regardless of belief. Nonetheless, if one man believes that it is right or legitimate for another man to issue commands, in the expectation of obedience, he has, in essence, as Hobbes' author, conferred the right to exercise power. This does not necessarily oblige him to accept the unbounded use of this right because the framework of legitimacy should adequately clarify the boundaries of acceptable action. Yet if a community has given someone the power to command and expect obedience under certain conditions, for example, under the terms of a set of rules or a contract, then people will be rewarded for obedience (often just not punished) or punished for disobedience within the given framework. But to go further, if one also believes in the legitimacy of this power, that power is thus enhanced by the development of a belief pattern and occupies a position of belief-authority. In the end, however, one cannot judge the form of the relationship unless there is a response to the edicts of the so-called authority. Even in a command-authority

238

relationship the one who is asked to obey has clearly some form of influence over the situation, and though there is not equality of reciprocity (in terms of actual influence on either side), reciprocity is still of primary importance where the right to command and the execution of obedience are not basic assumptions. The reciprocity of influence comes to the fore in those situations where a power, in the form of probable sanctions, is absent -- namely, in the case of what I have called belief-authority.

Belief-authority, much more common and hence more social than its regularly politicized counterpart, is but one kind of influence relation. Unlike the command-authority relation, it is possible that a person could be influenced without their being aware of it.[3] But they must be sufficiently aware of the influence to assign it legitimacy if an authority relation is to be perceived. The influenced person is thus important; for without influence, there is no response, and without response, there is no evidence of any influence. A person's awareness, and his judgment of legitimacy are both necessary for there to be an authority relation. But the assignment of legitimacy here is much more an act on the part of the one being influenced than it is in the case of command-authority. This is so because there is no command, no imperative, which demands obedience as a matter of right whether that right has been assigned or not. There are, of course, forms of communication which one might believe to be commands, such as strong suggestions, but they do not imply sanctions which can be enforced as a matter of right. Emotional blackmail or the disclosure of privileged information by or on behalf of the source of the influence may well be called a form of sanction, but its effects are not nearly as obvious as is disobedience to the law or the failure to comply to the wishes or orders of someone in the position of command-authority. Belief-authority is a type of legitimate influence which exists when the person being influenced sees fit to behave in a manner in which he otherwise would not have acted, and it legitimizes his response because of the qualities or characteristics of the source. Although it has often been claimed that it is the <u>intentions</u> of the source which must be complied with, as does Russell when he defines power as the 'production of intended effects,' this does not have to be the case. It is the respondent's beliefs about the intentions or desires of the source which are important, for it is these beliefs which prompt the granting of legitimacy.

If we take authority generally to refer to that type of relationship wherein the person influenced believes the influence upon him to be legitimate, we are not far from the Latin meaning of the word. For although the <u>actor</u> is the authority, it is the one who is influenced, who ascribes the legitimacy, who is the <u>author</u> of it. Clearly, many cases of command-authority are also cases of belief-authority. But what is important is that libertarian criticisms of authority are virtually without exception based upon their rejection of command-authority as legitimate power and not of belief-authority as legitimate influence. I believe it can be shown that the libertarians are not, in reality, against all forms of authority as they are assumed to be and indeed as they so eagerly claimed to be. On the contrary, their theories rest upon a highly complex system of belief-authority.

What the libertarians in effect are saying is that command-authority ought not to be necessary in the conduct of human affairs. To them it is illegitimate because they do not believe in the legitimacy of the power which is being wielded by those who claim to be 'in authority'. They do not accept that anyone should have the power to prolong inequality, to dictate behaviour by law, protect monopoly or private property, or make men into 'wage-slaves' in the name of economic progress. And when the libertarians speak of their opposition to authority, it is opposition to the form of command-authority which they believe to be responsible for the 'artificial' system of economic tyranny which deprives the majority of the populace of a more complete form of freedom. In other words, they claim that man would be freer if he were not compelled to submit, as a result of his belief, to the legitimacy of command-authority since that is a form of compliance ultimately based on force. It is 'bad' or illegitimate because it is a form of external authority which seeks to consolidate internal authority in its own likeness. The libertarians regard this as no better than 'brain-washing'.

On the other hand, if authority is understood as legitimate influence, it can, I believe, be shown to be in accord and not in conflict with the libertarian notion of freedom. This form of authority does not make use of command, coercion, or obedience, either in a one-to-one or one-to-many relationship. It does require the judgment of the persons who are influenced that the influence upon them is legitimate. In effect, this means that this form of authority is consciously granted rather than begrudgingly accepted. It is a matter of belief, of judgment being made by the recipient of the influence, who is in the true sense the 'author' of the relationship. Much belief-authority could be said to have its roots in emulated behaviour, that is, in people simply following the example of those others who 'command' respect. Such emulative response to authority is in opposition to the compliant response which is demanded in the command-authority relationship. It is worth noting that, for the libertarians, the emulation of authority is not only acceptable but often desirable. It is the emulative response in a belief-authority relation which makes the need for command and coercion unnecessary since the response itself, or the emulation, arises out of beliefs the influenced person has about the quality of the source. Such influences, to the extent that they are authoritative, bind together the two or more persons involved in the relationship as a result of respect, admiration, or belief. It is a form of social bond which is dependent upon the knowledge and participation of all the actors in the relationship and not entirely upon a framework of legitimacy which is often beyond people's control. Belief-authority relations become a part of interpersonal and social relations rather than an adjunct of a larger and more formalized legal or political construct.

The libertarians held that this form of belief-authority, which resulted in emulative behaviour rather than intentional behaviour,[4] was inimical to freedom in an inegalitarian or monopolistic society since it seemed to foster an attitude of paternalism within the existing authoritative structures. They had a certain fear, which is readily understood, about the wrong type of behaviour being emulated. Paternalism, in a 'corrupt' society, would end up as little more than manipulated hero-worship, giving carte blanche to persons in positions of superior strength or ability. It was necessary that people emulate the 'good' as opposed to the 'evil' side of man as a social animal. The libertarians did not want people to look to the law as a panacea or to perpetuate the legal-constitutional system as it existed in nineteenth-century England. They did not believe that the framework of legitimacy of that system could be altered by making use of the system itself. In other words, they felt that the system had to be thoroughly revolutionized before emulative behaviour could be considered a constructive part of social relationships. They believed that emulated action, that is, emulated intended behaviour on the part of the one who was influenced was necessary in the normal state of society, and that it was likely to be unconventional. Emulated behaviour was likely to be the reverse — it would be conservative and stultifying. However, in the libertarian society of the future, mores having changed as they did in Morris's News From Nowhere, emulated behaviour would be more acceptable and would be in effect a part of that social habit which would be the binding force of the new society.

Peter Kropotkin, one of the more 'scientific' of the anarchist theorists, who considered himself to be a libertarian, saw that, — "The best of men is made essentially bad by the exercise of authority."[5] He was obviously speaking here about command-authority. Although the libertarians tend not to use the term 'authority' in the exposition of their own case, the libertarian doctrine, to my mind, does contain a concept of authority. Libertarian authority or, what I have called, belief-authority is made acceptable by a morality which is wholly opposed to the use of force as a means to an end. According to Kropotkin, this morality verges on the commonsensical.

> it is a morality of a people which does not look for the sun at midnight (it is instinctual) - a morality without compulsion or authority, a morality of habit.[6]

Kropotkin argued that that form of morality would be enough to supplant the liberal system of liberty which was supposedly to be guaranteed by law in the way that Mill hoped it would. People would be moral if they were 'placed in a position' whereby they could emulate the right kind of authorities.

> Men are to be moralized by placing them in a position
> which shall continue to develop in them those habits
> which are social, and to weaken those which are not so.
> A morality which has become instinctive is the true
> morality, the only morality which endures while religions
> and systems of philosophy pass away.[7]

The idea of a morality of habit is in a strict sense what
Edward Carpenter was referring to when he spoke about the necessity for
mankind to 'do without rules'.[8] Carpenter, like Morris before him,
had a strong sense of hope and a vision of the future without
authority.

> My contention, then, is that our hope for future society
> lies in its embodiment of these two great principles
> jointly: (1) The recognition of the Common Life as
> providing the foundation-element of general morality, and
> (2) the recognition of Individual Affection and
> Expression -- ...as building up the higher groupings and
> finer forms of the structure.[9]

These were the desires which Carpenter wished to see fulfilled
"...for the solution of all sorts of moral and social progress."[10]
Authority would be replaced by custom, habit, or instinct or a moral
rule which is, in effect, an emanation of conscience, for it is
conscience which legitimizes habitual action. According to most
libertarians, the influence of the will on the agent in the presence of
any external influence makes, what I have called, belief-authority,
acceptable. He is an influencer as well as the influenced, for the
agent in his external actions who can legitimately influence without
recourse to coercion may find himself in a position of authority.
Nonetheless, internal-authority or what is basically an already
ingested moral sense is the foundation of all social life or what
Carpenter called 'Common Life'.

The libertarians believed that the individual in society ought to be able to choose for himself unhampered by law or institutionalized command-authority. They were convinced that most conflict arose from the inequalities which were exemplified in the distribution of wealth and the actual necessity of working more often for the selfish interests of another than for oneself and one's community. Like Morris, they believed that the capitalist system created a state of misery for the vast majority of the populace. The libertarians claimed that inequality favoured the person who could obtain either economic or coercive means (in effect, positions of command-authority) which would permit them to command the labour of others. The offshoot of such behaviour was an inculcated moral code which condoned the justice of a competitive system where, in the end, the acquisition of power, in few ways morally encumbered by law, gave rise to powerful and authoritative interest groups. Those who had sought power in the hope of attaining greater freedom would find themselves defending their positions in a society which was morally as well as physically hierarchical. And the hierarchical scale of power, which granted stability at the expense of equal freedom, was to the libertarian, unjust.

They claimed that the only freedom allowed by those in positions of authority in the modern state essentially related to the quantity rather than to the quality of choice. Modern man had a multiplicity of choices as compared to his forefathers, but the efficacy of these choices was often without substance as the inequity of the system itself pointed out. The conception of freedom as a multiplication of choice outside those areas which were dominated by powerful political and economic forces was too narrow. It was in no real way conducive to moral action as the boundaries of choice had already been predefined by the type of economic system under which the people lived, and the constitutional system which most had grown to accept. The libertarians claimed that without a notion which defined the quality of the choice to be as relevant as the quantity, the individual in society was, in no meaningful sense a free person.

In order to give a moral quality to the idea of freedom as choice it was essential that the notion of command-authority be eliminated because of its restrictive nature. Jean Grave, a Frenchman much read and admired by the libertarians, saw very clearly that the elimination of such authority was but the beginning point towards a permanent change in social relations.

> The total elimination of the principle of authority and of institutions, the powers in which it is manifested; these are the **means** and the **end** of Scientific Anarchy, the aim of which is the realization of the common good by the suppression of competition and the harmonizing of interests.[11]

The identification of both ends and means as being synonymous is extremely important to the libertarians, for it is one of the major prerequisites to the building of a moral society. But again, without 'moral force' society would remain "...nothing but an incoherent mass of obedient subjects of a central authority..."[12] as would be the case if the state socialist solution to society's ills were accepted. Kropotkin believed that this 'force,'

> ...can only act on society under one condition, that of not being crossed by a mass of contradictory immoral teachings resulting from the practice of institutions.[13]

Institutional or command-authority was anathema to the libertarians because it 'blunted man's moral sense' to the degree that he was not allowed to make many of the choices which were 'meaningful' to him. Locke's notion of 'tacit consent' would to them be the epitome of institutional and state rationalization and could be used in such cases as justifying going to war as a patriotic or even moral duty. Institutional leadership deprived persons of living up to their own responsibilities to themselves and their communities. It was,

> ...the taking away from the individual his direct interest in life and in his surroundings...blunting his moral sense;...teaching that he must never rely on himself...[but]...upon a small party of men who are elected to do everything. [This]...destroys to a large extent his perception of right and wrong.[14]

Without authority, the individual, to be a functioning moral agent, must have a sense of self-reliance and must make this decision for himself although he could abrogate the right to do so. The individual, according to the libertarians, must not be fooled by the powerful and influential who are loathe to account for genuine anti-institutional interests and opinions which cannot be solved within the legal-constitutional framework of a capitalist society.

The term 'individual' means, in the first instance, no more than a single human unit who has both physical and mental faculties. But as a moral agent, this unit, for the libertarians, was to become an integral part of some group (and not just one group) with whose hopes and expectations they would identify with whilst remaining a member. There is no contractual arrangement here, but something which one might call an 'affiliation' whereby the individual concerned applies their personal criteria in the affirmation of a particular choice of influence relation as do those who come into contact with them. This is meant to guarantee a form of voluntary association with its total cohesive factor ultimately dependent upon each and every individual. The cohesion of the group is linked to the depth and duration of the individual relationships.

> The individual is a compound of a certain number of thoughts, of remembrances, of wills, corresponding one to

the other, and of forces of equilibrium. This
equilibrium can only exist in a certain intellectual and
physical environment which is favourable to it. Now this
environment can only be supplied at a certain time. Man,
as he is constituted cannot predict eternity. There is
no indefinite progress in every sense, either for the
individual or for the species; individual and species are
only middle terms between past and future.[15]

The libertarians believed that, as a receptor of information,
it is in the final analysis the individual who feels and must think and
act in accordance with these feelings as they are tempered by the
morality of conscience. One of these feelings is 'happiness' and, like
Morris and Carpenter, Guyau, the young French philosopher, noted that,

We come to this conclusion - that a certain amount of
happiness is a necessary condition of existence.[16]

Happiness, although obviously shared with others, is a
sentiment of personal being and belonging as much as are the sensations
of pleasure and pain. Yet while happiness comes to the individual in
various ways, it is the indifference of the institutional structure to
individual concerns -- to "good and evil" -- which is important in the
libertarian concept of morality. It is man, the individual in group
contact, who lays down the fundamental bases for moral thought and
action. And the major criteria of judgment in moral concerns, be they
concerned with individual behavioural guidelines or social
relationships, can be summed up in the notions of 'usefulness' and
'hurtfulness'. As guidelines, these would lead to a series of social
habits or customs which the libertarians believed could easily supplant
the all-prescriptive systems of law and command-authority. This is
what was meant by Kropotkin in his desire for 'a morality which has
become instinctive'.[17]

Thus, to the libertarian, socialization was the outward
expression of a frame of mind which regulated everyday behaviour in

conformance with the continual action of the 'moral' habit. But the assimilation of such a habit, insofar as it was perceived to be an inculcated trait, did not act as a substitute for the initiative and choice which were so vital to the psychological well-being of the individual even though man was first and foremost a moral agent. The accepted habits which regulated normal forms of behaviour were, in effect, emulative responses to particular sources of influence. They were the result of a form of authority relation, that I have called belief-authority, which did not require a legal-constitutional framework of legitimacy. In the libertarian society there was still much room for dissent, for any challenge to the source of influence was possible, although clearly unlikely in most instances. Challenge would bring about forms of action which would result in changes. These were supposed to be accommodated within the moral framework which, viewed simply, brings to mind the idea of the 'Golden Rule'.

> "I do not follow my conscience; I am driven by it."
> According to this very delicate distinction, the impulses
> of the moral and social order may be divided into two
> classes. By the one we are liberally drawn forward by
> the sentiment of duty without having the time to discuss,
> to deliberate, to reason; by the other, we allow
> ourselves to be dragged along in its course with a more
> precise consciousness of a possible and already real
> resistance of a certain independence.[18]

Here we have a good example of two different facets of belief-authority without any hint of the necessity of command-authority. Social order is maintained first by an unconscious effort on behalf of the agent. This may take into account emulative behaviour wherein influences either perceived or not have become habitualized to such a degree that the reaction or duty verges on the instinctual. One could compare this to a normal course of events, say, where it would not enter one's mind in the course of social intercourse to inflict physical pain upon another. Yet this 'habit,' in the extreme, must lead to pacifism while its rejection could end in death. For in the second class of 'the impulses leading to social and moral order,' emulated behaviour does not necessarily demand either acceptance or lack of deliberation. This class of belief-authority links itself to the realization of individuality where one has the independent ability to make a choice in the face of conflicting alternatives. To the extent that this is so, the individual is able to accept or reject the influences acting upon him. Or in relation to the example above, having acquired the 'habit' of pacifism or non-violence, he may in the extreme choose to reverse his posture for the sake of some more important role such as resisting aggression.

There are of course great dangers in this simple dichotomy, for the individual's reasons or best interests may not be acceptable to those around them even though, in such cases, 'to discuss, to deliberate, and to reason' would be well advised. In the end, the individual must suffer the consequences of their own actions which, if they severely affect the freedom of others, might be dire indeed. The libertarian individual is fully responsible for their own actions.

But the libertarians argue that without command-authority the individual's 'habits' are more likely to conform to the social mores on the grounds that he has already accepted the ultimate responsibility for his actions. Cooperation and harmony being the normal course of life, he will not have the 'primitive habits' of those individuals reared in a society which uses competition and conflict as a means to personal advancement and fulfilment. To the libertarian, man is not just the expression of his individuality, not primarily a creature of habit, but a moral agent who must exercise his own will by putting his thoughts into action and thus make, in his opinions and behaviour, a living contribution to the relationships in which he is involved. The individual teaches and is taught by his community of like beings; he is morally bound to express his desires and thoughts whether they are found to be acceptable or not. The individual in all his mental and physical attributes is the indispensable source of primary unity, for he is never in isolation. As an expression of libertarian doctrine the social ethics, "...instead of demanding that the social customs should be maintained by the authority of a few, demands it from the continued action of all."[19] Kropotkin himself constantly fell back into the quasi-utilitaran phraseology and insisted that "...social customs must be looked to for establishing such relations between men that the interest of each should be the interest of all...."[20]

Clearly the libertarian framework is able to accommodate many variations of belief-authority because belief-authority unlike command-authority is not necessarily tied to the functioning of governmental or economic institutions. On the other hand, hierarchical organization and command-authority, based as they are on deference and the role of power in human relationships, are rejected as means to the harmonization of social interests. The libertarians are therefore not against all forms of authority nor are they essentially negative in their attitudes towards organization, individualism, or economic progress. As George Woodcock writes in his book on Anarchism,

> ...the very nature of the libertarian attitude - its rejection of dogma, its deliberate avoidance of systematic theory and above all its stress on extreme freedom of choice and on the primacy of individual judgment - creates immediately the possibility of a variety of viewpoints inconceivable in a closely dogmatic system.[21]

The principle of authority, as important as it is in

251

libertarian doctrines, is expressed by them as an almost entirely negative concept. In their criticism of institutions, leadership, government, and the state, this is obviously the case. As a concept posited against their notion of freedom, the concepts of authority and power acting in concert are, in essence, the common and simplistic view embodied in ordinary language. Just as the term 'authoritarian' conjures up images of harsh discipline almost amounting to slavery, so 'authority' is commonly seen to be in total opposition to freedom. But there are forms of authority which are, if not complementary to freedom, at least compatible with it. Belief-authority is one of these forms, and although the libertarians are loathe to use the term 'authority' at all in describing future social relations, it is without doubt an aspect of those relations, as the libertarian view of freedom in no way negates this assertion. This notion of freedom, which is central to the whole of libertarian thought, must next be examined.

CHAPTER FIVE

LIBERTY AND FREEDOM

Liberty and the Libertarian

In etymological terms the word 'liberty' has been with us longer than the word 'freedom.' The libertarians of English extraction, whose central concern was with the notion of freedom and its practical application, choose nonetheless to adopt the anglicized version of 'libertaire' as a name for their doctrine. But in borrowing from the French a term which does not distinguish between the usages of the words 'liberty' and 'freedom,' the student of English political theory is at once beset with the problem as to whether any distinction ought to be made at all between the two words.

In libertarian literature, when the two words are representative of conceptual formulations, they are found upon analysis to connote two basically different concepts. Although the concepts are used in a similar fashion at times, such as when they are posited as being the antithesis of authority, they are in most instances used to denote different attitudes and circumstances. This conclusion, although a matter of interpretation, is borne out by usage of these concepts in both the doctrinal and propaganda sources of libertarian writings. Basically, the concept of liberty connotes an attitude or posture of resistance to some source of power or authority or it suggests a situation whereby the individual is unhampered in his ability to make choices. To gain liberty becomes the pre-requisite of individual autonomy. The distinction between this and freedom, in the libertarian view, relates to the fact that freedom is more an attitude of mind than the result of physical circumstances, that it is not so much a form of resistance to external sources, but an affirmation of individual autonomy exemplified by the notion of choice. In the crude first instance, to be able to choose is to be free. Therefore, while liberty is judged in terms of lack of restraint, freedom is judged by the ability to choose.

The word 'liberty' derived from the Latin term 'libertas' seems to connote a negative sense although, as an aspiration, it is usually regarded in a positive manner. The concept of liberty suggests a state of physical existence which, in terms of observed behaviour, can be described as a situation where constraint is absent, albeit in many differently defined circumstances. In modern times, in the state structure the bounds of liberty are circumscribed by the particular social, political, and legal system under which one lives. For even when one is 'at liberty to,' the suggestion is that some overriding impediment has been legitimized, pacified, or eliminated. Liberty seems to be epitomized by the form of behaviour which results when a person who had previously been hindered by some force is suddenly able to behave in a manner which is conducive to his own desires and intentions. If, through this intended behaviour, his actions are themselves the result of his own choices, his liberty will make him free to the extent that he makes use of his own autonomy. If, on the other hand, he chooses to submit to new authorities while still being in a state of liberty, his freedom is diminished to the extent that he has abrogated his own power of decision-making. As far as the libertarians could see, this latter form of behaviour was not necessarily bad, for it could provide a person with a sense of security and obligation which he might require to be happy. It would be a different matter, however, if there was any legal or contractual arrangement which would eventually result in the loss of liberty, for then there could be no possibility of choice and hence freedom.

A person at liberty is a person unrestrained by imposed contractual arrangements, command-authority, or physical force. For it is generally accepted that one who has liberty has broken away from some externally imposed pattern of behaviour, not just to place himself in physically different circumstances, but to allow him to pursue his own interests by making choices and acting upon them.[1]

Someone therefore who sought liberty, in the libertarian sense, would in most circumstances consider himself to be already physically restrained and would consider such restriction to be illegitimate. It is the physical restriction which is important in the concept of liberty because even though rebellion or escape is possible, the superior forces of restraint are able to impose greater sanctions. Thus while one has the freedom or the choice to rebel, the restrictions themselves make it all but meaningless until one is 'at liberty' to make an unimpeded choice.

Therefore, in simple and purely descriptive terms, it could be said that a libertarian is one who seeks or advocates liberty, in that he deplores the existence of socially imposed behavioural restrictions which emanate from institutional authorities. For the libertarian claims that although the individual may well be free to think and in many circumstances to behave as he intends, he would consider the physical restrictions of law and command-authority to be very burdensome. He feels this way because the governmental structure prevents him from taking forms of action which he considers a proper response to social injustice.[2] He feels oppressed and although he is personally without adequate liberty, he still does not contend that he is without the capability or freedom to resist whether or not the results are inconsequential or of a more dire nature.

The libertarian believes that he is only truly free to do those things which he is at liberty to do. Although the freedom which he already has includes the ability to think (if necessary), in many cases it is not allowed expression in speech, print, or action due to social pressures or economic burdens which appear to be beyond his control. He is free to undertake certain actions but not at liberty to do so because of the risk of further restrictions. He is free to break the law but he must suffer the consequences even though the law may have been made to restrict his specific form of action.[3]

As a result of their views, one must note that the distinction between freedom and liberty is of some importance to the libertarians. The two terms are not entirely interchangeable even though one may have a certain amount of freedom without having liberty, or indeed liberty without having freedom or basic freedoms, i.e., legally protected rights. The conceptual ambiguities are pronounced, for freedoms, although an aspect of freedom, are better described as legitimate claims in a structurally defined state of liberty or particular rights granted by the authorities who have designated these rights as legal claims based upon a converse set of stipulated obligations.

Liberty is used as a descriptive expression of opposition to the status quo and, by direct implication, to command authority. The French revolutionaries demanded 'liberte' which meant in the overt sense both liberty and freedom. However, the English, on the whole, were interested primarily in freedom, the libertarians being but one example. In ethics and metaphysics the libertarians agreed with the notion of freedom as being similar to 'l'esprit de liberte.'

Yet, what usually opposed freedom was authority or what I have called command-authority, as its very existence seemed to bring it into conflict with the broad sense of liberty as an absence of physical restraint. Command-authority did not allow for the conditions which would encourage change outside of a rigidly defined political and social code. For liberty, in Berlin's familiar conception, could be indeed considered a negation -- freedom from something, a something identified, as far as it was institutionalized, as authority.[4]

Freedom, however, in other instances meant essentially the power or ability to choose. And the essence of the concept of freedom to the libertarians hinged around the ability to make this choice in an atmosphere devoid of compulsion or the threat of it. These factors, I believe, are inherent in the notion of command-authority.

On the negative side, as an opposing force, it could be said that the libertarians were desirous of a revolutionary change -- a change in the form of authority relations which would bring out the humanitarian 'instincts' in man once his life was no longer so reliant upon the dictates and actions of institutions. Man was no longer to be dominated by the government or the chauvinism of state loyalty. Insofar as power was necessary, the state, as an authority, was viewed simply as the supreme coercive institution. For, in the end, its ability to enforce compliance rested on legitimized methods of coercion because the ultimate legal sanctions included the ability to deprive one of the necessary conditions of life as well as life itself. The libertarians believed that the society in which they were living legitimized 'might as right' by fostering and enforcing the legal distinction between necessary coercion and properly enforceable sanctions.[5] They did not accept this situation but neither did they entirely concede that the attainment of an adequate amount of liberty would involve the use or threat of coercion. In their fight for liberty they accepted -- depending on how they viewed the nature of the oppression -- the inevitability of physical confrontation, but they never sanctioned the use of violence for the sake of a principle although they did view it as the ultimate form of self-defence. But, for the libertarians, it was not coercion which held society together. Rather it was a form of social morality which thrived only in a condition of freedom for all. They believed the condition of freedom to be a constructive and affirmative situation whereby society revolved around the practical implementation of cooperative effort and mutual aid.

Thus, in upholding the need for more liberty, the libertarians decreed coercion to be an undesirable force and since they saw this as the foundation upon which governmental rule rested, there was little room for government, as we understand it, in society as it ought to be.

They believed that the authority of the state had been legitimized in non-libertarian political theory on at least four grounds: the political, the legal-moral, the physical, and the economic, -- all of which they challenged.

The political justification, although in many ways a mixture of the other three, was exemplified in the legislature with the House of Commons and the House of Lords representing the interests (to a debatable degree) of different sectors of the population which, it might be remembered, at this time did not include women. The executive of the House of Commons, in terms of its policy and lawmaking powers and because of its governmental responsibilities, was, in reality, the final court of appeal. It had the power to deal with those whose actions threatened the security of the state as it was perceived by the government or else it could frustrate those of a revolutionary ilk who were desirous of certain forms of change. This so-called political actuality and the whole ethos which kept it alive was attacked by the libertarians under an umbrella definition of government.

The statutes passed by the Houses of Parliament, even those which in the opinion of John Stuart Mill were ostensibly enacted to enhance liberty, often did no such thing. Most laws were restrictive in their scope and, although they obviously aided certain sectors of the community, they failed to destroy the inequalities inherent in the British class structure. As we well know, there were debates as to the merits of 'positive law' based on Social Darwinism, Malthusian theory, universal suffrage, and social services, which all too well served to point out the interests of different segments of the population and the 'freedoms' which were being pondered. Most libertarians would say that it was within the realm of property relations that freedom, as right, was being most often abused. Yet statutes relating to property and its use were almost always upheld by the 'establishment,' who gave moral as well as legal-traditional reasons for their implementation.

As a second justification for the necessity of strong and ultimately coercive governmental authority, the judiciary, as guardians and interpreters of the law, reinforced the 'establishment' position. Proper and moral, i.e., legal behaviour for the individual in society was thus laid down in the law. The Rule of Law as well as a belief in the 'spirit of the law' was held in far greater sanctity, according to the libertarians, than that of the simple collective interests of a governing body. Both government and law had to be rigidly accepted.

The rules, customs, and habits, once made into law, were enforced as a result of prior law, i.e., as a result of the notion of law itself. Unpopular laws were enforced by those who relied totally on their physical capacities coupled with the ability to elicit compliance through fear -- the police and the army. In England, even in the latter part of the nineteenth century, coercion was not a method which the governors preferred to use except in the most (as they saw it) dire of circumstances. But when it was used, as in the case of the notorious 'Bloody Sunday' of 1887, it epitomized to the libertarians the hypocrisy and ineffectiveness of legally constituted rights.

Lastly, liberty was restricted in a less overt but more insidious manner by those who possessed capital. The libertarians believed that the wealth of any country ought to be owned by those who produced it and that the returns on capital investment should revert to those who produced the capital in the first place. They claimed that the great landowners and entrepreneurs of Victorian England, far from contributing to the 'national interest,' were actually the root cause of social misery and poverty. For in the end, the workers were ruled more by the material conditions under which they lived than by the myths which were foisted upon them by the hierarchy of politicians, judges, and policemen. It was in the economic sphere that the term 'wage-slave' epitomized the lack of liberty enjoyed by the working-poor.

Of course the libertarians were not the only ones who were concerned with injustice and oppression and thought they were fighting in the name of liberty.

In attempting to categorize the term 'libertarian,' an American author who edited an anthology entitled <u>Liberty and the Great Libertarians</u>, said

> The question we have to consider is whether they have proved that liberty in particular human relations is a logical deduction from correct reasoning ...[6]

Now this will clearly not suffice as a definition of libertarian writing, for it misses the major point which is endemic to the libertarians who see liberty as but a part of the wider, affirmative doctrine to which freedom is the primary adjunct -- that the tradition itself is one entirely built upon a particular ethical viewpoint peculiar in political and economic criticisms. For were this ethical consistency not present, we could classify such diverse sources as Max Stirner's anarchistic book <u>The Ego and Its Own</u> along with Auberon Herbert's <u>Anti-Force Papers</u> as being part of the libertarian tradition. We cannot, in terms of classification, pair Marx and Bakunin or Kropotkin and Spencer, for it would lead to representations and anomalies which would serve to cloud the issues even further. The whole consanguinity question in relation to what is or what is not libertarian must rest on more specific and, in particular, ethical criteria, and for this we must look at the concept of freedom. For, to the libertarians, freedom is a value and it is because of the ethical components subsumed under the name of freedom that freedom is at the centre of the whole question relating to who and what contributes to libertarian ideas and tradition in England.

Libertarians, true to the literal lexicon, oppose command-authority and, hence, the authority of the law and the legal-constitutional system. To the extent that they viewed liberty as basically the absence of physical or mental impediment, they did not believe that law, which was ultimately backed by coercion, guaranteed more liberty than it took away. To them, law was basically a restrictive device which, because it limited choice and actually restricted liberty, could not guarantee or foster freedom, especially if freedom was viewed initially as the ability to make an intentional choice. The attainment of a state of liberty by the removal of impediments placed in the path of the individual did not in itself guarantee freedom. As a result, there must be constant vigilance and a continuation of the struggle if liberty was to be preserved. The elimination of sanctions and legalized coercion from society is not a positive act, for it requires the suppression of a more forceful opponent, i.e., the legally constituted authorities. On the other hand, the state of liberty having been attained represented a great positive achievement and one which can only be accomplished by the combined forces of revolutionary opposition. The attainment of liberty was seen as the pre-requisite for enhanced freedom.

Liberty, outside a particular moral framework, -- transplanted into the same social value system which existed in nineteenth-century England, does little more than enhance the 'power to do' of the liberated. It is, in many cases, the beginning of a new form of oppression. The struggle for power, say the libertarians, is why most revolutions of a political nature have failed to bring about change extensively enough to get rid of all oppressors, i.e., institutionalized authorities. Political revolution is a concept based on the mechanistic notion that liberty is literally the freeing of the prisoners, a changing of the rules, and a consolidation of new roles. This is the liberty of the poor man to sleep under any bridge, of the strong man to rule the weak, or of the smart man to beguile the dumb.

To change mere liberty into freedom, it must be based upon an ethical system conducive to its maintenance for all and not limited, as it seems at present to be, to the privileged children of inequality.

Freedom, when connected to an ethical standard exists where non-coercive power, as influence, becomes an ability, -- the flowering of self-determination and autonomy -- which aids those involved to benefit their community and society in the best possible manner. And this state of affairs will not occur in what Morris has called a 'mechanical revolution'; it must go hand in hand with a transvaluation of values which allows moral precepts to be inculcated into a rational framework.[7] As a result, the libertarians claim that without constraint everyone will have the ability (using power as influential affirmation) to make choices.[8] Freedom then becomes synonymous with choice, both in relation to material circumstances and the development of the 'inner self' as represented by the mind and conscience. To choose, they say, regarding the criteria of a moral and rational nature is to be free. But choice is not the only operative feature.

Thus understood as a moral concept, it is freedom without what could be categorized as 'licence.' For licence would mean a form of irresponsibility which is the antithesis of the libertarian view of the world. The cornerstone of the new-found, yet inculcated sense of freedom, would be the dual precepts of respect and responsibility neither of which rely upon coercive or authoritative methods to make them realizable. Such values are the social obligations which arise out of the communalistic life-style of persons living in cooperation rather than competition. The so-called 'competitive instinct' is repudiated; it is seen not as an instinct but as an instrument of force and, as long as the world concedes to its legitimacy and gives accolades accordingly, so then will the 'will to power' play a dominating role in community life.[9]

In libertarian terms, the community itself becomes the belief-authority to whom the individual ought to give his respect. It is the authority of moral suasion based both on an appeal to conscience (moral force) and reason (rationality). For unless there was an identity of interests, a genuine community, free cooperation would be impossible at the beginning and there would be no common bond between individuals, groups, communities, and federations. As biggest is not viewed as best, there is no hierarchical view in a federated structure; leadership becomes a skill and not a position of power; equality a possibility and not an abstraction; authority, a right habit; freedom, a right choice; right, a moral precept; and society, a state of affairs not imposed by a legal-political construct.

Libertarian Freedom

The categorization of the libertarian belief in freedom is grouped around two main ideas which enable one to view the concept in separate but compatible ways. Freedom is an affirmation of intentional behaviour (action) and it involves relations between people. As an affirmative disposition, freedom could be described as being 'positive.'

> Freedom ... is not merely negative; it is not merely an absence of arbitrary restraints imposed by the will of some upon others. It is also positive, it is active, voluntary cooperation amongst men who have mutually agreed to associate for the common purpose of obtaining for themselves and each other the fullest, widest, intensest life of which their nature is capable. All association is a seeking after this, however imperfect, however misguided in its methods and partial in its intention.[10]

In this sense, it goes beyond the negative idea of liberty as the lack of physical constraint, for as an affirmation of intentional behaviour, there comes a creative potential. Whether, in fact, this potential is used and regardless of how it is used, is, in the first instance, not particularly relevant.

As a method of action, libertarian freedom goes beyond the mere 'seeking for liberty' in the form of ridding society of coercive and authoritative institutions. It is, in effect, a form of power, an influence which acts as an inner force and allows the individual to act in a manner conducive to their needs.[11] But it is also a restraining moral force which makes that same individual realise the scope and repercussions of their decisions (choices) in relation to other people. Thus we have in intentional behaviour, or action, a requirement of making a choice, and when this choice is affected, we have a situation wherein the ability (power) to make that choice (to be free) comes outside the self into contact with other individuals. This latter aspect makes the whole process relational; the choices involved can be seen as a relation wherein the results of certain forms of action affect other individuals. For others must be present in order to give any moral context to the notion of freedom. To be free in isolation would, in the libertarian view, not give rise to any important moral questions. Libertarian freedom suggests not only the negation of the actions of coercive powers or institutions but the substitution for this force of a doctrine which would justify one being able to continue the battle over a protracted period even in changed circumstances, e.g., the state of liberty.

> When we speak of human freedom we speak of a relation
> between man and man, of that social relation which allows
> and actively promotes the fullest possible individual

self-development, whereof the principle is: Space and opportunity for the individual initiative, the individual activity of each by the mutual agreement of all.[12]

The relational aspects of this concept of freedom are of the utmost importance here because they do not give a hard and fast definition as to 'what the relations will be' but only that they will exist in accordance with the spirit of cooperation, mutual help, and self-realization.

> Either the state will be destroyed and a new life will begin in thousands of centres, on the principle of an energetic initiative of the individual; of groups and of free agreements; or else the state must become the master of all the domains of human activity, must bring with it its wars and internal struggles for the possession of power, its surface revolutions which only change one tyrant for another, and inevitably at the end of this revolution, -- death![13]

There are virtually no limits to the extent of the multiplicity and kinds of relationships, for, in the relational context, it is the persons so involved who define both the content and quality of the endeavour given that they are mutually agreed as to its place and necessity in terms of their own actions. For it is, " ... the protestants of liberty who have been and are as yet only able to take the preliminary step towards freedom and, conceiving it more a social separation than a social relation, go about preaching a gospel of hate ..."[14]

According to the libertarians, to protest against liberty is to deny the opportunity of freedom affirming as do the laws, a social cynicism as to the 'nature' of man, a nature which, they maintain, is infinitely malleable in relation to how man apprehends the universe and the way in which this act of apprehension brings him towards thought, action, and belief as to his own capabilities. In many instances the so-called 'enemies of liberty' arise in the guise of the laissez-faire liberal who is concerned about a particular type of individual freedom safeguarded by a legal-constitutional system or the Social Darwinist who is concerned with the 'natural' allocation of rewards. To the libertarians, these attitudes and the doctrines which they gave rise to exemplified the sort of cynicism about the forms of liberty which most likely lead to a situation of greater freedom.

Some who have written on law and its questionably moral foundation have categorized freedom without institutionalized structures as moral anarchy, but this in itself presupposes a view of the world as a place which can only be 'improved,' by the use of coercive measures.[15] For, as the libertarians attempted to show, in opposition to the liberal ideas of someone like John Stuart Mill, the essence of individualism was a state of being in a free society where one was able to express their 'individuality' in a manner which was complementary to that society.[16] Such expression does not include the freedom to assert oneself (whether backed by the force of law or not) in a manner which actuated the legitimacy of command-authority. As this form of 'self assertion' was not conducive to harmonious relations, it was unacceptable and only befitting of one whose "... social instinct has been withered or warped, or perhaps had little chance to grow."[17] Thus there was no entitlement to command-authority. For, as the libertarians were quick to point out, it was generally the powerful who were self-assertive in the face of great opposition. Libertarian individuality concerned all people, and its consequences applied to all people. One individual was as free as the other, and constant vigilance was necessary to sustain freedom in a society of equals.

We ... conceive that true freedom necessarily

implies active social cooperation for the purpose of obtaining and maintaining it ...[18]

Now although it is relatively clear what the libertarians are saying in these statements, the statements themselves may be criticized for the way in which they obscure the original concept, i.e., freedom, by introducing such metaphysical ideas as 'nature,' 'social instinct,' and 'social cooperation.' As the history of political thought shows, there are no easy nor perhaps fully adequate means to deal with like notions which are rife with ambiguity. The only way to clear up such problems is to attempt, along the way, an explanation of the way libertarians wrote of these ideas. Perhaps their use appears too simplistic to warrant comment at times, but it is nonetheless imperative to a study such as this that one should not take presupposed notions as either obvious or wholly commonsensical. In this respect, the clarification of secondary terms is necessary to avoid misunderstanding the more fundamental and central themes of libertarian theory.

Both Kropotkin and Carpenter believed that habit, as a personal attribute, and custom, as a social attribute, were both desirable social 'instincts.' That is, because they both existed in a communal context, they were potentially amenable to social change. Social instincts, in contrast to the more individually variable physiological instincts like appetite and sexual drive, were not biologically orientated. Social instincts were the result of the inculcation of belief to such an extent that it defied rational explanation by those individuals who accepted it as possessing inalienable qualities. For although most people described or would describe their social instincts differently, they usually agreed upon one common point, namely, that they believed or reacted to many situations without rational deliberation. Carpenter linked the two ideas of social instinct and moral action or 'intuition.'[19] In this way he suggested that,

> ... The New Morality ... [is] ... to look within, to feel and refer to the needs of others as instinctively as to one's own ...[20]

According to the libertarians in general, even the positive law of governments when it could claim to rest on moral premises was, in most cases, an affirmation of already established customs or openly expressed ideas. But this was not necessarily the case with many prescriptive laws which attempted to enhance freedom through 'progressive' positive legislation. Positive lawmaking worried the libertarians, for they believed that such laws were really a reflection of the mores of the legislature and not of the society in which they functioned. This was not to wholly deny their merit or the sincerity of their application but rather to assert that they took away from the individual much of his autonomy and imposed restrictions on the area of choice.

By attempting to undermine the authority of law, the libertarians sought to reverse the trend towards governmental paternalism. They wanted cooperative and mutually reinforcing habits to be the moving force in a society operating as a homogeneous and harmonious whole and committed to the belief in the necessity for equal freedom for all. Carpenter expressed a similar optimism in reference to marriage relations in future society. He believed that social customs could prevail even over existing law to the ultimate benefit of the community. For much of what already exists is not sanctioned by law and is indeed positively discouraged. Carpenter, as a homosexual, was obviously much concerned with personal relations between consenting adults and believing that legal marriage amounted to little more than prostitution, he held that common-law marriage was preferable.

> More likely it is that, underneath the law, the common practice will slide forward into newer customs.[21]

However, custom, as a social expression of instinct, is entirely relative. It is what is believed to be the case at a certain time and place; it is not necessarily what ought to be but what is acceptable for the maintenance of a communal identity. Even so, it is still related to morality:

> And then to come to the subject of morals. These also are customs, — divergent to the last degree among different races, at different times or in different localities; customs for which it is often difficult to find any ground in reason, or the 'fitness of things.'[22]

Customs are not classified as good or bad but only as useful or hurtful to the community and its members; they can be useful only to a community which has shunned the necessity for command-authority and its coercive attributes, a community which is maintained around the general consensus that each individual can only be as free or as unfree as their comrades and neighbours.

Kropotkin was the most vociferous advocate, amongst the libertarians, of such a view of morality, and no doubt this opinion was closely related to his sociological and biological interests. Having opposed many of the conclusions which the popular image of Darwin had encouraged, he said in <u>The Place of Anarchism in Socialistic Evolution</u>, that,

> A morality which has become instinctive is the true morality.[23]

Because,

> It is the morality ... of habit.[24]

Instinct, then, for Kropotkin, is wholly identified with the interests, whatever they may be, of a community of people who are never compelled to act in a manner to which they do not entirely assent. The harmony of such a community was expressed through the development of social cooperation.

Social cooperation is a form of relation between members who live in proximity to one another. Cooperation becomes social at the moment that it includes those people who are engaged in a cooperative effort merely not for the sake of their own personal ends. The notion of social cooperation in libertarian society is universalized to the extent that it is a shared belief held by those who are attempting to work in harmony. Most individuals live amongst people whom they do not know. To act in a social context is to act in concert, on various levels, with those who are strangers, but potential friends. The medium of intercourse in a 'free' society is, therefore, cooperation or something which the liberal might more cynically define as 'mutual tolerance.'

> Morality in its essence is not a code, but simply the realization of the Common Life: ... To liberate this instinct of the Common Life, freeing it from hard and cramping rules, and to let it take its own form or forms -- grafted on and varied of course by the personal and selective elements of Affection and Sympathy -- is the hope that lies before the world today for the solution of all sorts of moral and social problems.[25]

To cooperate assumes a multiplicity of views that are potentially incompatible but which can with effort and understanding be accommodated. When a man cooperates, he, in effect, yields some of his autonomy and his desires to the somewhat similar inclinations of others in the community. Cooperation is an individual compromise with the social being. It is a compromise which leads to an agreement over some general rules of conduct. The first and foremost is that everyone agrees to discuss the possibility and the necessity of cooperation for the purpose of the pursuit of the 'Common Life,' i.e., life within the community. A community assuming, as the libertarians do, an absence of coercion and hierarchical structures must stand or fall on its spirit of social cooperation. This means that cooperation must be voluntary and depend for its perpetration on shared mores which have themselves been categorized as the communal instinct. The libertarians maintain that we can survive, in such circumstances, on "... our increasingly social habits rather than the prescriptions of our laws."[26]

Nature, another important term for the libertarian, is simply the perception of the inner being of man. Yet nature can also be what man professes to desire and, in this way, it could be said that nature characterizes one's particular existence at any particular time. The libertarians feel that those traits in individuals which are considered innate but are undesirable are, in fact, the result of institutional corruption. They would maintain that what is natural is good to the degree that it is not corrupted by other forces. This is rather a convenient way of ascribing all bad things to 'unnatural' forces and thus this libertarian 'rationalization' makes their notion of nature very straightforward. The nature of man is, consequently, those good intentions which appear to be of universal desire. In libertarian terms, there seem to be only two -- happiness and freedom.

The desire for happiness in all its manifestations seemed endemic to mankind but it, despite the calculus of Bentham, was for the most part not amenable to rational calculation, for it included a predisposition towards the libertarian 'ideals' of freedom and equality. Indeed, the notion of equality does not seem to have any 'natural' derivation and it was for this reason that it was usually described as a necessary moral virtue, i.e., a belief in its rightness. Freedom, on the other hand, was often seen as complementary to happiness as it was something which could be individually expressed and interpreted as a means to a desired end. What libertarians were reasonably sure of was that everybody aspired to a condition which they personally considered to be -- freedom. They began with the premise that freedom, as they saw it, would fulfill the Benthamite dream of 'the greatest happiness,' not just for the greatest number, but for all.

The libertarians would argue that man is, if not consistent, at least capable of responding to a community and environment which he has been able to comprehend for himself. However, the important thing is that there is not a "... fixed pattern or level of human behaviour."[27] It often seems fixed only because it cannot be affirmatively expressed under an already existing condition of liberty or in a social situation in which the individual is an integral part of his environs, i.e., in a libertarian community. Otherwise the individual is unable to express his individuality because of the authority of the law and its complementary institutions. Libertarian thought, like some forms of anarchism,

> ... recognizes and values individuality, which means, character, conduct and the springs of conduct, free initiative, spontaneity, ... [and] ... autonomy.[28]

In other words, only those who have gained liberty and are free can be individual and representative of what is patently their own self-imposed 'nature.'

> Is not the best way of becoming free to make use of liberty, acting up to the best of its inspirations, rejecting the tutelage of no matter whom?[29]

Freedom, as a condition which flows out of the acquired state of liberty, is in turn strongly linked to certain forms of 'right' action.

> Freedom of the people, complete freedom in all their modes of action is all we ask.[30]

And this is 'asked' for as the necessary means required in gaining the 'hoped for' end. As Jean Grave put it on behalf of many libertarians,

> ... We believe that universal harmony will result from the free action of all men.[31]

To think and to choose is to act, i.e, freedom as choice distinguishes action from mere behaviour, as action is the result of some form of intention. This intention is the reason for choice, for without choice transferred into action there would be, in effect, no freedom. For again the distinction is made between the purely physical attainment of a state of liberty which is linked to the hoped for or desired product — a condition of freedom.

> We recognize the full and complete liberty of the individual; we desire for him plentitude of existence, the free development of all his faculties.
> Provided that you yourself do not abdicate your freedom; provided that you yourself do not allow others to enslave you; and provided that to the violent and anti-social passions of ... [any] ... person you oppose your equally vigorous social passions, then you have nothing to fear from liberty.[32]

The separation of freedom from liberty is essential. Although the libertarians aspire to both freedom and liberty, they realize that nothing of positive value can arise until they liberate themselves. It is at this point that the libertarian critique of society, on the political level, re-adjusts itself, first to questions or moral concern and then ultimately to matters of psychological speculation. For once people are emancipated, it is only the aspirations of freedom in association that will preserve society from lapsing again into the 'trammels of obedience.'

The idea of freedom, however, presumes to encompass the notion of equality, for "... the principle of equality sums up the teaching of the moralists ..." and supposedly guarantees "respect for the individual."[33]

Yet, for some reason, although the libertarians emphasize the concept of freedom and the manner in which it will be employed, they do not regularly give the same attention to the notion of equality. Their demand for equality of condition and opportunity arises out of their belief that freedom itself must come from shared beliefs incorporating respect and responsibility towards other individuals in the community. The issue of equality seems somehow to arise 'naturally' from the libertarian desire for a communistic as opposed to an individualistic society.[34] Since the basic tenet of communism is first and foremost the need for equality in social relations, one would assume that the libertarian social order must be in many ways similar. Even though freedom and equality are often viewed as incompatible notions when put into practise, the libertarian notion of freedom presupposes a situation of practical equality. The libertarians somewhat naively assume, on the basis of their particular notion of freedom, that the individual will not be in conflict with the rest of his community but will be a relatively stable and vital element of it. But this assumption is understandable only if we view their ideas on freedom in relation to their particular ideas about the role of authority, individuality, and the effective equality of communism. We are led to the conclusion that the principle of equality, to the libertarians, is a necessary counterpart to the moral aspect of freedom. Kropotkin considered the pursuit of equality as a duty of the liberated being.

> This is all we have the right to do, this is all the duty we have to perform, to keep up the principle of equality in society. It is the principle of equality in practice.[35]

For if to be free is to have the ability to make meaningful choices, could 'meaningful' simply denote equal? I think not. 'Meaningful' refers to a state of mind which can only be active under a condition of equal liberty, so that each person has the potential to make the initial choice. Where liberty is first a condition of physical and not mental reality, freedom is a perception of what can be, for the libertarians, and is not to be confused with the acceptance of a free-will philosophy. Freedom should be seen as an ability to elicit change of both a physical and intellectual kind. As a perception of the choices made available to the individual, it is for the individual to make his own future. According to Sebastian de Grazia,

> Perception is ... not passive, but active, seizing upon the world with intent, and at once half perceiving it and half creating it.[36]

So it is with libertarian freedom. It is the act of creation which leads even the anarchist "... to insist that the idea of human liberty, which cannot be made absolute, must be maintained as the highest of all human values."[37] A state of freedom is the moral context in which the emancipated individual must learn to survive in his relations with his fellow man. For,

> Without the idea of a free man, the anarchist idea falls to the ground; because the future society cannot exist, or its beginnings nurtured without him.[38]

Freedom, as responsibility, choice, and the assumption of

social obligations, is also a necessary part of the libertarian view of the future, no matter how 'non-planned' or unpredictable their literature depicts it.[39] Libertarian thought rests on the fundamental assumption that a society of free people will spontaneously and invariably create a 'Common Life' which (itself) reflects the notion of freedom which they uphold.[40] This is true of many authors who could not consistently be referred to as libertarians.

Proudhon, one of the favourite philosophers of the individualist anarchists, was mainly concerned with the liberty of conscience rather than freedom. His ideas on freedom included a concept of free will as well as the right of the individual to coordinate his own life free from external authority.[41] But he was not a communist and his notions of freedom were in many ways similar to John Stuart Mill's concept of individuality.[42]

Max Stirner, another individualist anarchist who wrote in the middle of the nineteenth century, regarded freedom as the power to accomplish a task, but set it in a very egoistic framework.[43] Yet in spite of this, one cannot imagine a libertarian objecting to such a statement as,

> Regard yourself as more powerful than they allege you to be, and you have more power; regard yourself as more and you are more.[44]

It is this 'regarding of self' which is one of the main methods of attaining freedom in the libertarian sense, but it says nothing of the ethical base, a base without which one could not distinguish between Stirner and a consistent libertarian.

Bakunin, on the other hand, while not always discerning differences between liberty and freedom, again had the idea that there were norms to be taken into consideration when one spoke of emancipation, even though he based them on a form of 'general will'.[45]

> I myself am a free man only insofar as I recognize the humanity and liberty of all the men who surround me. In respecting their humanity I respect my own.[46]

But the most internationally famous and respected of all the anarchists at the turn of the century was Kropotkin. As a propagandist of the libertarian ethic he, on several occasions, expounded upon the libertarian view of freedom. In the first issue of _Freedom_ he and his co-editor, C. M. Wilson, set out what they perceived freedom to be.

> We dream of the positive freedom which is essentially one with social feeling, of free scope for the social impulses, non-distorted and compressed by property, and its guardian, the law; of free scope for the individual sense of responsibility, or respect for self and for others .... of free scope for the spontaneity and individuality of each human being, such as is impossible when one hard and fast line is fitted to all conduct.[47]

'Free scope' in this sense is both a predisposition of the intent to act, and an affirmation of the physical circumstances under which one is able to carry out those actions. That is, positive freedom, i.e., libertarian freedom, is 'non-distorted' because people are presumed to have achieved a condition of liberty, i.e., they are no longer oppressed. Thus one is able, both mentally and physically, to make good his choices providing one accepts the role of the necessity for responsibility and respect.

It is the social revolution and the way in which it is brought about which gives credence to types of future action which are deemed necessary. "It ... is _liberty_ which is to be established by the social revolution."[48] For as Alexander Berkman later pointed out in his handbook, _The A.B.C. of Anarchism_,

> The main _aim_ of the social revolution is therefore to

establish   liberty   on   the   basis   of   equal
opportunity.[49]

However, he added, this was not enough, for, just as Kropotkin
stated that one had a duty towards the realization of 'practical
equality', so Berkman argued, ethical values had to be maintained:

> To forget ethical values, to introduce practises and
> methods inconsistent with, or opposed to the high moral
> purposes   of   the   revolution   means   to   invite
> counter-revolution and disaster.[50]

Therefore, the social revolution, according to this communist
anarchist and libertarian, had to be carried through in conformance
with libertarian principles. In particular, new authorities would not
replace the old and the notion of command-authority would become
obsolete.[51]   The   social   revolution,   and   the   abolition   of
command-authority was the first major step in establishing freedom, for
it was meant to bring about a condition of equal liberty for all.
However, this was just the beginning, for,

> Far greater and more significant will be the results of
> such liberty, its effect upon man's mind, upon his
> personality. The abolition of the coercive external
> will, and with it of the fear of authority, will loosen
> the bonds of moral compulsion, no less than of economic
> and physical.[52]

In a libertarian society,

> Instead of 'thou shalt not', the public conscience will
> say, 'thou mayest', taking full responsibility.[53]

Hence we have the necessary conditions in which one is able to be, as
an actor, free. Emma Goldman, another communist anarchist and a close
associate of Berkman as well as the Freedom Group, was also quick to
point out that 'true liberty' was literally a condition of freedom.

> 'True liberty' ... is not the negative theory of being
> free from something, because with such freedom you may
> starve to death. Real freedom, true liberty, is
> positive; it is freedom to something; it is the liberty
> to be, to do, in short; the liberty of actual and active

opportunity.[54]

This statement in effect is derived from the distinctly non-liberal notion that freedom, or 'true liberty' "... is not derived from the non-reality known as 'the state'."[55] The libertarian form of freedom "... cannot be given; it cannot be conferred by any laws or government. The need for it is inherent in the individual."[56]

In order that such a notion of freedom be more than a theoretical abstraction, it must in every practicable sense be a mode of action, a means to the end, and in particular a means to the emancipation of the individual from the coercive forces which inhibit him from pursuing a satisfying and harmonious role within the community.

> Man's true liberation, individual and collective, lies in his emancipation from authority and from his belief in it. All human evolution has been a struggle in that direction and for that object.[57]

Freedom, then, as distinct from liberty, is clearly the end of libertarian ethics. But this brings us to an interesting point of which we must take account if we are to adequately separate the two. For the libertarians claim that liberty, although a condition of positive benefit in terms of emancipation, is in essence the result of a reactive process. That is, it is the successful culmination of the fight against coercion of institutional authority. It arises from the desire to make the rule of one person over another both unnecessary and immoral. And perhaps, insofar as they view the abolition of command-authority as 'right action', they cannot (if they want to abolish government) be accused of being nihilists or destructionists.

The libertarians have always maintained that the ends do not justify the means if those means are incompatible with the conditions of the ultimate end, i.e., the future society. For this reason they were very wary of calling for violent action as one method for bringing about the social revolution. Violence was used in the most intolerable and illegitimate forms of oppression and was the method employed to effect political revolutions. The libertarians were not interested in political revolutions which they believed would merely exchange one set of masters for another. They believed that if man were to use coercion to achieve their ends, it would be not only logical but ethically justifiable for opponents or counter-revolutionaries to use the same methods. Rather unconvincingly at times, they suggest that violence ought only to be employed in a defensive situation or for the protection of self. Yet the bounds of violent action are not so easily discerned much less justified by a simple interpretation of what is or what is not defensive or aggressive behaviour. It will suffice to say that the libertarians did not adequately come to terms with the problem of defensive violence except to the extent that they believed it could be justified in the end. It is for this reason that the most consistent of them were driven into the fold of pacifism. Yet others could still say with full conviction that,

> ... to secure liberty, you must learn to do without authority and compulsion.[58]

The question which inevitably comes to mind is: Is opposition to all forms of institutionalized authority, and in particular government, a negative belief based on despair, hatred, or nihilism?

The libertarians cannot be accused of having such a pessimistic outlook. On the contrary, they would say that their belief entailed a total affirmation of the important ethical problems central to political philosophy as a whole. They posit a unique solution to an old problem of who should rule when they by critical and prescriptive means suggest that no one should rule. In this they obviously affirm their undying optimism with regard to the possible role of the individual in society. It is imperative that the individual _feel_ that he is free. He must be free to do with his life what he wills, to make his own decisions based on personal knowledge, conviction, or belief. This makes him more 'natural' in that he is not coerced into obedience by any external source and not, at any rate, living under an impersonal and incomprehendable governmental authority.

If man, even before he had won his liberty, was to act _as if_ he were free and by doing so manifestly react against those legal and traditional restrictions of his age, which the libertarians see as illegitimate constraints on his personality, then he would have initiated the battle for physical emancipation, i.e., liberty.

In choosing, man can be free psychologically and it is not for any central authority to subject those choices to an institutionally decreed set of laws and rules. Choice has meaning in the libertarian sense only insofar as it matters, to the person who makes the choice. It is not the _range_ of choice which matters, but the value placed upon the various alternatives by the individuals concerned. To be free is to create. Since values such as responsibility and respect are meant to be internalized, choice, i.e., freedom, becomes a matter in the creative context of internal inspiration and deliberation for the individual who, in being able to make the choice in the first place, must accept the obligations created by his choices. In other words, the responsibility implied in making a choice entails responsibility for the consequences of that choice whether they are unintended or not. Other people's choices and reactions to your choices must be respected and accepting ultimate responsibility even for unintended consequences facilitates conciliation and social cohesion.

In a discussion about the ability of an individual to view the logical aspects of being forced to be free, Benjamin R. Barber makes some very interesting points as to what freedom means to him. He distinguishes between two schools of thought with regards the analagous formulations with which one may view freedom in a conceptual manner. Referring to them as models he calls these two conceptions The Abstract Physical-Mechanistic Model and The Concrete Psychological-Intentionalist Model.[59] And although he is using them both to argue against what he perceives to be an anarchist view of freedom, he in fact paints a picture of freedom which is in virtual agreement with libertarian thought and ethics.

Hobbes, J. S. Mill and I. Berlin are all classified by Barber as belonging to that school which explains freedom in mechanistic terms or, to put it in Barber's terms, " ... as a physical problem of vector analysis."[60] To the degree that the libertarians would accept this view of freedom, they would apply it only to the notion of liberty. But their view of freedom would be classified under Barber's Concrete Psychological-Intentionalist Model. In the latter grouping Barber includes such people as Montesquieu, Sartre, and Ardent, whom, he suggests, would agree that,

It is only the man who acts intentionally who acts freely.[61]

The psychological model centres around the idea that choices, to be 'meaningful', must arise from the intentional behaviour of the individual.

A man is unfree in behaving impulsively, not because he necessarily would have chosen to act otherwise, but

because he did not choose to act at all, his behaviour
was not really his action at all ...[62]

To the libertarian and, even to a great extent, the
existentialist, it is of the utmost importance that freedom be linked
with choice not only as an ability but as a positive predisposition in
the face of all traditional and social custom which does not fulfill
the criteria of individual being. It must be so linked even if, in the
extreme, it means solitude and exile although this is not the intended
end in mind. The individual becomes a free agent, insofar as it is he
who, given the time and circumstances and given the befitting
situation, creates or gives to those circumstances or situations a new
dimension which is due almost entirely, in the ensuing change, to the
existence of the agent himself.

> In consciously choosing then, man does not select among
> given alternatives, rather he brings them into being. By
> intending, he creates ends — just by meaning, he gives
> meaning. The free man is neither the path-finder, nor
> the path-chooser; he is the path-maker.[63]

But in his discussion, much in the manner of Mill in his essay
On Liberty, Barber says that habit confounds freedom, since it
betrays the active mind by making it divorced from the process of
rational decision-making. For the so-called liberated being who is
'ruled' by habit will not account for the fact that, " ... freedom
entails struggles and anguish and is marked by activity rather than
passivity."[64]

Edward Carpenter, for one, would not disagree nor would most
libertarians who were convinced of the probability of struggle and
anguish in both making and maintaining the social revolution. The
disagreement here is about habit and not, as Barber makes out, about
freedom.

To say that habit is nothing other than a form of passive response or a stultifying condition of existence bespeaks an intolerably dogmatic attitude. Although it could be said for several reasons that habit and even Kropotkin's instinct were manifestations of sterility and stagnation, one could for other reasons maintain the opposite. The libertarians argued that habit promoted stability, reduced anxiety, and reinforced expectations. To view habit as a passive response is to deny that there are choices between habits or reasons for having made these choices. The libertarians saw habit as a form of behaviour based on previous choices and hence prior intentional action. Those habits which were more generalized and were inculcated as customs or instincts were, in themselves, part of the ethical framework of a society at any given time.

Since Kropotkin and Carpenter believed that habit would allow for order in a community without a formal law structure, they did not suggest that this was in itself a major aspect of freedom but only that certain forms of habit, e.g., greater responsibility and respect, would be the result of freedom. The same conditions that created habits could destroy them. It is a great error to confuse the libertarian conception of habit and custom with what we would now distinguish as outmoded habit and custom based on force, myth, or inadequate information.

It is their conception of habit which links the libertarian concept of freedom with the ethical components of libertarian society. For morality consists in the discovery of rules of conduct arrived at under conditions of non-coercive and mutual cooperation. Such rules or norms that appear are characterized in the way in which they are accommodating to the demands of free individuals living within their

285

own comprehendable social milieu. Their behaviour, which becomes a
matter of habit, is no less than the collected and intermingled facets
of a well understood social compatability which is known to be a
guarantee of communal solidarity. The knowledge that habitual or
customary behaviour of immutable or ill-defined past decisions
contributed to the cohesion of a community without law and, in fact,
regulated its very existence. As far as the libertarians are
concerned, no one suggests that all habits will be good or even the
same at different times and places, but they are optimistic enough to
believe, or at the very least hope for, a situation whereby the best
aspirations of men can be regulated from within. What then exists are
social as well as individual habits which serve a purpose, like myths,
but which can also be called into question by either deviant
individuals or succeeding generations who have acknowedged that they
are able to think for themselves.

In theory, nothing is sacred, and it is possible that people
will have no expectations of a legitimate nature outside of their
customary behaviour. But the conditions which gave rise to such
notions do continue to operate. The condition of freedom, as an ethic
imbued in the social nature of the individual, is part of the
cooperative force which defines the boundaries of the community without
which it would cease to function in the libertarian mould. Freedom is
an aspect of social cohesion; equality, responsibility, and respect are
strands of moral force which allow for the accommodation of fluctuating
influences -- in effect, those influences of a non-coercive nature,
where command-authority disappears.

CONCLUSION

I have argued that there is a body of knowledge which can be called libertarian thought. Furthermore, if one can speak of a tradition as an ongoing set of ideas, then it is clear that a libertarian tradition has existed, and continues to play a significant role in revolutionary literature. This is especially true when one considers critics of the state. I have sought in this book to bring together common ideas and theories from hitherto neglected sources. This primary material is meant to provide insight into the social and political milieu of late nineteenth-century Britain and illuminate the political ideas of political and social agitators and propagandists who refused to accept the possibility of change by working within the legal-institutionalized order. Not only did these individuals refuse to acknowledge the contemporary means of participation as relevant, but they also rejected the then growing tide of solutions as put forward by the state socialists. It is partially due to the acceptance by most of the radical elements of the state socialist idea that libertarian literature was for so long dismissed in most discussions of socialist theory. Clearly this literature does not fit comfortably into the simple formulations provided by the all-too-familiar left-right continuum, and this is perhaps one reason why this important material has not received the serious attention it deserves.

With the advent, in the United States and Canada, of an active libertarian movement which engages in electoral politics, there has been a renewed effort to characterize libertarian ideas with individualism. As would be the case if the logical progression of Mill's ideas were instituted, these groups eschew state control, but concentrate on the virtues of private property, individual contract, tax revolt, and freedom from state authority.

Consequently, there is much confusion as to what the term 'libertarian' designates. This examination of the British libertarian movement shows that it was unequivocally socialist in nature. Individualists such as Auberon Herbert and Wordsworth Donisthorpe recognized that their anti-statism was not of a form which would incur the sympathy of people like Morris or Kropotkin.

The anarchists' prediction of the "omnipresence of the state" has proved to have had considerable merit, and those in Britain who made contributions to libertarian thought in the late nineteenth century have in many ways been vindicated. If state power has triumphed, it has been in large part because of the practical success of the state socialists. To change or ameliorate the all-pervasive power of the state remains part of the continuing struggle of the libertarians who seek not an autonomous form of individual liberty, but an egalitarian society which provides for social justice for all classes.

FOOTNOTES TO CHAPTER ONE

1.   Mill, J. S., On Liberty, as reprinted in The Utilitarians, Dolphin Books, Doubleday and Co., Garden City, New York, 1961, p. 484.

2.   Ibid.

3.   "Those who admit any limit to what a government may do, except in the case of such governments as they think ought not to exist, stand out as brilliant exceptions among the political thinkers of the Continent." Ibid., p. 477.

       "The limitation...of the power of government over individuals loses none of its importance when the holders of power are regularly accountable to the community, that is, to the strongest party therein." Ibid., p. 478.

4.   Mill, J. S., On Liberty, op. cit, p. 482.

5.   Ibid., p. 479.

6.   Ibid.

7.   Ibid.

8.   Ibid., p. 485.

9.   Ibid., pp. 483-4 (underlining mine).

10.   Aldred, G. A., The Possibility and Philosophy of Anarchist Communism (Reprinted from Freedom, August-September 1907), Bakinin Press, London, 1907, pp. 7-8.

11.   Fox, Jay, Trade Unionism and Anarchism - A letter to a Brother Unionist, Social Science Press, Chicago, 1908, p. 10.

12.   Mill, J. S., op. cit., p. 485.

13.   The Anarchist (March 1888) 'Anarchistic Queries'.

14.   Ibid., (April 1885) 'Notes'.

15.   Ibid., (August 15, 1885) 'The Anarchists' Catechism 1'.

16.   Ibid., (June 1885) 'The Unruly Majority Rule'.

17.   Mill, J. S., op. cit., p. 543, 586.

18.   Ibid., p. 485.

19.   Ibid.

20.   Ibid.

21.   In reference to democratizing trends Mill said that we were fast
        coming to a situation whereby, "...the only power deserving the name is
        that of the masses, and governments while they make themselves the
        organ of the tendencies and instincts of the masses". _Ibid._, p. 542.

        Public opinion is "...always a mass, that is to say, 'collective
        mediocrity.'" _Ibid._, p. 542. He did however recognize the main
        source of public opinion - "...in England chiefly the middle class".
        Ibid., p. 542.

22.   "I do not mean that they choose what is customary in preference to what
        suits their own inclination. It does not occur to them to have any
        inclination at all, except for what is customary." _Ibid._, p. 537.
        This refers to those individuals "...from the highest class of society
        down to the lowest". _Ibid._, p. 537.

23.   _Ibid._, p. 534.

24.   _Ibid._, pp. 548-9.

25.   _Ibid._, p. 547.

26.   _Ibid._, p. 536.

27.   _Ibid._, p. 546.

28.   "...the tyranny of opinion is such as to make eccentricity a reproach".
        Ibid., pp. 543-4.

29.   "Genius can only breathe freely in an _atmosphere_ of freedom." _Ibid._,
        p. 541.

        But Mill also added, "I am not countenancing the sort of 'hero-worship'
        which applauds the strong man of genius." _Ibid._, p. 543.

30.   _Ibid._, p. 536.

31.   _Ibid._

32.   "Energy may be turned to _bad_ uses;..." _Ibid._

33.   _Ibid._

34.   _Ibid._, p. 539.

35.   "In proportion to the development of his individuality, each person
        becomes more valuable to himself, and is therefore capable of being
        more valuable to others." _Ibid._

36.   _Ibid._

37.   _Ibid._, p. 540.

38.   _Ibid._, p. 537.

39.   Ibid.

40.   Ibid., p. 541.

41.   "And even to himself there is a full equivalent in the better development of the social part of his nature." Ibid., p. 539.

42.   Ibid.

43.   Ibid.

44.   Ibid.

45.   Ibid. See pp. 536-7 with reference to the growth in states of
society.

46.   Ibid., pp. 534-5.

47.   Ibid., p. 535.

48.   Ibid., p. 532.

49.   Ibid., p. 535.

50.   Aldred, G. A., op. cit., p. 6.

51.   Kropotkin, P., Anarchism: Its Philosophy and Ideal, Freedom Pamphlet
No. 10, Second Issue, Freedom Press, London, 1897, p. 20.

52.   Ibid., p. 25.

53.   Ibid, p. 26.

54.   Burns-Gibson, J., Essays in Communist Anarchism as reprinted from
issues of Freedom, 'Anarchism Kills Individualism', p. 1.

55.   Mill, J. S., op. cit., p. 552.

56.   Ibid.

57.   Ibid., p. 553.

58.   "The same strong susceptibilities which make the personal impulses
vivid and powerful are also the source from whence are generated the
most passionate love of virtue, and the sternest self-control." Thus,
for Mill, the selfish person, one who lacked self-control or respect
for others, would not be virtuous. Ibid., p. 536.

59.   Burns-Gibson, J., op. cit., p. 1.

60.   See for example: Carpenter, E., Civilization; Its Cause and Cure and
other Essays, (15th Ed.), Geo. Allen and Unwin Ltd., London, 1921.

       Reid, Geo. W., The Natural Basis of Civilization, Proletarian
Publishing Co., Pamphlet No. 1, n.d.

Morris, W., Signs of Change" Seven Lectures, Longmans Green and Co., New York, 1903. Note especially the one entitled 'The Hopes of Civilization'.

61. "Anarchism recognizes and values individuality which means character, conduct and the springs of conduct, free initiative, creativeness, spontaneity, autonomy." See Burns-Gibson, J., op.cit., p. 2. Compare this to Mill's words about the worth of spontaneity in On Liberty, op. cit., pp. 532-33.

62. Burns-Gibson, J., op. cit., p. 2.

63. Mill, J. S., op. cit., p. 554.

64. Ibid., p. 573.

65. Ibid., p. 576.

66. Ibid., p. 577.

67. Ibid., p. 583.

68. Ibid., p. 560.

69. Ibid., p. 582.

70. Ibid., p. 578.

71. Ibid., pp. 578-79.

72. Ibid., p. 575.

73. Ibid., p. 481.

74. Ibid., p. 585.

75. Ibid., p. 552.

76. Ibid., p. 567.

77. Ibid., p. 575.

78. Ibid.

79. Ibid., p. 566.

80. Mabbott, J. D., The State and the Citizen, Hutchinson University Library (2nd ed.), London, 1970, p. 75.

81. See Mill, J. S., op.cit., pp. 475-80.

82. Ibid., p. 552.

83. See my Section entitled 'The Individual and Society'.

84.   This is turning around Mill's quote referred to in footnote 82.

85.   Mill, J. S., op. cit., p. 552.

86.   We could of course mix things up further by saying that even if the
       two senses of individual are different, it by no means leads one to
       the conclusion that the two uses of the term society have to be
       different. This may be true, but I think it could be argued as to
       why Mill so cunningly made it look like they were both to be taken in
       the same sense while still making use of different words.

87.   For example, as he said, "Such oppositions of interest between
       individuals often arise from bad social institutions, but are unavoid-
       able while those institutions last; and some would be unavoidable under
       any institutions." Mill, J. S., op. cit., p. 574.

       Or again, in a very libertarian vein, he said, "It is only because
       the institutions of this country are a mass of inconsistencies, that
       things find admittance into our practice which belong to the system of
       despotic, or what is called paternal, government." Ibid., p. 582.

88.   Ibid., p. 485.

89.   Ibid., p. 478.

90.   "There are still in this country large bodies of persons by whose
       notions of morality and religion these recreations [dancing, public
       games, etc.] are condemned; and those persons are chiefly of the middle
       class who are the ascendant power in the present social and political
       condition of the kingdom." Ibid., p. 565.

91.   Ibid., p. 480.

92.   Kropotkin, P., op. cit., p. 16.

93.   Kropotkin, P., Law and Authority: An Anarchist Essay, International
       Publishing Co., London, 1886, p. 16.

94.   Kropotkin, P., The State; Its Historic Role, Freedom Pamphlet No. 11,
       Freedom Press, London, 1898, p. 4.

95.   Mill, J. S., op. cit., p. 543.

96.   Ibid., p. 481.

97.   Reid, Geo. W., op. cit., p. 3.

98.   The International Anarchist Congress - Amsterdam, August 26-31,
       (Proceedings), Freedom Office, London, 1907, p. 9.

99.   Mill, J. S., op. cit., p. 543.

100.   Kropotkin, P., Anarchism: Its Philosophy and Ideal, op. cit.,
       p. 21.

101. *Ibid.*

102. Mill, J. S., *op. cit.*, p. 542.

103. *Ibid.*, p. 552.

104. *Ibid.*, p. 556.

105. Mabbott, *op. cit.*, see pp. 77-84. Indeed he suggested that there would be much less confusion if the term 'society' were dropped.

106. *Ibid.*, p. 531.

107. See in particular the argument which begins, "An opinion that corn-dealers are starvers of the poor, or that private property is robbery..." *Ibid.*, p. 531.

108. *Ibid.*, p. 485.

109. *Ibid.*, p. 581.

110. Carpenter, E., 'Private Property', in *England's Ideal; And Other Papers on Social Subjects*, Swan Sonnenschein and Co., (rev. ed.), London, 1895, p. 143.

111. Mill, J. S., *op. cit.*, p. 587.

112. *Ibid.*, p. 593.

113. *Ibid.*, pp. 591-92.

114. *Ibid.*, pp. 590-91.

115. See my Section on 'The Rulers and the Ruled'.

116. Mill, J. S., *op. cit.*, p. 585.

117. *Ibid.*, p. 574.

118. Sampson, R. V., *Equality and Power*, Heinneman, London, 1965, pp. 96-97.

119. Carpenter, E., *Marriage in a Free Society*, Labour Press Society Ltd., Manchester, 1894, p. 8.

120. "The third and most cogent reason for restricting the interference of government is the great evil of adding unnecessarily to its power." Mill, J. S., *op. cit.*, pp. 591-93.

121. *Ibid.*, p. 532.

122. *Ibid.*, p. 492.

123. *Ibid.*, p. 532-33.

124. *Ibid.*, p. 531.

125. "The usefulness of an opinion is itself a matter of opinion; as disputable, as open to discussion, and requiring discussion as much as the opinion itself." *Ibid.*, p. 497.

126. *Ibid.*, p. 529.

127. For example, what benefit is the law of copyright or patent, to most ordinary people. It does little more than give the inventor security at the expense of the persons who must cater to his monopoly position in order to attain any benefit from the invention.

128. De Grazia, S., 'Authority and Rationality' in *Philosophy*, Vol. XXXVII, No. 101, April 1952, pp. 108-9.

129. "Whenever there is an ascendant class, a large portion of the morality of the country emanates from its class interests, and its feelings of class superiority." Mill, J. S., *op. cit.*, p. 480.

130. See footnote 60 for relevant references.

131. Reid, Geo. W., *op. cit.*, p. 10.

132. Mill, J. S., *op. cit.*, p. 571.

133. *Ibid.*, p. 540.

134. *Ibid.*, p. 490 (underlining mine).

135. *Ibid.*, p. 579.

136. *Ibid.*

137. *Ibid.*, p. 580.

138. *Ibid.*, p. 580 (underlining mine).

139. *Ibid.*, p. 581 (underlining mine).

140. Carpenter, E., 'The New Morality' in *Civilization: Its Cause and Cure*, *op. cit.*, p. 261.

141. De Grazia, S., *op. cit.*, p. 99.

142. That is, by having set out certain goals, like cooperation, they believed that the means to attaining the goal could only be legitimized by behaving cooperatively. By living their 'ideals' they would thus set an emulative example so that the final end or goal would not be unlike the means used to reach it. This could be explained in libertarian terms as in footnote 143.

143. "No revolution can ever succeed as a factor of liberation unless the MEANS used to further it be identical in spirit and tendency with the

PURPOSES to be achieved. Revolution...is the destroyer of dominant values upon which a complex system of injustice, oppression, and wrong has been built up... It is the herald of NEW VALUES, ushering in a transformation of the basic relations of man to man, and man to society... It is first and foremost the TRANSVALUATOR, the bearer of new values. It is the great teacher of the NEW ETHICS inspiring men with a new concept of life and its manifestations in social relationships; It is the mental and spiritual regenerator." As quoted by R. Drinnon in Rebel in Paradise - A Biography of Emma Goldman, Toronto, Beacon Press, 1970, p. 261.

144.   As Kropotkin commented: "We again take up the current which led men in the twelfth century to organize themselves on the basis of a free understanding, of free initiative of the individual, of free federation of those interested." The State: Its Historic Role, op. cit., p. 41.

145.   Emerson, R. W., 'Essay on Fate', Basic Selections from Emerson; Essays Poems and Apothegms, New American Library, New York, 1971, pp. 359-60.

146.   Fromm, E., Man for Himself - An Inquiry into the Psychology of Ethics, Fawcett Premier Books, New York, 1969, p. 95. This passage of course refers to the dispositional aspects of power which tend to lead to relationships of a similar nature.

147.   Mill, J. S., op.cit., p. 485.

148.   Ibid., p. 579.

149.   Malatesta, E., as quoted by V. Richards in the Introduction to Anarchy, Freedom Press, London, 1974, p. 8.

150.   Ibid., p. 596 (underlining mine).

151.   Ibid.

152.   Ibid., p. 595.

153.   See Geo. Plechanoff's criticisms in Anarchism and Socialism, New Times Socialist Publ. Co., Minneapolis, Minn., 1912.

154.   The liberal individualism can exist only under a law-bound and regulatory political system. The individual is forced into a relationship with a governing body. According to one libertarian this is "...taking away from the individual his direct interest in life and in his surroundings...blunting his moral sense;...teaching that he must never rely on himself...[but]upon a small part of men who are elected to do everything...[which]...destroys to a large extent his perception of right and wrong". Smith, J. B., Direct Action Versus Legislation, Freedom Press, London, 1909, p. 3.

Or, in terms of the individual and property, Ed Carpenter seemed convinced of the role of law. "Clearly the sooner we get rid of all mere law in the matter of property the better. The good sense of mankind...will always allow a man his claim in the product of his own hands, or his own labour; and the same good sense will never dispute a man's right in that which he puts to good human use." From Private Property, op. cit., p. 162.

155.   One could not consider anarchist individualists in many cases to be libertarian because they maintained that individualism and competition were essential to their philosophy. One can see this in the anarchist press, in particular, the journals Liberty and The Anarchist.

156.   See the Introduction of Liberty and the Great Libertarians by C. T. Strading (1913 Reprint), Arno Press and The New York Times, New York, 1972.

157.   Godwin was much the same at times. "But what is to hold men together in 'society without government'? Not a promise, at any rate. No promise can bind me; for either what I have promised is good, then I must do it even if there had been no promise; or it is bad, then not even the promise can make it my duty." W. Godwin, as quoted by P. Eltzbacher, Anarchism – Exponents of the Anarchist Philosophy, Freedom Press, London (2nd ed.), 1960, pp. 29-30.

158.   "I am an anarchist, declaring by this word the negation, or better, the insufficiency, of the principle of authority." As quoted in Edwards, S., (Ed.), Selected Writings of Pierre-Joseph Proudhon, MacMillan and Co., Ltd., London, 1970, p. 91. As taken from Proudhon's Philosophy of Poverty, 1853, p. 74.

FOOTNOTES TO CHAPTER TWO

1.   Spencer, H., **First Principles**, on the section dealing with Equal
     Freedom, as reprinted in **Liberty and the Great Libertarians**, Los
     Angeles, 1913, reissued as **The Right-Wing Individualist Tradition in
     America**, Arno Press and the New York Times, New York, 1972, p. 219.

2.   This quote of Spencer's was embodied as the aim of the Party of
     Individual Liberty. A. Herbert, **The Right and Wrong of
     Compulsion by the State**, Anti-Force Papers No. 2, Williams and
     Norgate, London, 1885, p. 4.

3.   Although a reading of Herbert's works will show that he was not an
     anarchist, the press of the day was not at all consistent in its
     understanding of his philosophic position, which was in effect the
     same as that of Herbert Spencer.

     As **Freedom** said in 1888 - "The Auberon Herbertites in England are
     sometimes called Anarchists by outsiders, but they are willing to
     compromise with the inequity of government to maintain private
     property." **Freedom**, Vol. II, No. 17 (Feb.) 1888. Yet only two
     months later this same anarchist journal reported that - "Individualist
     Anarchists...like the State Socialists...are perfectly prepared to
     pursue a policy in utter contradiction with their profession of faith
     - vide Mr. A. Herbert's 'Right and Wrong of Compulsion by the State'
     and Mr. W. Donisthorpe's criticism thereon in the last two numbers of
     Jus." **Freedom**, April 1888.

     In January 1892 the **Fortnightly Review** stated, "Auberon Herbert has
     some sound Anarchistic remarks upon politics and morals in his article
     'Under the Yoke of the Butterflies'."

     It is interesting to note however that Herbert's books and pamphlets
     were advertised in **The Commonweal**, **Freedom**, and the **Anarchist**.

4.   As described by Wordsworth Donisthorpe in his pamphlet, **Liberty or
     Law**, Liberty and Property Defense League, London, 1885, p. 60.

5.   For the aims and principle programme of this Party, see **Anti-Force
     Paper No. 1 - The Free Mind in the Free Body: A Statement of
     Principles and Measures**, Women's Printing Society Ltd., London,
     1885.

6.   See Herbert, A., **Anti-Force Papers, No. 2, op. cit.** After one
     has law, or general principles in politics, freedom means in essence
     absence of restraint, or as he called it, 'Force'. He pitted Force
     against liberty.

     "...the side of Force...strong governments and interfering
     departments...protection and regulation...of socialism and life divided
     between rulers and ruled.

     "...the side of Liberty...of self-dependence and self-response, of
     free thought, free religion, free enterprise, free trade, of every free

moral influence that grows where Force is not..." (p. 17).

7.   Herbert, A., <u>Anti-Force Papers No. 2</u>, <u>ibid</u>., p. 6.

8.   "...the foundation of all morality is respect for the free choice and
      free actions of others, the essence of a true offence against person or
      property seems to be the violent interference with a man's faculties,
      the constraining of his will and actions...prevented...from doing those
      actions which he is physically and morally competent to do;..."
      <u>ibid</u>., p. 35.

9.   Donisthorpe, W., <u>Democracy</u>, read before the Fabian Conference of
      1886. Printed in <u>The Anarchist</u> of August 1886, under the heading of
      'Anarchy'. William Morris said in the same month in <u>The Commonweal</u>
      (reprinted in <u>The Anarchist</u> of September 1886) in reference to
      Donisthorpe, that he was a man "...whose aim would seem to be the
      destruction of the meaning of language".

      A year prior to this Henry Seymour of <u>The Anarchist</u> had already taken
      up the cudgels on the side of the anarchist's by denouncing an article
      in <u>Justice</u>. Seymour said in his 'Notes' of July 1885: "<u>Justice</u>
      of the 11th describes the members of the 'Liberty and Property Defense
      League' as Anarchists. Mr. Hyndman knows well enough that the members
      of this League are <u>not</u> Anarchists, and that they would as quickly
      resent the imputation against Anarchists as Anarchists would against
      them. If Mr. Hyndman has read Proudhon's 'What is Property' or knows
      anything at all about Anarchists he knows that they hold that property
      and liberty are absolutely irreconcileable and contradictory terms."

10.   For the programme of the Liberty and Property Defense League see the
      pamphlet <u>Liberty or Law</u>, by W. Donisthorpe, published by the Liberty
      and Property Defense League, 4 Westminster Chambers, Victoria St.,
      London, 1885.

11.   Burke, E., <u>A Vindication of Natural Society</u>, as reprinted in
      Strading, <u>op.cit</u>., p. 69.

12.   Mill, J. S., <u>Political Economy</u>, London, 1848.

13.   Paine, T., <u>The Rights of Man, Part II</u>, as quoted in Strading, H.,
      <u>op.cit</u>., p. 75.

14.   Mill, J. S., <u>op.cit</u>., p. 10.

15.   Paine, T., <u>op.cit</u>., p. 76.

16.   Godwin, W., <u>An Inquiry Concerning Political Justice</u>, as reprinted
      in Strading, H., <u>op.cit</u>., p. 102.

17.   <u>Ibid</u>., pp. 94-95.

18.   Spencer, H., <u>op.cit</u>., p. 220.

19.   Mill, J. S., <u>On Liberty</u>, as reprinted in <u>The Utilitarians</u>, Dolphin
      Books, Doubleday and Co. Inc., New York, 1961. See especially

pp. 491-96 which refer essentially to his views on 'truth and opinion'.

20.   This term 'Interregnum' is used by Raymond Williams to describe the
      intellectual and social history of England from 1880 until 1914. See
      Culture and Society, 1780-1950, see chapter entitled 'The
      Interregnum', Chatto & Windus, London, 1967.

21.   See in particular the following works of Morris: Signs of Change;
      Hopes and Fears for Art; Architecture, Industry and Wealth; Four
      Letters on Socialism; Communism; and A Factory as It Might Be.

      Raymond Williams came to a general conclusion. "In the middle of the
      twentieth century Morris remains a contemporary thinker for the
      directions which he indicated have become a part of a general social
      movement. Yet, he belongs, essentially, with the great Victorian
      rebels, sharing with them an energy, an expansion, a willingness to
      generalize which marks him, from our own period of critical specialism
      as an historic figure." Ibid., p. 161.

22.   Shaw wrote, shortly after Morris's death in 1896 that, "He remained
      unchanged in his Socialism but he practically adopted the views of the
      Fabian Society as to how the change would come about... His latest
      important act in the Socialist movement was to try to unite all of
      the Socialist Societies into a single party. He did not initiate the
      plan, but he did his best to carry it out; and he was certainly the
      best man for the purpose, since 'the societies were all agreed in
      having' a deep regard and respect for him." As quoted by Vallance,
      A., William Morris, His Art, Writings, and Public Life, Geo. Bell
      and Sons, London, 1897, p. 357.

      Neither Morris, nor Shaw, who made up the drafting committee for this
      united action could agree with Hyndman who was the member representing
      the S.D.F. As Shaw commented in 1936, "Morris soon saw that we were
      irreconcilable... Morris's draft, horribly eviscerated and patched,
      was subsequently sold for a penny as the Joint Manifesto of the
      Socialists of Great Britain [on May 1, 1893]. It was the only
      document any of the three of us had ever signed and published that
      was honestly not worth a farthing." Shaw, G.B., Morris as I knew
      Him, in Morris, May, William Morris, Artist, Writer, Socialist,
      Basil Blackwell (limited edition of 750 copies), Oxford, 1936,
      pp. xxxv-xxxvi.

      For further insight into this attempt at reconciliation on the part of
      Morris, see Edward Pease's account of what he called 'The Manifesto of
      English Socialists' in The History of the Fabian Society, Frank Cass
      and Co. Ltd., (third ed.), London, 1963, p. 203.

23.   Commenting on Morris's withdrawal from the Socialist League in
      November of 1890, apparently due to the anarchist takeover, L.E. Grey,
      one more political interpreter of Morris, said,

      "It has been claimed sometimes, that these Anarchists were mild docile
      men, for the most partial ideologists rather than real Anarchists. Yet
      the manner in which they threw caution to the winds after Morris's
      withdrawal hardly supports this view." William Morris, Prophet of

England's New Order, London, 1949, p. 305. However, the examples Grey gives, especially with reference to the Walsall plot of 1892, or the writing in a later Commonweal do not bear this out. Morris's disagreements were ones of principle, but theirs were more of tactics.

24. See the Freedom article entitled 'George Bernard Czar' of February 1909 (Vol. 23, No. 238).

25. See Chesterton, G. K., William Morris: An Appreciation, Walthamstow, The Library, 1934.

"Modern England will never exhaust her debt to William Morris. He was a very great Distributionist. There seems to be a curious idea prevalent that he was a Socialist. Indeed, it was so prevalent that he was partly deceived by it himself." As cited by Grey, L. E., op.cit., p. 320. (One must feel that the seriousness of this comment is in doubt.)

See footnote 22 for Shaw's comments regarding Morris's attitude to Fabianism.

26. "Revolution...means a change in the basis of society." Morris, W., Signs of Change: Seven Lectures, from "How We Live and How We Might Live", Longmans Green and Co., New York, 1903, p. 2.

27. See in particular, J. W. MacKail, The Life of William Morris, Vol. II, Longmans Green and Co., London, 1898. Also one must note the relationships with his wife Jane and Rossetti, and the letters which survive to and from Edward Burn-Jones's wife 'Georgie' to and from Morris.

28. Morris, W., 'Anarchism and Socialism' see Commonweal, May 18, 1889 (Correspondence).

29. Morris, May, op.cit., p. 9. Also see Thompson, E. P., op.cit., pp. 272-3, and Vallance, A., op.cit., pp. 21, 307, 311.

30. "His art and his Socialism were, to Morris's mind, associated integrally with one another; or rather they were but two aspects of the same thing. Those well-meaning apologists, then, who try to explain away William Morris's share in the movement are not doing him a real service, nor such for which he would have thanked them." Vallance, A., op.cit., p. 305.

31. This was clearly illustrated in the letters he wrote to family and friends at the time Hyndman was seeking to gain personal control of the Social Democratic Federation in 1884. See The Letters of William Morris to His Family and Friends, Edited by P. Henderson, Longmans Green and Co., London, 1950, pp. 218-29.

Thompson confirms this, and uses it as an excuse for much of Morris's so-called deviations from the Marxist line. He says, "...after the 'split' Hyndman's claim to be the only true disciple of Marx, and his doctrinaire use of Marx's name, prompted Morris to be especially careful to avoid this kind of dogmatism." op.cit., p. 895.

Referring to one of his last meetings with the S.D.F. Morris mentions
in a letter that, "I plainly expressed my opinion as to Hyndman's
absolutism and self-seeking." Letter to Robert Thompson, Jan. 1,
1885. The Letters..., op.cit.

32. Morris, to J. L. Joynes, December 25, 1884, as reprinted in Morris,
May, op.cit., pp. 587-92.

33. Ibid.

34. "I put some conscience into trying to learn the economical side of
Marx, though I must confess that, whereas I thoroughly enjoyed the
historical part of Capital, I suffered agonies of confusion of the
brain over reading the pure economics of that great work." See The
Letters..., op.cit., p. lv.

35. See Morris's diary for period of Jan. 25 to April 11, 1887. British
Museum Add. MSS. 45335.

36. Grey, L. E., op.cit., p. 237.

37. For a fuller description of Bax, see Morris, May, op.cit.,
pp. 173-74.

38. Shaw, G. B., op.cit., p. xi.

39. Every book on Morris's socialism seems to have a different account of
the whole futile attempt at reconciliation. Shaw's is certainly the
most amusing version. See, ibid., pp. xxxiv-xxxvi.

40. Grey, L. E., op.cit., p. 319.

41. In December 1890 the Commonweal became a monthly, and was subtitled
'A Journal of Revolutionary Socialism'. In May 1891 it was subtitled
'A Revolutionary Journal of Anarchist-Communism'. Since February 1891
it claimed to represent the newly constituted London Socialist League.
In 1892, from 145, City Road, E.C., the publishers of Commonweal
issued a series of Revolutionary Studies. David Nicoll, later to be
arrested for 'Incitement to Murder' was its editor, and Charles Mowbray
was publisher. For an account of the trial see The Public Records
Office, DPP 4/26: Nicol [sic] and Others - 1892.

The few existing examples of the legally offending material published
under this subtitle see The Public Records Office, DPP 4/26
containing pieces of the Commonweal for March 5, 12, 19, 26; April 2,
19, 16, 1892.

42. Founded by Morris as an independent organization on November 23, 1890,
two days after he left the Socialist League.

43. See Morris, May, op.cit., pp. 310-27. Vallance, A., op.cit.,
pp. 348-52. Grey, L. E., op.cit., pp. 282-307. MacKail, J. W.,
op.cit., pp. 152-154. Thompson, E. P., op.cit., pp. 638-41.

44. Grey, L. E., op.cit., p. 282.

45. "The work that lies before us at present is to make Socialists, to cover the country with a network of associations composed of men who feel their antagonism to the dominant classes, and have no temptation to waste their time in the thousand follies of party politics." Morris, W., Socialism and Politics, Commonweal (Supplement), July 1885.

46. Grey, L. E., op.cit., p. 265.

47. British Museum Add. MSS. 45335, February 20, 1887.

48. "On March 18th we had a meeting in Commemoration of the Commune at South Place: that was a great success, the place crowded. Kropotkin new come from prison spoke, and I made his acquaintance there: I like him very much: had a long talk with him yesterday evening at a gathering of the S.D.F." Morris to Carruthers, March 25, 1886. Morris, May, op.cit., pp. 595-99. Kropotkin had previously been in London in July 1881 for a few weeks, returned in autumn of 1881 until May 1882, finally he returned to stay 30 years in the early part of 1886 when Morris met him for the first time.

49. Morris, May, op.cit., p. 320.

50. Ibid.

51. Carlyle, T., Works of Thomas Carlyle, Vol. II, as quoted by Thompson, E. P., op.cit., Works, p. 234.

52. Ibid., p. 233.

53. Morris, W., op.cit., Works of William Morris, 'Art and Its Producers', Vol. XXII, p. 352.

54. Carlyle, T., Works, p. 247.

55. Morris, W., Art, Labour and Socialism - with a modern assessment. Original title Art Under Plutocracy, lecture in Oxford, 1884, Pamphlet, n.d., p. 24.

56. Ibid., p. 29.

57. Carlyle, T., op.cit., pp. 244-45.

58. Morris, W., The Letters..., op.cit., p. 151.

59. Carlyle, T., op.cit., pp. 244-45.

60. Williams, R., op.cit., p. 83.

61. Morris's essay, 'Useful Work Versus Useless Toil' in Signs of Change, op.cit., pp. 141-73.

62. Morris, W., ibid., p. 155.

63. In a letter to the Rev. Geo. Bainton on April 10, 1888, Morris gave his views on government in socialist society. "But to return to our 'government' of the future, which would be rather an administration of things than a government of persons... Nations as political entities would cease to exist; civilization would mean the federalization of a variety of communities great and small, at one end of which would be the township and the local guild, in which administration would be carried on perhaps in direct assemblies in more majorum, and at the other some central body whose function would be almost entirely the guardianship of the principles of society, and would when necessary enforce their practice; e.g. it would not allow slavery in any form to be practised in any community." The Letters..., op.cit., p. 287.

64. Morris said that "Wealth is what Nature gives us and what a reasonable man can make out of the gifts of Nature for his reasonable use." 'Useful Work Versus Useless Toil', op.cit., p. 149. In the 1840s Morris's father had in excess of 200,000 pounds. Morris himself received an annuity of 900 pounds a year on his twenty-first birthday. See MacKail, op.cit., Chapters 1 and 2.

65. See his letter to the Daily News of 20 November 1885 relating to the vulgarization of Oxford, and also his letter on art and society in the Manchester Examiner of 14 March 1883. Both are reprinted in Briggs, A., William Morris: Selected Writings and Designs, Penguin, 1962.

66. See 'Useful Work Versus Useless Toil', op.cit., for protractive definitions and descriptions of the upper, middle and working classes. He usually refrained from referring to the workers as a singular class.

67. See Morris, W., Monopoly: Or How Labour is Robbed, a pamphlet by The Hammersmith Socialist Society, 1893. Reprint of 1891 Socialist League pamphlet. Also, Art, Labour and Socialism, op.cit.

68. Thompson, E. P., The Communism of William Morris, a lecture to the William Morris Society, London, 1965, p. 12.

69. From How I Became a Socialist, as quoted by E. P. Thompson, op.cit., p. 153.

70. Williams, R., op.cit., p. 136.

71. Ibid., p. 135.

72. Ibid., Chapters 4 and 7.

73. Thompson, E. P., William Morris..., op.cit., p. 214.

74. Kropotkin, P., The State: Its Historic Role, Freedom Pamphlet No. 11, Freedom Press, London, 1898, p. 42.

75. Williams, R., op.cit., p. 214.

76. Morris, W., Art, Labour and Socialism, op.cit., "I hold that the condition of competition between man and man is bestial only, and

that of association human." (p. 20).

"...All art, even the highest, is influenced by the conditions of labour of the mass of mankind, and that any pretentions which may be made for even the highest intellectual art to be independent of these general conditions are futile and vain; ... any art which professes to be founded on special education or refinement of a limited body or class, must of necessity be unreal and short-lived. 'Art is man's expression of his joy in labour.'" p. 22.

77.   *Ibid.*, p. 22.

78.   *Ibid.*

79.   Ruskin, J., *Stones of Venice*, especially the chapter entitled 'The Nature of Gothic'.

80.   Morris, W., *Art, Labour and Socialism*, op.cit., p. 24.

81.   *Ibid.*, p. 23.

82.   *Ibid.*, p. 22 (underlining mine).

83.   *Commonweal*, April 1885, *The Worker's Share of Art*.

84.   Morris, W., *Art, Labour and Socialism*, op.cit., pp. 22-23.

85.   *Ibid.*, p. 24.

86.   Morris, W., *Letters*, p. 206.

87.   Morris, W., *Art, Labour and Socialism*, op.cit., p. 30.

88.   Morris, W., *Art and the People*, as reprinted in Briggs, A., op.cit., p. 142.

89.   Morris, W., *Art, Labour and Socialism*, op.cit., pp. 33-34.

90.   Morris, W., *Useful Work Versus Useless Toil*, op.cit., p. 142.

91.   See *Commonweal*, April 1885, *The Worker's Share of Art*.

92.   *Ibid.*

93.   Morris, W., 'The Aims of Art' in *Signs of Change*, op.cit., p. 127.

94.   Morris, W., *Useful Work Versus Useless Toil*, op.cit., p. 142.

95.   *Ibid.*, p. 144.

96.   Morris, W., *The Worker's Share of Art*, op.cit.

97.   Morris, W., 'The Aims of Art' in *Signs of Change*, op.cit., p. 121.

98.   *Ibid.*, p. 133.

99.   Upon the formation of the Socialist League he commented: "The worst of
       the new body, as far as I am concerned, is that for the present at
       least I have to be editor of the paper, which I by no means bargained
       for, but it seems nobody else will do." MacKail, J. W., Vol. II,
       op.cit., p. 128.

100.   Letter in The Daily Chronicle of 10 November, 1893.

101.   From Four Letters on Socialism, privately printed in 1894, from
       Morris to the Rev. Geo. Bainton. Reprinted in Briggs, A., op.cit.,
       p. 152.

102.   Ibid., p. 153.

103.   Morris, W., The Worker's Share of Art, op.cit.

104.   Morris, W., 'The Aims of Art' in Signs of Change, op.cit., p. 132.

105.   Morris, May, op.cit., p. 318.

106.   Ibid., p. 314.

107.   "As to the matter of majority rule, let us look at the matter again.
       All rule must be...majority rule - i.e., of the effective majority. If
       at any time the minority rules, it is because they are better
       organized, better armed, less stupid, more energetic than the mere
       nose-counted majority: this effective majority therefore coerces the
       minority; and as long as it can coerce it, it will." May Morris,
       ibid., p. 318.

108.   Morris to Rev. Bainton, 2 April 1888, The Letters..., op.cit.,
       p. 282.

109.   "The land, factories, machinery, means of transit, and whatever wealth
       of any sort is used for the reproduction of wealth and which therefore
       is necessary to labour and can only be used by it, must be owned by the
       nation only, to be used by the workers (who will include all honest
       men) according to their capacity." Ibid., p. 284. Morris himself
       has a footnote to this statement: "I ask you to keep well in mind the
       distinction between the ownership of wealth which implies no
       corresponding duties, and the possession of it for use which implies
       full responsibility towards other people."

110.   "...As to the class of rich people doing no work, we all know that they
       consume a great deal while they produce nothing. Therefore, clearly,
       they have to be kept at the expense of those who do work, just as
       paupers have, and are a mere burden to the community." Morris, W.,
       Useful Work Versus Useless Toil, op.cit., p. 145.

111.   Ibid., p. 147.

112.   "The means whereby this is to be brought about is first, educating
       people into desiring it, next organizing them into claiming it
       effectually." Morris to R. Thompson, 24 July 1884, in The

Letters..., op.cit., p. 207.

113. Morris, W., 'How We Live and How We Might Live' in Signs of Change, op.cit., p. 2.

114. Carlyle, T., op.cit., p. 248.

115. The closest Morris ever came to advocating a force similar to a 'proletarian vanguard' came in an interview in the Daily News of January 8, 1885, just a few weeks after the foundation of the Socialist League. As far as I can ascertain this sentiment was never repeated.

"I do not care for a mechanical revolution. I want an educated movement. Discontent is not enough, though it is natural and inevitable.

"The discontented must know what they are aiming at when they overthrow the old order of things. My belief is that the old order can only be overthrown by force; and for that reason it is all the more necessary that the revolution...should not be an ignorant but an intelligent revolution. What I should like to have now by far more than anything else, would be a body of able high-minded men, who should act as instructors of the masses, and as their leaders during critical periods of the movement."

116. Morris, W., 'Dawn of a New Epic' in Signs of Change, op.cit., p. 177 (underlining mine).

117. Ibid., p. 193 (underlining mine).

118. Morris, W., 'Communism and Anarchism', Correspondence in Commonweal, 17 August 1889, reprinted in Morris, May, op.cit., p. 318.

119. Morris, W., Monopoly: Or How Labour is Robbed, op.cit., pp. 11-12.

120. Morris, W., A Factory as It Might Be, Preface by Jas. Leatham, Twentieth Century Press Ltd., London, 1907, p. 11.

121. For Morris's own justifications as to the working of his 'factory' he answered those who referred to him as a 'Capitalist Socialist' by writing to the Evening Standard in January 1885. See, Grey, L. E., op.cit., p. 248. See in particular his letter to 'Georgie' Burne-Jones of 1 June, 1884, where he discusses his employer-employee relationships in general. The Letters..., op.cit., pp. 196-200.

122. Morris, W., The Letters..., op.cit., p. 198.

123. Ibid.

124. Letter from Morris to the Daily Chronicle, 10 November 1884.

125. Morris to Burne-Jones, op.cit., p. 198.

126. Morris, W., Useful Work Versus Useless Toil, op.cit., p. 129.

127. See letter of Morris to Burne-Jones, op.cit., pp. 196-200. In his
book on Morris, Briggs has subtitled this letter as 'Self-Help No
Remedy', op.cit., pp. 149-150.

128. Morris to C. E. Maurice, 1 July 1883, The Letters..., op.cit.,
p. 176.

129. On January 14, 1884 Morris gave his first committed political lecture,
on 'Art and Democracy' for the Russell Club, University Hall,
Oxford, with Ruskin in the Chair. The lecture is better known as
'Art Under Plutocracy'. Morris became publicly involved in
politics as early as 1877 when he was the Honorary Treasurer to the
Eastern Question Association, which opposed Disraeli's involvement in
Turkey. For details see Morris, May, Chapter III, op.cit.,
pp. 51-72.

130. This was not an open declaration of socialist principles as was the one
of January 1884. The one at Manchester was entitled 'Art, Wealth And
Riches', and is reprinted in the Collected Works Vol. XXIII.
Thompson's description of the whole ordeal can be found in William
Morris..., op.cit., pp. 357-59.

131. Morris, W., 'Whigs, Democrats and Socialists' in Signs of Change,
op.cit., p. 41.

132. Thompson, E. P., William Morris..., op.cit., p. 272.

133. Morris, W., 'The Art of the People', Collected Works, Vol. XXII,
p. 48.

134. Morris established the Society for the Protection of Ancient Buildings
in 1877. (He always referred to it as 'Anti-Scrape'.) He was its
secretary, and on December 4, 1877 he delivered his first important
public lecture at the Trades Guild of Learning, to raise money for this
cause. It was always very close to his heart throughout his life. The
first lecture was entitled 'The Lesser Arts'.

135. See Briggs, R. C. H., A Handlist of the Public Addresses of William
Morris to be Found in Generally Accessible Publications (The William
Morris Society), Dolmen Press, Dublin, 1961.

See Vallance, A., for a chronological list of the printed works of
William Morris, Appendix I, op.cit., pp. 447-52.

136. Morris, May, William Morris: Artist, Writer, Socialist, Volume Two,
Morris As A Socialist, Basil Blackwell, Oxford, 1936.

137. Vallance, A., op.cit., pp. 305-366.

138. MacKail, J. W., Vol. II, op.cit., p. 152. For confirmation of this
see Thompson, E. P., William Morris..., op.cit., pp. 736-37,
886-87.

139. The Daily News: 'A Talk with William Morris on Socialism' (January 8
1885); 'Celebrating the Commune' (March 18, 1887).

140.   London Echo, 'Editorial' (October 1, 1884).

141.   Morris, W., 'Why Celebrate the Commune of Paris', Commonweal,
        (March 1886).

142.   Morris, W., 'The Policy of Abstension', first delivered at Hammersmith
        at the end of July, 1887. Extensive quotes from Thompson, E. P.,
        William Morris..., op.cit., p. 543.

143.   Morris, letter to C. E. Maurice, 1 July 1883, The Letters...,
        op.cit., p. 175.

144.   Morris, letter to C. E. Maurice, 22 June, op.cit., p. 173.

145.   Clarke, W., 'Individualism in Masquerade — A Critique of Shaw by a
        Fabian', Seed-Time, October 1889.

146.   Morris, W., 'A Talk with William Morris on Socialism', op.cit.

147.   From a review of the Fabian Essays by Morris in Commonweal,
        January 25, 1890.

148.   See Shaw, G. B., Morris as I Knew Him, op.cit.

149.   Morris, W., Whigs, Democrats and Socialists, op.cit., p. 54.

150.   As early as 1884 Morris pronounced judgment upon certain forms of mass
        organization: "...where the very combinations, the Trades Unions,
        founded for the advancement of the working class, have already become
        conservative and obstructive bodies, wielded by the middle-class
        politicians for party purposes..." Art, Labour and Socialism,
        op.cit., p. 35.

151.   Morris, W., 'Whigs, Democrats and Socialists', op.cit., p. 54.

152.   Morris, letter to J.L. Joynes, February 3, 1885, British Museum
        Add. MSS. 45345.

153.   "In the view of Lane and Scheu, a 'truly democratic party' would have
        no personal president at all. The Executive Council ('a chosen elite')
        electing a different Chairman each session." See Thompson, E. P.,
        William Morris..., op.cit., p. 399.

        In a letter of July 1888 Morris wrote to Burne-Jones: "I have always
        felt that it was rather a matter of temperament than of principle."
        This was in direct reference to the 'troubles' in the Socialist League.

154.   Ibid., p. 526.

155.   As May Morris later remembers Joseph Lane, one of the anarchists in the
        Socialist League: "Joe Lane was an uncompromising anarchist, but a
        dear." op.cit., p. 180 (ff.). He was the author of the
        Anti-Statist Communist Manifesto and confirmed his opposition to
        'propaganda by the deed'.

156.   Thompson, E. P., <u>William Morris...</u>, <u>op.cit.</u>, p. 527.

157.   Glasier, J. B., <u>William Morris and the Early Days of the Socialist Movement</u>, London, 1921, p. 128.

158.   Kitz, who was a leading member in the Labour Emancipation League, decided to merge with the Socialist League to this end. "The purely propagandist and non-parliamentary objects of the League appealed to our members and we joined it at once...and we finally decided to merge our work into the League's, with its possibilities of a wider field of propaganda." 'Recollections and Reflections', <u>Freedom</u>, April, 1912.

159.   <u>Ibid.</u>, <u>Freedom</u>, May, 1912.

160.   "If he could not win the Socialist movement as a whole to his view, still he believed it necessary for the League to exist alongside the parliamentary movement, keeping alive the propaganda of 'principle'. Increasingly between 1887 and 1890 he came to see the role of the League as being educational and propagandist within a larger Socialist movement." Thompson, E. P., <u>William Morris...</u>, <u>op.cit.</u>, p. 545.

161.   Morris, letter to Rev. J. Glasse, 19 May 1887. As quoted in Thompson, E. P., <u>ibid.</u>, p. 531.

162.   <u>Ibid.</u>, p. 353.

163.   Morris, W., 'Correspondence', <u>Commonweal</u>, May 18, 1889. Answering attacks on his integrity from 'Comrade Blackwell'.

164.   See Morris's reaction to the 'Anti-Statist Communist Manifesto' in Thompson, E. P., <u>William Morris...</u>, <u>op.cit.</u>, pp. 527-8.

165.   Dr. Creaghe and H. Davis.

166.   Morris, letter to R. Thompson, <u>op.cit.</u>, p. 206.

167.   Are related by Thompson, E. P., <u>William Morris...</u>, <u>op.cit.</u>, p. 437.

168.   <u>Ibid.</u>, pp. 638-41.

169.   <u>Ibid.</u>, p. 639.

170.   Shaw, G. B., 'The Impossibility of Anarchism', <u>Fabian Tract No. 45</u>.

171.   <u>The Hammersmith Socialist Record</u>, May 1892.

172.   Morris letter to R. Thompson, <u>op.cit.</u>, p. 207.

173.   When trying to patch up the split in the Socialist League Morris said,

       "I may as well say here that my intention is if possible to prevent the quarrel coming to a head between the two sections, parliamentary and anti-parliamentary, which are pretty much commensurate with the Collectivists and Anarchists: and this because I believe there would

be a good many who would join the Anarchist side who are not really
Anarchists, and who would be useful to us: indeed I doubt if, except
one or two Germans, etc., we have any real Anarchists amongst us: and
I don't want to see a lot of enthusiastic men who are not very deep in
Socialist doctrines driven off for a fad of the more pedantic part of
the Collectivist section..." Br. Museum Add. MSS. 45335.

174. Vallance, A., op.cit., pp. 351-2.

175. Morris, letter to R. Thompson, 20 June 1884, Letters..., op.cit.,
      p. 201 (underlining mine).

176. It is interesting to note here that Thompson makes a great number of
      accusations and assessments of the anarchists in the League, but does
      not back them up with his usual scholarly barrage of footnotes. His
      generalizations do not fit with the evidence. See his comments on
      pp. 657-58 of William Morris..., op.cit. Compare these with any
      statements made by Lane, in the Anti-Statist Communist Manifesto,
      or by Nicoll and Co. when they produced their 'Revolutionary Studies'
      at the height of the anarchist phase of the Commonweal.

      Letter of Morris to Tochatti, December 12, 1893, as reprinted by
      Thompson, E. P., William Morris..., op.cit., p. 686.

177. Ibid., p. 657. This is quite true, but it has not been established
      by Thompson that the League was representative of this general
      spectrum.

178. Morris was certainly conscious of the anarchistic side of the League.
      In April 1890 he wrote to Bruce Glasier stating,

      "Otherwise I can't say that I call the League prospects good. Outside
      the Hammersmith branch the active(?) members in London mostly
      consider themselves Anarchists, but don't know anything about Socialism
      and go about ranting revolution in the streets, which is about as
      likely to happen in our time as the conversion of Englishmen from
      stupidity to quick-wittedness." Letters..., op.cit., p. 322.

      Kitz, commenting on the breakup of the League, gave a very different
      view of the so-called anarchistic elements.

      "There existed...in the League itself opposing elements which
      eventually led to its disruption.

      "The merely negative policy of Anti-Parliamentarians could be endured
      by the West End branches of which Hammersmith was the strongest and in
      which Morris's personality was dominant; but the East End comrades
      confronted by a fierce struggle for existence and in the midst of
      gigantic labour conflicts, drifted towards a definitely Anarchist
      attitude.

      "Many of the West End members would have found a more suitable
      environment and method of exposition of their ideals within the ranks
      of the I.L.P. or the Fabian Society... They seemed to be afflicted
      with the timidity of anaemic respectability.

311

"...a climax was reached occasioned by an article in Commonweal by my
co-editor D. J. Nicoll on the question of tactics. The publication of
a second instalment of it was made a test question by the Hammersmith
Branch and as he refused to withdraw it, they severed their connection
with the League."

"As indicative of the attitude of this Branch...at a meeting held in
the East End...the Hammersmith choir refused to render the whole of the
'Carmagnole' and deleted the verse containing the line, 'Their gods to
hell may fly', as repugnant to West End respectability and Hammersmith
orthodoxy." Kitz, F., Freedom, July 1912.

179.   Morris, W., 'Socialism and Anarchism', Commonweal, May 18, 1889.
       'Communism and Anarchism', Commonweal, August 17, 1889.

180.   Morris, W., 'Why I Am A Communist' in The Why I Ams, Liberty
       Press, London, 1894.

181.   Morris, W., 'Four Letters on Socialism', op.cit., p. 152.

182.   Morris, W., Commonweal, November 15, 1890.

183.   Morris, W., as quoted by Thompson, E. P., William Morris...,
       op.cit., p. 798.

184.   Morris, W., Commonweal, 'Looking Backward', June 22, 1889.

185.   Ibid.

186.   Morris, W., Useful Work Versus Useless Toil, op.cit., p. 156.

187.   Morris, W. and Bax, E. B., Socialism: Its Growth and Socialism,
       op.cit., p. 285.

188.   Commonweal, April 13, 1889.

189.   Letter from Morris to C. Faulkner, October 16, 1886. As quoted by
       Thompson, E. P., op.cit., pp. 818-820.

       And Morris also claimed that without social conscience "...there can be
       no society; and further...man without society is not only impossible
       but inconceivable". Commonweal, May 18, 1889.

190.   Commonweal, April 13, 1889.

191.   'The Deeper Meaning of the Struggle', Morris's letter to The Editor of
       The Daily Chronicle, 10 November 1893, as reprinted in Letters...,
       op.cit., p. 356.

192.   Morris, W., 'The Society of The Future' as reprinted in Morris, May,
       op.cit., pp. 453-68. See pp. 466-68.

193.   Morris, W., ' The Deeper Meaning of the Struggle', op.cit., p. 356.

194.   Morris, W., From a lecture on 'Communism', Kelmscott Ho., March 10,
        1893, as quoted by A. L. Morton in The Political Writings of William
        Morris, Lawrence and Wishart Ltd., London, 1973, pp. 201-2.

195.   Morris, W., 'The Dawn of a New Epoch' in Signs of Change, op.cit.,
        p. 178.

196.   Morris, W., 'True and False Society', Collected Works, Vol.
        XXIII, p. 215.

197.   That is, the non-producers.

198.   See 'Dawn of a New Epoch', op.cit. "No, it is not Absolutism and
        Democracy as the French Revolution understood those two words that are
        the enemies now: the issue is deeper than it was; the two foes are now
        Mastership and Fellowship. This is a far more serious quarrel than the
        old one, and involves a much completer revolution. The grounds of
        conflict are really quite different." p. 176.

199.   Ibid., p. 193.

200.   See Footnote 107.

201.   Commonweal, May 18 and August 17, 1889.

202.   Morris, W., 'Socialism and Anarchism', Commonweal, May 18, 1889.

203.   Ibid.

204.   Ibid.

205.   Ibid.

206.   Ibid.

207.   Ibid.

208.   Ibid.

209.   Morris, W., 'Communism and Anarchism', Commonweal, August 17, 1889.

210.   Ibid.

211.   Morris, W., 'Socialism and Anarchism', op.cit.

212.   Morris, W., 'The Society of The Future', op.cit., p. 456.

213.   Ibid., p. 459.

214.   Ibid., p. 456.

215.   Ibid., p. 457.

216.   Ibid.

217. Morris, W., News From Nowhere, or an Epoch or Rest: Being Some Chapters from a Utopian Romance, 1891. Appeared serially in The Commonweal from January 11 to October 4, 1890.

218. As quoted by Hulse, J. W., Revolutionists in London: A Study of Five Unorthodox Socialists, Clarendon Press, Oxford, 1970, p. 99.

219. Vallance, A., op.cit., p. 346.

220. A Note, in Letters on Socialism, William Morris to The Reverend Geo. Bainton, Privately Printed (34 copies), London, 1894.

221. The Socialist Ideal appeared in the New Review, January, 1891. Reprinted as a pamphlet in January 1891. See also Collected Works, Vol. XXIII, pp. 255-63.

222. How I Became a Socialist was printed in Justice, May 5, 1894. See also Collected Works, Vol. XXIII, pp. 277-81.

223. Communism, a lecture given at the Hammersmith Socialist Society in 1892, and at the Fabian Society in 1893. See also Collected Works, Vol. XXIII, pp. 264-76.

224. Kropotkin, P., Law and Authority, International Publishing Co., London, 1886, p. 18.

225. Morris, W., The Socialist Ideal, Collected Works, Vol. XXIII, op.cit., p. 258 (underlining mine).

226. Ibid., p. 261.

227. Commenting upon his conversion to Socialism Morris said in his article How I Became a Socialist, "Such finish to what an education of practical Socialism as I am capable of I received afterwards from some of my Anarchist friends, from whom I learned, quite against their intention, that Anarchism was impossible, much as I learned from Mill against his intention that Socialism was necessary." op.cit., p. 278.

228. "For I must here repeat what I have often had to say, that the pleasurable exercise of our energies is at once the source of all art and the cause of all happiness; that is to say, it is the end of life." The Socialist Ideal, op.cit., p. 260.

229. Morris believed that the rich, in different ways were as infected by the commercial system as the poor. In reference to the rich man Morris said, "He can go where he likes and do what he likes outside the realm of art but there he is helpless. Why is this? Simply because the great mass of effective art, that which pervades all life, must be the result of the harmonious cooperation of neighbours. And a rich man has no neighbours, nothing but rivals and parasites." The Socialist Ideal, ibid., p. 259.

Two years later (1893) he reiterated his hopes on the rich and poor.

"In short, there would be no very rich men: and all would be well-off; all would be far above the condition of satisfaction of their material necessities." Communism, op.cit., p. 272.

Or, to put it more bluntly, "If there were no poor people I don't see how there could be any rich..." Ibid., p. 274.

230. Morris, W., The Socialist Ideal, op.cit., p. 261.

231. "To the Socialist, a house, a knife, a cup, a steam-engine or what not, anything I repeat, that is made by man and has any form, must either be a work of art or destructive to art. The Commercialist, on the other hand, divides 'manufactured articles' into those which are prepensely works of art, and are offered for sale in the market as such, and those which have no pretence and could have no pretence to artistic qualities. The one side asserts indifference, the other denies it." Ibid., pp. 256-7.

232. Ibid., p. 261.

233. For the most comprehensive theoretical appeal for Socialism by Morris see his article Communism, which was written in 1893 and is reproduced in the Collected Works, Vol. XXIII, pp. 264-76.

234. Ibid., pp. 273-74.

235. Morris, W., The Socialist Ideal, op.cit., pp. 261-2.

236. Ibid.

237. Morris, W., letter to the Rev. Geo. Bainton, op.cit., 1888.

238. Morris, W., Communism, op.cit., p. 274.

239. Shaw, G. B., 'Morris As I Knew Him', op.cit., p. 18.

240. Ibid., p. 11.

241. Thompson, E. P., op.cit., p. 660.

242. Ibid., p. 899. It is interesting to note that he takes this particular quote from Shaw in Morris As I Knew Him (p. 11) but avoids using the previous quote which is on the same page. See Footnote 240.

243. British Museum Add. MSS. 45335.

244. Thompson, E. P., op.cit., p. 795.

245. Morris, W., Letter to Rev. Geo. Bainton, op.cit.

246. Thompson, E. P., op.cit., p. 790 (underlining mine).

247. Ibid., p. 895 (underlining mine).

248. Ibid. (underlining mine).

249. Ibid.

250. Ibid., p. 896.

251. Ibid.

252. Ibid.

253. Ibid., p. 897.

254. Freedom, December 1911.

255. Kitz, F., Freedom, July 1912.

256. Manifesto of the Socialist League. A New Edition, annotated by W. Morris and E. B. Bax, Socialist League Office, London, 1885.

257. "Philanthropy has had its day and is gone, thrift and self-help are going, participation in profits, parliamentarianism and universal suffrage, State Socialism, will have to go the same road, and the workers will be able to face at last the fact that modern civilization, with its elaborate hierarchy and iron drill, is founded on their intolerable burdens and then the employer will make their labour hours short enough. They will see that modern society can only exist as long as they bear their burden with some degree of patience; their patience will be worn out, and to pieces will modern society go." See the article 'Unattractive Labour' in the Commonweal Supplement, July 1885.

258. "Equality will speedily make itself felt by the consciousness of its necessity being impressed upon the working people, and that they will consciously and not blindly strive for its realization. That in fact is what we mean by the education into Socialism of the working classes. And I believe that if this is impossible at present, if the working people refuse to take any interest in Socialism, if they practically reject it, we must accept that as a sign that the necessity for an essential change in society is so far distant, that we need scarcely trouble ourselves about it. This is the test: and for this reason it is so deadly serious for us to find out whether those democratic tendencies and the schemes of new administration they give birth to are really of use in educating the people into direct Socialism. If they are not, they are of use for nothing else; and we had best try if we can't make terms with intelligent Tories and benevolent Whigs, and beg them to unite their intelligence and benevolence, and govern us as kindly and wisely as they can, and to rob us in moderation only. Communism, op.cit., p. 268.

259. "Even the crudest form of State Socialism (which I do not agree to) would have this advantage over the individual ownership of the means of production, that whereas the State might abuse its ownership, the individual owners must do so." Morris to the Rev. Geo. Bainton, April 4, 1888, Letters on Socialism, op.cit., p. 13.

260. Letter of Morris to the Rev. Geo. Bainton, April 10, 1888, _ibid._, p. 18.

261. _Ibid._, p. 17.

262. _Ibid._, p. 18.

263. _Ibid._

264. _Ibid._, p. 21.

265. Shaw, G. B., _op.cit._, p. 40.

266. From the review of 'Looking Backward' by Morris printed in the _Commonweal_ of June 1888.

FOOTNOTES TO CHAPTER THREE

1. For full details of Kropotkin's life one of the best books is Woodcock,
    G. and Avakumovic, I., The Anarchist Prince; A Biographical Study of
    Peter Kropotkin, Boardman, London, 1950.

2. Richards, V., Errico Malatesta; His Life and Ideas, Freedom Press,
    London, 1965. Also, Woodcock, G., Anarchism, A History of Libertarian
    Ideas and Movements, Pelican, London, 1962.

3. Rocker, R., The London Years, translated by J. Leftwich, Robt.
    Anscombe and Co., for Rudolph Rocker Book Committee, London, 1956.

    Fishman, W. J., East End Jewish Radicals, 1875-1914, Duckworth,
    London, 1974.

    Rudolf Rocker (1873-1951), a German Catholic bookbinder, came to London
    in January 1895 and by 1898 was the editor of the Jewish (Yiddish)
    anarchist paper Der Arbeter Fraint until his internment in 1914 by the
    British authorities. His best known work is Nationalism and Culture,
    published in London in 1938.

4. Edward Carpenter (1844-1929) was a vegetarian homosexual poet and
    sociologist. He wrote in Walt Whitman's manner, was a nature lover and
    interpreter of Hinduism. In 1868 he took orders and acted as a curate
    under F. D. Maurice; but in 1874 he relinquished both his curacy and
    his Fellowship of Trinity Hall, Cambridge. In 1884 he put forth a
    large sum of money to begin Justice and founded the Sheffield
    Socialists (allied with the Socialist League) in 1886.

5. Charlotte M. Wilson, a radical aesthete, was married to a London
    stockbroker who owned Wildwood Farm in Hampstead. She lived in a small
    house in one corner of the farm and let it be used as a meeting place
    for all manner of London Radicals. She was an anarchist and early
    member of the Fabian Society, and a founding member of the Freedom
    Group who worked in close collaboration with Kropotkin. She edited
    Freedom from 1886 until 1894. She remained a member of the Fabian
    Society throughout and was elected to its executive in 1911. See
    references to her in Pease, E. R., The History of the Fabian Society,
    Frank Case and Co. (third edition), London, 1963, and the chapter "Mrs.
    Wilson and Henry Seymour" in Oliver, H., The International Anarchist
    Movement in Late Victorian England, St. Martin's Press, New York,
    1983, pp. 24-32.

6. Kitz, Frank (1848-1923), was brought up by his mother who was in
    service in the West End, and lived in and around Soho. He was a dyer
    by trade, and early on became a member of the Manhood Suffrage League.
    He edited the English edition of Freiheit after its Austrian editor,
    the individualist anarchist Johann Most, was imprisoned for 18 months
    in 1881. A member of the radical Rose St. Club he worked with foreign
    elements in the East End in the Local Rights Association for Rental
    and Sanitary Reform before joining the Socialist League in 1885. See
    his Recollections in Freedom, January-July 1912.

318

7.   Joseph Lane (1850-1920), born in Wallingford, came to London as a
     carter in 1867. He attended the First International in 1871, was a
     member of the Manhood Suffrage League and founder of the Labour
     Emancipation League. In 1881 he formed the Homerton Social Democratic
     Club in Hackney and in that year was a delegate to the International
     Anarchist Congress in London. British Museum Add. MSS 46345 (Burns
     Collection). Leader of anti-parliamentary group in the Socialist
     League in 1887 Council meeting. See the Reminiscences of Ambrose
     Barker in Freedom, May 1931.

8.   Read, Herbert, from the Foreword of The London Years, op.cit.,
     p. 13.

9.   In 1881 Johann Most was convicted of scandalous libel. From the Office
     of the Director of Public Prosecutions, Public Record Office,
     D.P.P. 4-14. As a result Freiheit, the first anarchist paper in
     Britain (1879), was suppressed. In 1892 David Nicoll and another, were
     convicted of incitement to murder for an article in Commonweal,
     ibid., D.P.P. 4-26. As a result of this Commonweal soon ceased
     publication.

10. Guy Aldred was convicted in 1909 for seditious libel. An account
     however is given in his autobiography, No Traitor's Gait, The
     Strickland Press, Glasgow, 1955, Vol. I, 1957, Vols. 2 and 3. Aldred
     claimed to be an anarchist and was Secretary in 1907 of the Industrial
     Union of Direct Actionists. Their Manifesto History (I.I.S.H.),
     catalogue under Bro. An. 1475/40. Perhaps what Aldred was could be
     gleened from his 1908 pamphlet, From Anglican Boy-Preacher To
     Anarchist Socialist Impossibilist. He published and edited the
     Herald of Revolt in 1912.

11. See for example the papers around the time of the trial of the Walsall
     Anarchists: The Daily Telegraph, May 7, 1892; The Chronicle,
     April 11, 1892; The Evening Standard, April 22, 1892, or the
     reproduced article in Fishman's book, op.cit., entitled 'The Haunts
     of the East End Anarchists' from The Evening Standard of October 2,
     1894.

12. Freedom, June 1892, 'The Authoritarian Press'.

13. See the article in Encounter, December 1971, "Havelock Ellis and
     Company", by Arthur Calder-Marshall. With reference to a certain
     Detective Inspector Sweeney of Scotland Yard in the 1890s who wanted
     to suppress The Adult, the sexually oriented journal of the
     Legitimation League. He said,

     "Sweeney conferred with his superiors and between them they concocted
     a plan worthy of the libertarian principles of the late nineteenth
     century Britain. In a country proud of giving political asylum to
     Marx, Engels, and Prince Kropotkin, it was impossible to arrest
     anarchists for what they thought and said. But it was possible to
     limit their opportunities for propaganda. The Legitimation League had
     to be smashed, because it was an anarchist front-organization, but no
     mention must be made of politics." Henry Seymour, who had earlier been
     the editor and publisher of The Anarchist was active in this whole

business, as was Edward Carpenter and Bernard Shaw. In the third issue of the Commonweal (April 1885 Supplement) Andreas Scheu, a close friend of Morris's expressed his frustration at trying to get their socialist opinions across to the public.

"Much harder to bear is the censure of those who are aware of our aims and wilfully misunderstand them in order that they may lecture us from the pinnacle of superior knowledge, and appear before the superstitious world as our guides and teachers. In that hypocritical endeavour the public press occupies the most prominent position. Newspapers are, like all saleable articles today, not made for use but for profit; not, as they pretend, to enlighten the community, but to enrich those who undertake their production. The public press is, in short, an eminently commercial institution, and hence a mercenary agent of commercialism. As a fashioner of people's opinion it is a most powerful machine for evil and a fountain-head of corruption.

"Woe to us who dare to have ideas and ideals of our own! We are decried by them daily and loudly with every manner of names. We embody everything that is wrong, hurtful, and mistaken. There is no notion too preposterous, no imputation too absurd and no lie too palpable to be employed against us by the wholesale purveyors of 'news' and sensational food for the multitude. Have we any way to meet them? By sternly and unflinchingly opposing them;..." From an article entitled 'Sincerity and Devotion'.

14. Justice, April 30, 1892; Commonweal, April 1885; Freedom, September 1887; The Anarchist, July 1885.

15. The case which was internationally famous was the trial and execution of the anarchists in the 'Haymarket Affair' in Chicago in 1887. In England it was that of the Walsall Anarchists in 1892. For an account of the whole issue see David Nicoll's pamphlet, The Walsall Anarchists, D. J. Nicoll, London, 1893. See also his speech Anarchy at the Bar, delivered at the Old Bailey, May 5, 1892 in defence of the article he wrote in the Commonweal on April 11, 1892, about the trial of the Walsall Anarchists. It was published by D. Nicoll, London, 1892.

16. Dod Street in Limehouse was a traditional site for radical open-air propaganda sessions. It was popular with the S.D.F. and with the Socialist League. One of their speakers, Jack Williams, was arrested for 'obstruction' in 1885, found guilty and served one month's hard labour. This was the first of many arrests in the 'fight for free speech'.

At a mass rally on September 20, 1885, Mowbray and Kitz among others were arrested there. They were found guilty and fined. Morris was arrested for 'disorderly conduct' at their trial but subsequently discharged.

The Daily News, September 22, 1885; Commonweal, October 1885.

17. The first police 'raid' took place at the premises of the International Club in Stephen's Mews, on May 9, 1855. Commonweal, June 1885.

Kitz was arrested in Stratford in August 1885, but acquitted.
Mainwaring and Williams were arrested for giving an open-air speech at
Bell St. near Edgware Road, on July 11, 1886. Freedom, August, 1886;
Commonweal, August 21, 1886. The 'Unemployed Riots' took place on
February 8, 1886. For details see Thompson, E. P., op.cit.,
pp. 480-86.

18.   The Times, November 14, 1887; Vallance, A., op.cit., p. 338;
        Commonweal, November 19, 1887.

19.   Most's Die Freiheit lasted from 1878 until 1881 when Most was sent to
        prison for 'scandalous libel'. The English version, edited by Kitz,
        was suppressed by the police in 1882 after they declared support for
        the assassins of Lord Cavendish. This was the first English anarchist
        newspaper. Commonweal ceased publication in October 1892 after the
        trial of its editor, David Nicoll, and its publisher, Charles Mowbray,
        for 'incitement to murder'. (Commonweal appeared sporadically until
        mid-1894 as a broadsheet edited by H. B. Samuels, but bore none of the
        hallmarks of its predecessor.) The Walsall Anarchists - The Truth
        About the Walsall Plot, Printed and Published by D. J. Nicoll,
        London, n.d.

        Freedom suspended publication in 1894 until May 1895 as a direct result
        of constant police harassment. During the First World War its editor,
        Thomas Keell, was imprisoned because they published anti-war
        propaganda.

        Arbeter Fraint was suppressed during the First World War and its
        editor, Rudolf Rocker, was interned as he was of German extraction.
        It was shut by the police in 1915.

20.   Cole, G. D. H., A History of Socialist Thought, Volume II, Marxism and
        Anarchism 1850-1890, Macmillan, St. Martin's Press, New York, 1969.
        See especially the Chapter entitled: 'The Revival of British Socialism
        - William Morris', pp. 379-424.

21.   Fishman, W. J., op.cit., pp. 163-311.

22.   The libertarians even set up their own school of sorts to combat what
        they considered to be the biases of state education. Freedom, 'The
        International School', Vol. 5, No. 58 (1889) and Vol. 6, No. 63 (1890).

23.   Rocker, R., The London Years, op.cit., p. 37.

24.   For some good examples see William Morris on: The Society of the
        Future; The Socialist Ideal, or A Factory as It Might Be. See
        Kropotkin's pamphlet, The State - Its Historic Role, Freedom Pamphlet
        No. 11, 1898, and his Law and Authority - An Anarchist Essay, London,
        1886. See also Edward Carpenter's collection of essays entitled
        Civilization: Its Cause and Cure, Geo. Allen and Unwin Ltd. (15th
        edition), London, 1921.

25.   See, for the individualist position, another paper edited by Henry
        Seymour called The Revolutionary Review which was printed in London in

1889. From November of 1890 until 1892, there was The Herald of Anarchy edited by Albert Tarn, a member of the London Group of Individualist Anarchists who issued it as a monthly organ 'of social, political and economic free-thought'.

For the Marxist revolutionary viewpoint see Justice, the organ of the Social Democratic Federation.

26.   See the lecture lists which offer speakers on certain topics in the various copies of Freedom or Commonweal.

27.   Kitz, F., 'Recollections and Reflections', Freedom, May 1912.

28.   See British Museum Additional MSS 46345 (Burns Collection).

29.   Thompson, E. P., William Morris: Romantic to Revolutionary, op.cit., p. 398.

30.   Morris, May, William Morris: Artist, Writer, Socialist, Vol. II, Morris as a Socialist, op.cit., p. 180.

31.   Lane left the Socialist League in 1889 and according to Thompson, "...had long resisted in the League Council any permanent Chairman or acknowledged leader", Thompson, E. P., William Morris: Romantic to Revolutionary, op.cit., p. 641.

32.   Kitz, F. op.cit., Freedom, January 1912.

33.   Kitz, F., Freedom, April 1912.

34.   Ibid.

35.   See the following pamphlets: The Sheffield Outrages, 1896; The Greenwich Mystery, Sheffield, 1897; Anarchy at the Bar, London, 1893; The Walsall Anarchists, London, 1895; The Featherston Massacre, n.d., and The Ghosts of Chelmsford Gaol, Sheffield, 1896.

36.   Nicoll, D. J., The Walsall Anarchists - Trapped by the Police - Innocent Men in Penal Servitude - The Truth About the Walsall Plot, Printed and Published by D. J. Nicoll, London, 1895.

37.   The Public Record Office, Nicol [sic] and others, D.P.P. 4/26.

38.   In a letter to Freedom in February 1891, W. Bailie reminds the readers that anarchists must not confuse "...the desire to excel, emulation, with competition".

39.   'The Logic of Communism', Freedom, May 1887; 'Act For Yourselves', Freedom, January 1887; 'What's to be Done', Freedom, February 1892.

40.   As translated by V. Richards and contained in his book, Errico Malatesta - His Life and Ideas, Freedom Press, London, 1965. From an article in l'En Dehors, August 17, 1892.

41.   'The Jerry Builder' by Frank Kitz in Commonweal, May 1885; 'Bastille,

Bourgeoise and Bumble', F. Kitz, Commonweal, November 1885; and 'Poor Human Nature', T. MacGuire, Commonweal, July 24, 1885.

42.   See his autobiography, Prison Memoirs of an Anarchist, Schocken Books, New York, 1970. For the clearest statement of his communist-anarchist principles see The A.B.C. of Anarchism, Freedom Press, London, 1964. For supporting details, see Emma Goldman's, Living My Life, Vols. I & II, Dover Publications, New York, 1970.

43.   Berkman, A., Prison Memoirs, op.cit., p. 417.

44.   Barrett, G., The Anarchist Revolution, Freedom Press, London, 1920. This pamphlet gives a good detailed outline of the methods used and the ends sought 'come the revolution'.

45.   Roller's pamphlet Direct Action caused some concern to Guy Aldred who suspected his reasons for writing it. "I never liked Roller personally. ... He did not spend all his time in London but often disappeared mysteriously and as mysteriously reappeared in his old London haunts.... When I understood the full character of Roller's argument, I dismissed it as much too violent... It might have been written by a police agent and was dangerous only to the person who had it in his pocket... His account of what constituted direct action was menacing and absurd." Aldred, G., op.cit., p. 290.

46.   Roller, A., The Social General Strike, translated from the German by F. K., Geo. Bauer, New York, 1905?

47.   The Letters of William Morris to his Family and Friends, op.cit., p. 215.

48.   Ibid., p. 193 and Morris, May, op.cit., p. 91.

49.   Morris, May, ibid., p. 92.

50.   Delavenay, E., D. H. Lawrence and Edward Carpenter: A Study in Edwardian Transition, Heinemann, London, 1971.

51.   Carpenter gave money to help start Justice in 1884, was an active member of The Fellowship of New Life, contributed funds to Freedom, founded the Sheffield Socialist in 1886, had links with the Legitimation League and volunteered for a case study of homosexuals for Havelock Ellis's study of the phenomena, Studies in the Psychology of Sex: Volume One: Sexual Inversion.

52.   Morris, May op.cit., p. 89.

53.   See Delavenay, op.cit.

54.   For sketches on the characters and influence of these men see Aldred, G., No Traitors Gait, op.cit.

55.   The Anarchist, March 1885.

56.   The Commonweal, February 1885.

57.   In Europe there was The Anarchist in Holland, Idee Ouvriere (Le Havre), Ca Ira (Paris), Le Drapeau Noir (Belgium), La Critique Sociale (Geneva).

       In Australia: Radical and Honesty.

       In America: Liberty (Boston), Lucifer and the Sun (Kansas), Alarm (Chicago), Libertas, Fair Play and Alarm (New York).

58.   Barrett, G., op.cit., p. 13.

59.   Ibid.

60.   See the section in Vernon Richards where Malatesta discusses 'The Occupation of the Factories', op.cit., pp. 134-37.

61.   'The Wild Beasts of Society', Freedom, May 1892.

62.   Ibid.

63.   John Turner (1864-1934) was one of the exceptions to this. He was in the 1880s and 1890s a member of both the Socialist League and the Freedom Group, being the publisher of Freedom from May 1895 until 1907. He reestablished it in 1929, working for it until his death. He formed the first Shop Assistants' Union, and served as its General Secretary for twenty five years after it had amalgamated with a larger more reformist and parliamentary body.

64.   Most and Malatesta went to America, then to France and Italy, Kropotkin died in Russia, Dr. Creaghe went to Mexico.

65.   D. J. Nicoll, G. Aldred, and Fred Charles.

66.   Kropotkin, Malatesta, Berkman.

67.   Nicoll died deranged and in poverty; Lonthrop Withington was on the Lusitania; Stepniak tried to outrun a train; Berkman committed suicide.

68.   Carpenter went to Yorkshire; F. Charles married a wealthy Suffolk widow; H. Seymour committed himself to the Francis Bacon Society.

69.   Guyau, J. M., A Sketch of Morality Independent of Obligation or Sanction, Translated by G. Kapteyn, 2nd edition, Watts and Co., London, 1898, p. 66.

70.   Malatesta, E., in Vernon Richards, op.cit., p. 9.

71.   Ibid.

72.   Nicoll, D. J., The Walsall Anarchists, op.cit., p. 9.

73.   Ibid.

74.   'The Wild Beasts of Society', Freedom, May 1892; 'The Force

Question', The Anarchists, February 1888; 'The Philosophy of Force', The Anarchist, January 1887.

75.   "What's In A Name? - or How An Anarchist Might Put It", was written by G. B. Shaw for the first edition of The Anarchist in March 1885. According to the editor of Shaw's letters this was the first piece of writing of Shaw's which ever appeared in the United States, in the individualist anarchist paper Liberty.

76.   Pease, E., op.cit., p. 43.

77.   For Shaw's own recollection of this see Shaw, G. B., Morris As I Knew Him, op.cit.

78.   Ibid.

79.   The Anarchist, April 1885.

80.   The Anarchist, June 1885.

81.   Fishman, W. J., op.cit.

82.   See Rocker, R., The London Years, together with the 'testimonials' of Herbert Read and Joseph Leftwich. As Rocker himself concluded in his book: "The fact is that all the Jewish trades unions in the East End, without exception, were started by the initiative of the Jewish Anarchists. The Jewish labour movement grew largely out of the cease-less educational work that we carried out year in year out." p. 168.

        Fishman, W., 'Rudolph Rocker, An Anarchist Missionary to the Jews', History Today, January 1966.

83.   See: 'A Society Without Government', Freedom, June 1891; 'Must We Pass Through State Socialism', Freedom, February 1892; and 'Work', Freedom, July 1888.

84.   Woodcock, G., Anarchism, op.cit., p. 416.

85.   A book in which a paper called The Bomb was discussed is A Girl Amongst the Anarchists by Helen Meredith. It was thought to be auto-biographical, but is, I discovered, semi-fictional. Helen Meredith was Olive Rossetti, one of the sisters who published The Torch, and it is likely that her reference to The Bomb was the result of this link. See 'Some Little Known Anarchists', Freedom, April 1934.

86.   Edward Carpenter was connected with this endeavour. For a short history and principle participants see Pease, E., op.cit., pp. 32-6.

87.   Calder-Marshall, A., Encounter, December 1971.

88.   Two of the most notable successes in the eyes of the revolutionary groups were 'The Match Girls Strike' against Bryant and May in 1888, and the London Dock Strike in 1889.

89.   Most of the accused had professed to be anarchists, although there
       seems to have been no conclusive proof in the light of such savage
       sentences of personal slander and libel. Victor Dave was denounced by
       The Anarchist and C. T. Reuss by Commonweal. The dispute continued
       off and on in the pages of both journals between August 1886 and June
       1888. See Commonweal for January 1888, 'Police Spies Exposed', an
       article for which Reuss entered an action for 1000 pounds damages
       against William Morris. The Anarchist, September, October 1886, May,
       June, August and October 1887; January and February 1888. The Pall
       Mall Gazette, July and August 1887. The charge against Coulon was
       made by David Nicoll in his pamphlet The Walsall Anarchists, and he
       also accused a former Commonweal comrade H. B. Samuels in The
       Greenwich Mystery - Letters from the Dead, D. J. Nicoll, 6 Windmill
       St., London, April 19, 1898.

90.   Commonweal, July 21, 1888; Freedom, November 1887; and
       Commonweal, November 6, 1886.

91.   See the 'Branch Reports' from any issue of Commonweal after January
       1887.

92.   British Museum MSS (Burns Collection), op.cit.

93.   'Work and the Workers in Sheffield', Freedom, April 1887.

94.   Commonweal, June 26, 1886.

95.   'Notes on the Socialist Movement', Freedom, September 1887.

96.   Kropotkin, P., Communist Anarchism, Freedom Press, London, 1912.

97.   As quoted by Pease, E., op.cit., from the Early History of the
       Fabian Society, under 'The Fabian Conference of 1886', p. 56.

98.   Ibid., p. 55.

99.   Kitz, F., 'Recollections and Reflections', Freedom, February 1912.

100.   The Anarchist, March 1885.

101.   See especially any edition of The Anarchist.

102.   Justice, March 7, 1885.

103.   Calder-Marshall, A., op.cit., p. 15.

104.   The Anarchist, March 1885.

105.   Ibid.

106.   'From a Friend Across the Channel', ibid.

107.   Appleton, H., 'What is an Anarchist', ibid.

108.   Malatesta, E., 'Anarchy', Freedom, September 1891.

109. *The Anarchist*, April 1885.

110. *Commonweal*, April 1885.

111. Letter of William Morris to May Morris, March 11, 1885, in *Letters...*, *op.cit.*, p. 234.

112. 'Notes', *The Anarchist*, April 1885.

113. 'Notes', *The Anarchist*, May 1885.

114. *The Anarchist*, June 1885.

115. *Freedom* was printed by The International Publishing Co. for a very short time then moved to the Offices of the Socialist League. The Freethought Publishing Co. printed it up until a disagreement over the Haymarket affair in 1887. It was then printed by the Cooperative Labour Press until acquiring its own type and premises in 1890.

116. *The Anarchist*, February 1885.

117. *The Anarchist*, June 1886; 'An Arrogant Sophist', August 1886.

118. *The Anarchist*, April 1885.

119. *The Anarchist*, December 1885.

120. *The Anarchist*, July 1885. Also 'Law and Justice', August 1885.

121. *The Anarchist*, September 1885.

122. *The Anarchist*, January 1, 1886 with a reply by Seymour in the same issue.

123. *The Anarchist*, 'Private Property – A Basic Principle of Anarchism', September 1886; 'The Warfare of Words', December 1886. Edgeworth was writing from America.

124. *The Anarchist*, October 15, 1885.

125. *The Anarchist*, August 15, 1885; October 15, 1885; December 1885.

126. 'Labour and Capital', *The Anarchist*, July 1885. See also, 'The True Theory of Value', January 22, 1886; 'The Malthusian Theology', December 1886.

127. *The Anarchist*, April 20, 1886.

128. *Ibid*.

129. *The Anarchist*, July 1, 1886.

130. *The Anarchist*, June 1, 1886.

131. *Ibid*.

132. *Ibid*.

133. *The Anarchist*, July 1, 1886.

134. *Ibid*.

135. In a pamphlet entitled the History of the Freedom Press, at the International Institute of Social History, it is claimed that the 'first associates' were: Kropotkin, Tchaikovsky, Dr. Merlino, Dr. Gibson, C. M. Wilson, and H. Seymour (1885).

136. *The Anarchist*, October 1886, 'Mr. Donisthorpe's Democracy', a reprint from a comment by William Morris which appeared in Commonweal. In the Commonweal of June 19, 1886, Shaw commented on the individualist A. Herbert, who was often mistakenly taken as an anarchist. In his article 'Mr. Auberon Herbert and Individual Liberty', Shaw concluded, "I am quite certain that my only difficulty as to the attitudes of Mr. Herbert and the Tsar towards Liberty arise when I try to decide which is the more dangerous enemy."

137. *The Anarchist*, 'Atheism and Anarchism'; 'Free-Love', November 1886. 'The Matrimonial Question - From an Anarchist Point of View', June 1887. 'Free-Love Defined and Defended', July 1887. 'The Logic of Free-Love', October 1887. 'Revolution and Religion', April 1888. 'The Anarchy of Love or the Science of the Sexes', July 1888.

138. *The Anarchist*, November 1886. He was also much impressed with the Polyopticon which he sold from his premises. October 1885. But one interest in which he was to later make money in was the phonograph whereby he claimed, "All errors are avoided because like the photo-camera, it cannot produce lies." *The Anarchist*, July 1, 1888.

139. *The Anarchist*, March 1887.

140. *The Anarchist*, March 1888. See also 'Anarchy and Communism', May 1887; June 1887; 'Is Anarchy Practical?', July-October 1887.

141. *The Anarchist*, 'Memoranda', 'Sickly Sentimentalism' and 'Freedom's Frolics', March 1888.

142. This is claimed by D. H. Lawrence, the editor of G. B. Shaw's Collected Letters 1874-1897, Max Reinhart, London, 1965, pp. 109-10. See also: Ellis, H., My Life, London, 1940, p. 364.

143. *The Anarchist*, May 1887.

144. "I will begin by saying that I call myself a Communist, and have no wish to qualify that word by joining any other to it." This was his view in May 1889. See Morris, May, op.cit., p. 313.

145. Donisthorpe, W., Liberty or Law, The Liberty and Property Defense League, London, 1885; Herbert, A., The Right and Wrong of Compulsion by the State, Williams and Norgate, (Anti-Force Paper No. 2), London,

1885.

146.   This attitude is most apparent in the comments made by Seymour in
       The Anarchist. One strange illustration is as follows:

       "I will not attempt to argue here the close connection and relationship
       of the Anarchy propounded by Kropotkin, with State-Socialism. It is
       true, he maintains with an inconvertible array of evidence the
       principle of personal liberty - but the representatives of the Liberty
       and Property Defense League do that with equal effect." The
       Anarchist, May 1887.

147.   Morris, W., 'Introductory', Commonweal, No. 1, February 1885
       (underlining mine).

148.   'Our Policy', Commonweal, March 1885; 'The Policy of the Socialist
       League', Commonweal, June 9, 1887; 'Where Are We Now?',
       Commonweal, November 15, 1890; Morris, W. and Bax, E. B., The
       Manifesto of the Socialist League - With Annotations to the Second
       Edition (Adopted at Annual Conference, July 5, 1885), London 1885.

149.   Commonweal, February 1885.

150.   Many examples of Bax's work can be seen in the pages of Commonweal:
       'Imperialism Versus Socialism', February 1885; 'Gordon and The Soudan',
       March 1885; 'At Bay', April 1885; British Foreign Policy', June 1885;
       'The Congo', August 1885. One of his less characteristic pieces was
       'The New Ethic' (in four parts) February-May 1888.

151.   'Where Are We Now?', op.cit.

152.   Glasier, J. B., William Morris and the Early Days of the Socialist
       Movement, op.cit., Pelling, H. M., The Origins of the Labour
       Party, 1880-1900, London, 1932.

       Thompson, E. P., William Morris, Romantic to Revolutionary, op.cit.

153.   A footnote in Thompson claims that "Sales of Commonweal (Hammersmith
       Minutes) 2400, March 21st 1887; 2600, July 25th, 1886; 2600 ("a
       decrease"), August 7th, 1887." At the end it became no more than an
       influential broadsheet. Thompson, E. P., op.cit., p. 488.

154.   This is pointed out in a letter by Binning to the Socialist League
       Council, on June 1886. Socialist League Correspondence, The
       International Institute of Social History.

155.   Commonweal, March 1888; November 1885. Engels was influential in
       having Commonweal come out as a monthly. The process is described to
       Andreas Scheu by Morris in a letter dated December 28, 1884. Morris
       himself wanted a weekly selling for 2d. or 3d. right from the
       beginning. See, The Letters of William Morris..., op.cit.
       pp. 224-26.

156.   For Nicoll's early contributions see Commonweal, 'The Benevolent
       Bourgeois' (May 1885); 'Moderation Canti' (September 4, 1886).

157.   A letter from C. Wilfred, Commonweal, March 1885.

158.   Kitz, F., 'The Jerry Builder', Commonweal, May 1885.

159.   Fred Charles was in reality F. C. Slaughter of Norwich who was
        sentenced to fifteen years for his part in the Walsall anarchist plot.
        When he came out of prison he married into money and retired to the
        country. See, Carpenter, E., My Days and Dreams, op.cit.; Nicoll,
        D., The Walsall Anarchists, op.cit.

160.   Sam Mainwaring was a Welshman, and an engineer by trade and for years
        served as a delegate on the London Trades Council. See Freedom,
        May 1934. He also founded the Swansea Socialist Society and remained
        active until his death in 1907.

161.   Tochatti, like Mowbray was a tailor and follower of Kropotkin in the
        anarchist wing of the Socialist League, and participated in the
        Hammersmith Socialist Society. He edited Liberty after 1893, and even
        got Morris to contribute articles to it. See Thompson, E. P.,
        op.cit., p. 685.

162.   Charles Mowbray was in the anarchist wing of the Socialist League and
        was imprisoned in Norwich for his part in an unemployed demonstration
        in 1887. For an account of this see J. L. Mahon to the Council of the
        Socialist League, Socialist League Correspondence, I.I.S.H. He was
        also tried with Nicoll in 1892 but was acquitted even though he was
        publisher of Commonweal at this time. He then left the movement. See
        Aldred, G., Dogmas Discarded, op.cit., p. 67.

163.   Dr. Creaghe of Sheffield was described as "...not commercially minded.
        Carrying on in a poor locality, he often returned his fees to
        impoverished patients, telling them to buy food, which he said was more
        necessary than medicine." He published the Sheffield Anarchist but
        later emigrated to Argentina and published the Anarcho-Syndicalist
        paper La Protesta ending up in Mexico after the revolution. See
        Freedom, June 1934.

164.   The claim of 'irresponsibility' is Thompson's. See his book,
        op.cit., pp. 657-59.

165.   Tom Cantwell was a member of the Hammersmith Branch of the Socialist
        League and an anarchist. He edited the Commonweal after Nicoll's
        imprisonment, and later helped publish Freedom. See Thompson, E. P.,
        ibid., pp. 684-85 and Aldred, G., No Traitor's Gait, op.cit.,
        pp. 302-7.

166.   Letters..., op.cit., pp. 324-25, regarding Morris's warning letter
        to Nicoll.

167.   The Public Record Office, op.cit.

168.   The only major indication in the pages of Commonweal that the anti-
        parliamentarians (together with Tochatti and Charles as the anarchist
        members) had gained control of the Council of the Socialist League in

May 1888, was a new League policy statement which was published on
June 9, 1888. It was drafted by Morris and reaffirmed the rejection
of parliamentary action or 'palliatives'. The chief aim was the
education of the workers. By this time the pro-parliamentarians had
left the League by seceding with the Bloomsbury Branch of the Socialist
League.

169. In particular with relation to views on parliamentary action, trade
unionism, elections, direct action and the general strike. Later the
whole issue was clouded over by what seemed to be the simple advocation
of violence.

170. History of the Freedom Press, an undated pamphlet in the
International Institute of Social History indexed under Bro. An.
1485/178.

171. The first associates were Kropotkin, Tchaikovsky, Dr. Merlino, Dr.
Gibson, C. M. Wilson, and H. Seymour, ibid.

172. "Mrs. C. M. Wilson was helped in the Freedom activity by Mr. Dryhurst,
Mrs. Hyde, and later Miss Agnes Henry. Among the men - Kropotkin, of
course; Sydney Olivier, later Lord Olivier, did a lot of writing for
Freedom. H. W. Nevinson also, while Hyde and W. Wess did what can be
described as the necessary drudgery work. Towards the end of 1894 and
at the beginning of 1895, Mrs. Wilson's domestic affairs made it
impossible for her to continue the editorial work." See Aldred, G.,
No Traitor's Gait, op.cit., p. 305.

173. Ibid.

174. 'The Commonweal Trial', Freedom, June 1892. In 1913 the figure was
about the same. See the letter of Kropotkin to Georg Hertzig written
on December 16, 1913, in the I.I.S.H.

175. See the article 'Another Turn of the Screw' which relates capitalist
monopoly to many of the laws passed by Parliament. Freedom, June
1889.

176. Freedom, October 1886.

177. Ibid.

178. 'Notes', Freedom, June 1891.

179. Freedom, June 1889.

180. 'Sticking to Principle', Freedom, July 1887.

181. Freedom, January 1887.

182. 'Names and Opinions', Freedom, February 1888.

183. Ibid. Contrast this with, What Socialism Is (Fabian Tract No. 4).
The second part of this was written from an anarchist perspective by
Wilson and essentially repeats what was said in 'Names and Opinions'.

For her earlier opinions of the subject see The Principles and Aims of Anarchists, which was the abstract of a paper Wilson gave before the London Dialectical Society on June 2, 1886. As reprinted in The Present Day, July 1886.

184.   Freedom, February 1888 (underlining mine).

185.   Ibid. (underlining mine).

186.   Ibid.

187.   The Fabian Parliamentary League was formulated in February 1887. Its Constitution is given in Fabian Tract No. 41. According to Pease, "Fabians could join or not as they pleased." op.cit., p. 68. According to the Constitution it had been agreed that,

"The League will take active part in all general and local elections. Until a fitting opportunity arises for putting forward Socialist candidates to form the nucleus of a Socialist party in Parliament, it will confine itself to supporting those candidates who will go furthest in the direction of Socialism. It will not ally itself absolutely with any political party..."

Annie Besant and the Rev. Stewart Hedlam standing as Progressives were elected to the School Board in November 1888.

The I.L.P. was founded in January 1893 in conjunction with the Fabian Society representation and support.

In 1892 six members were elected to the London County Council.

Pease, E., op.cit., p. 151.

188.   Freedom, February 1888. Auberon Herbert and associates would be classified as individualistic democrats, while Robert Harding and Henry Seymour would come under the title of individualistic anarchists.

189.   'Notes On the Socialist Movement', Freedom, September 1887.

190.   Ibid.

191.   Ibid.

192.   Freedom, February 1888.

193.   'Freedom Discussion Meetings', Freedom, April 1888 (underlining mine).

194.   'A Word For War', by George Bernard Shaw in Today, September 1888.

195.   As early as 1882 a young anarchist called Cyvogt was convicted of throwing a bomb into the cafe of the Bellecour Theatre in Lyons.

In Paris in 1886 a bottle of vitriol was thrown on the floor of the Stock Exchange by a young anarchist Carles Gallo who used his trial as a platform for his views.

In November of 1887 the Chicago Anarchists were executed for allegedly having thrown a bomb into a crowd of demonstrators.

Kedward, R., _The Anarchists - The Men Who Shocked An Era_, B.P.C. Unit 75, London, 1971.

196.   For an attack by _Justice_ and the Social Democratic Federation see, 'Ravachol - The Anarchist Hero', April 16, 1892. See also the leading articles in _The Times_, April 5, 7, 25 and 28, 1892.

197.   There were among others Peter Kropotkin, Mary Wilson, Joseph Lane, John Turner, and Frank Kitz. Shaw, G. B., _The Early History of the Fabian Society_, op.cit.; _To-Day_, October 1886.

198.   'The Commune of London', _Freedom_, April 1892.

199.   'The Chicago Anniversary', by Wilson, in _Freedom_, December 1888.

On October 14, 1887 there was a large protest meeting held at the South Place Institute. In London the speakers who condemned the sentences of death passed on the Chicago Anarchists were: The Rev. S. Headlam (Guild of St. Matthew); William Morris (Socialist League); J. Blackwell (S.D.F.); Annie Besant (National Secular Society); G. Standring (Radical Federation); Tarleton (Hammersmith Radical Club); H. George ('unemployed'); Stepniak ('Russian revolutionary and author'); and Kropotkin and Wilson (Freedom Group). Other meetings held were by: The London Anarchist Groups and the Socialist League at the Hall of the Communist Club; the Hackney Branch of the S.D.F.; the Tower Hamlets Radical Club; Peckham Reform Club; the Sheffield Socialists; the Clay Cross Socialists; the Scandinavian Workingmen's Club of London; and the Dublin Labour League.

'It Must Not Be', _Freedom_, November 1887, and after the execution, 'The Tragedy of Chicago', _Freedom_, December 1887. This issue had a black border.

'Murdered By Law' in _The Anarchist_, December 1887. This issue had a black front page.

200.   'Socialist Propaganda' a new section which was to become a regular feature. _Freedom_, October 1887.

201.   _Freedom_, October 1888.

202.   'The Red Indians and the American Government', _Freedom_, March 1891. See also 'Indian Troubles', _The Anarchist_, May 1885.

203.   From France came, '_Idee Ouvriere_' (Le Havre); _Ca Ira_ (Paris); from Switzerland came _La Critique Sociale_ (Geneva); from Australia, _Radical_, and from Holland the _Anarchist_ (in Dutch).

204.   _The Conquest of Bread_ began in _Freedom_ in September 1892. _Communism and the Wage System_ began in _Freedom_ in August 1888. _Mutual Aid_ was

first published in the <u>Nineteenth Century</u>, in September 1890.

205. <u>A Talk About Anarchist Communism Between Two Workers</u>, began in <u>Freedom</u> in February 1891. <u>Anarchy</u>, September 1891, in <u>Freedom</u>, lasting until June 1892.

206. In the issues of <u>Freedom</u> from February to July 1890 it appears that the original subscriber has penned in the names, or initials of the authors of articles. These issues are held at the <u>British Library of Political and Economic Science</u>, catalogued under R/D8 848.

207. 'William Morris on Communism', <u>Freedom</u>, May 1893.

208. 'Fabians on Anarchism', <u>Freedom Supplement</u>, November 1891.

209. 'Mr. Auberon Herbert's Voluntary State – Part 1', <u>Freedom</u>, July 1893.

210. 'Anarchism', <u>Freedom</u>, June and July 1893.

211. 'Anarchism According to Stepniak', <u>Freedom</u>, January and February 1893. Morris's last public speech was to a crowd gathered at Waterloo Station for Stepniak's funeral in 1896. Morris, May, <u>op.cit.</u>, p. 182.

212. A letter of Edward Carpenter's to the editor of <u>Freedom</u>, November 25, 1892.

213. <u>Freedom</u>, January 1891.

      Shaw's <u>Early History of the Fabian Society</u>, <u>op.cit.</u> Pease, E., <u>op.cit.</u>, pp. 66-71. <u>Today</u>, October 1886. All of these publications give accounts of the inter-radical meetings which took place, and Shaw claimed <u>Today</u> in particular made very enjoyable reading.

214. <u>Freedom</u>, January 1891.

215. 'The General Election', <u>Freedom</u>, July 1892.

216. 'Parliamentary Rule', <u>Freedom</u>, February 1887.

217. 'Face to Face with the Facts', <u>Freedom</u>, December 1887.

218. <u>Freedom Supplement</u>, November 1891.

219. <u>Ibid.</u>

220. 'Anarchy' by E. Malatesta, <u>Freedom</u>, September 1891.

221. <u>Ibid.</u>

222. <u>Ibid.</u>

223. 'Anarchist Literature', <u>Freedom</u>, August 1887.

224.	<u>Ibid</u>.

FOOTNOTES TO CHAPTER FOUR

1. Hobbes, T., _Leviathan_, Edited by M. Oakeshott, Blackwell, Oxford, 1955, pp. 105-106.

2. My use of the terms 'belief-authority' and 'command-authority' were initially derived from a colleague who has been working on the concept of authority for some years. I look forward to the publication of his book on the subject. Although I do not use these terms in the same way in which Dr. T. R. Sansom does, I am indebted to him for the terminology within which I can describe my own ideas.

3. As command-authority usually implies some form of order, and hence some form of obvious influence, there are many occasions when persons are unaware of the influences playing upon them. For example, do we buy a certain product because of the way in which it was advertised, or did we make the decision independent of that source?

4. The use of the term _action_, to connote _intended behaviour_ is described by B. R. Barber in his book _Superman and Common Man_, Pelican, 1972.

5. Kropotkin, P., _Anarchism: Its Philosophy and Ideal_, Freedom Press, London, 1897, p. 21.

6. Kropotkin, P., _The Place of Anarchism in Socialist Revolution_ (Translated by H. Glasse), International Publishing Co., London, 1886, p. 16.

7. _Ibid._

8. Carpenter, E., 'The New Morality', in _Civilization: Its Cause and Cure_, _op.cit._, p. 250.

9. _Ibid._, p. 255.

10. _Ibid._, p. 251.

11. Grave, J., _Anarchy on Trial_, Freedom Pamphlet No. 9, Freedom Publishing Co., London, 1901, p. 14.

12. Kropotkin, P., _Anarchism: Its Philosophy and Ideal_, _op.cit._, p. 23.

13. _Ibid._, p. 24.

14. Smith, J. B., _Direct Action Versus Legislation_, Freedom, 127 Ossulston St., N.W., London, 1909, p. 3.

15. Guyau, J. M., _A Sketch of Morality Independent of Obligation or Sanction_, Translated from the French by Gertrude Kapteyn (Second Edition), Watts and Co., London, 1898, pp. 19-20.

    In a pamphlet entitled _The Natural Basis of Civilization_ George W.

Reid, explained the individual in a similar fashion. Somewhat dog-
matically he exclaimed,

"Universal individualism is impossible, men are naturally communists,
and the communal desires must always dominate the selfishness of the
individual.

"True society, or communism, would be nothing more nor less than the
banding together of the members of the community into a cooperative
commonwealth, where each member, in order to facilitate the better
securing of the necessaries of life, to each other, would practically
surrender their individuality in order that others should benefit by
their exertions, and that the individual in return for such surrender,
would be enabled to partake of the combined productivity of the
community." This pamphlet was published by the Proletarian Publishing
Co., as Pamphlet No. 1, at 47, Corporation Row, London, E.C., n.d.,
p. 3. Reid was a Communist-Anarchist.

16.   Guyau, J. M., op.cit., p. 36.

17.   Regarding 'usefulness and hurtfulness' and 'instinctive morality' based
       on 'social habit' see Kropotkin, P., Law and Authority: An Anarchist
       Essay, The International Publishing Co., 35 Newington Green Road,
       London, N., 1886.

18.   Guyau, J. M., op.cit., p. 97.

19.   Kropotkin, P., Anarchism: Its Philosophy and Ideal, op.cit.,
       p. 25.

20.   Ibid.

21.   Woodcock, Geo., Anarchism: A History of Libertarian Ideas and
       Movements, Penguin, 1962, p. 15.

       Woodcock believes that the anarchist unlike the nihilist, "...believes
       in a moral urge powerful enough to survive the destruction of authority
       and still to hold society together in the free and natural bonds of
       fraternity". Ibid., p. 12.

337

FOOTNOTES TO CHAPTER FIVE

1. The term 'action' or one who is 'acting' is reserved for those forms of
    behaviour which are intentional, i.e., those which take into account
    deliberation and awareness regardless of the reasons for which they
    were undertaken. For a detailed discussion of this view see Barber,
    B. R., Superman and Common Man - Freedom, Anarchy and the Revolution,
    op.cit., pp. 53-57.

2. Not all libertarians were opposed to government as such although they
    were highly suspect of its authoritarian and centralizing tendencies.
    It was the anarchists, like Kropotkin and Rocker, who were
    uncompromising in their opposition to the institution. People like
    Morris, Carpenter, and C. M. Wilson were less inflexible in their
    approach to the problem and saved much of their critical comment for
    less all-pervading sources of social discord such as leadership,
    education, labour, and women's rights.

3. In the 1880's and 1890's there were restrictions on the freedom of
    assembly and speech in public places; on the rights of women,
    especially the vote; on strikes and picketing; on homosexuality in
    private; and on the dissemination of birth-control information. The
    libertarians were involved in all the campaigns which attempted to
    stamp out these restrictions.

4. Berlin, I., Four Essays on Liberty, Oxford University Press, 1971.

5. For criticism about the role and necessity of 'civilization' as it
    related to the libertarian conception of nineteenth century society
    see Morris, W., The Hopes of Civilization, as contained in his book
    of essays, Signs of Change, op.cit.; Carpenter, E., Civilization,
    Its Cause and Cure, in Civilization, Its Cause and Cure and Other
    Essays, op.cit.; Reid, G. W., The Natural Basis of Civilization,
    op.cit.

6. Strading, C. T., Liberty and the Great Libertarians: An Anthology on
    Liberty: A Hand-Book of Freedom, Los Angeles, 1913. Reprinted as
    part of the series called The Right-Wing Individualist Tradition in
    America, Arno Press and the New York Times, New York, 1972, p. 5.

7. The Revolution " ... is first and foremost the TRANSVALUATOR, the
    bearer of new values. It is the great TEACHER of the NEW ETHICS,
    inspiring man with a new concept of life and its manifestations in
    social relationships. It is the mental and spiritual regenorator."
    Emma Goldman, as quoted by Richard Drinnon in his biography on Goldman
    called Rebel in Paradise, Beacon Press, Toronto, 1970, p. 261.

8. For a more prolonged discussion on 'power' as an affirmation of self
    see Fromm, E., Escape from Freedom, Holt Rinehart and Winston, New
    York, 1967.

9. The 'will to power' here is not used in the sense that Neitzche
    presented it. It is designed as an attribute of modern man which is
    positively reinforced by the society and the institutions of that

society which are seen to be founded on dominance and submission. For
an excellent discussion of this view see Sampson, R. V., _Equality and
Power_, Heineman, London, 1965.

10.   'Freedom and Property' in _Freedom_, February 1891.

11.   " ... certainly _needs_ not _deeds_ will be the measure of the cost society
       will impose on itself to temper the principle of deeds." Kropotkin,
       P., _The Wage System_, Freedom Pamphlet No. 7, Revised Edition, n.d.,
       p. 14.

12.   _Freedom_, February 1891.

13.   Kropotkin, P., _The State: Its Historic Role_, Freedom Pamphlet
       No. 11, Freedom Press, London, 1898, p. 42.

14.   _Freedom_, February, 1891.

15.   Negley, G., _Political Authority and Moral Judgment_, Duke University
       Press, Durham, North Carolina, 1965.

16.   As a reaction against so-called bourgeoise individuality it was stated:
       "What, _then is individuality_? Individuality is contrast,
       speciality, distinction, difference, and not separateness. But
       individualism cannot distinguish without dividing, and on this
       separation loses the distinction it seeks after." From the essay
       Anarchism Kills Individualism in _Essays in Communist-Anarchism_, by
       J. Burns-Gibson. Originally printed in _Freedom_.

17.   'Freedom and Property', _Freedom_, March 1891.

18.   _Ibid._

19.   Carpenter, E., _Defence of Criminals: A Criticism of Morality_, in
       Civilization: Its Cause and Cure, op.cit., p. 156. In particular,
       " ... of those who regard morals as intuitive, there are few who have
       thought about the matter who would be inclined to say that any _act_ in
       itself can be either right or wrong. Though there is superficial
       judgment of this kind, yet when the matter comes to be looked into, the
       more general consent seems to be that the rightness or wrongness is in
       the _motive_."

20.   Carpenter, E., _The New Morality_, in _Civilization ..._, op.cit.,
       p. 258.

21.   Carpenter, E., _Marriage in a Free Society_, Labour Press Society,
       Manchester, 1894, pp. 44-5.

22.   Carpenter, E., _Custom_, in _Civilization ..._, op.cit., p. 213.

23.   Kropotkin, P., _The Place of Anarchism in Socialistic Evolution_,
       op.cit., p. 16.

24.   _Ibid._

25. Carpenter, E., <u>The New Morality</u>, <u>op.cit.</u>, p. 251.

26. Kropotkin, P., <u>Law and Authority</u>, <u>op.cit.</u>, p. 16.

27. Sampson, R. V., <u>op.cit.</u>, p. 229.

28. Burns-Gibson, J., <u>op.cit.</u>, p. 2.

29. Grave, J., <u>Moribund Society and Anarchy</u>, Translated by V. de Cleyre, Free Society Library, San Francisco, A. Isaak, 1899, p. 122.

30. <u>Ibid.</u>, p. 8.

31. <u>Ibid.</u>, pp. 54-5.

32. Kropotkin, P., <u>Anarchist Morality</u>, <u>op.cit.</u>, p. 27.

33. <u>Ibid.</u>

34. Reid, G. W., <u>The Natural Basis of Civilization</u>, <u>op.cit.</u>; Morris, W., <u>Communism</u>, <u>op.cit.</u>; Morris, W., <u>Four Letters on Socialism</u>, <u>op.cit.</u>; Kropotkin, P., <u>The Place of Anarchism in Socialistic Evolution</u>, <u>op.cit.</u>; Carpenter, E., <u>Private Property</u>, in <u>England's Ideal and Other Papers on Social Subjects</u>, Swan Sonnenschein and Co., London, 1895.

35. Kropotkin, P., <u>Anarchist Morality</u>, <u>op.cit.</u>, p. 27.

36. De Grazia, S., 'Authority and Rationality' in <u>Philosophy</u>, April 1952, p. 104.

37. Reichert, W. O., 'Anarchism, Freedom and Power,' in <u>Ethics</u>, January 1969, p. 142.

38. Weick, D. T., 'Essentials of Anarchism', <u>Resistance</u>, August 1953, p. 7.

39. 'From Politics to Social Revolution', <u>Resistance</u>, April 1954, p. 3.

40. Reichert, W. O., <u>op.cit.</u>, p. 144.

41. Eltzbacher, P., <u>Anarchism: Exponents of the Anarchist Philosophy</u>, Translated by S. T. Byington, Edited by J. J. Martin, Freedom Press (Second Edition) London, 1960. See in particular the criticisms of Proudhon and Stirner.

42. That is, they were considered by many libertarians and anarchists alike by the turn of the century, as being 'petit bourgeoise'.

43. "I too love men, not merely individuals, but everyone. But I love them with the consciousness of egoism; I love them because love makes me happy. I love them because love is natural to me, because it pleases me. I know no 'commandment of love'." Eltzbacher, <u>op.cit.</u>, p. 64.

44. <u>Ibid.</u>, pp. 73-4.

45. In Eltzbacher's interpretation, for Bakunin, " ... according to his expectation, norms will then prevail which 'are based on a general will' and which even secure obedience by forcible compulsion if necessary ..." Ibid., p. 81.

46. Ibid., p. 85.

47. 'Freedom' in Freedom, October 1886.

48. Berkman, A., The A.B.C. of Anarchism, Freedom Press, London, 1964.

49. Ibid., p. 74.

50. Ibid., p. 74.

51. Ibid., p. 62. " ... We have seen that the social structure rests on the basis of ideas, which implies that changing of the structure presupposes changed ideas. In other words, social ideas must change first, before a new social structure can be built."

52. Ibid.

53. Ibid.

54. Goldman, E., The Place of the Individual in Society, The Free Press Society Forum, Chicago, n.d., p. 14.

55. Ibid.

56. Ibid.

57. Ibid., p. 12 (underlining mine).

58. Berkman, A., op.cit., p. 49.

59. In the Abstract Physical-Mechanistic Model " ... the perspective is abstract because it neglects the concrete manifestations of coercion and freedom in human experience in favour of a philosophical generalization which Hobbes proposes 'may be applied no less to irrational, and inanimate creatures than to rational.' It assumes, further, that the relationship between liberty as motion, and coercion as the impeding of motion, is purely mechanistic ..." From, Barber, B. R., op.cit, p. 38.

"The psychological-intentionalist model, taking its analogies from psychology rather than from physics, begins then with the premise of human intentionality as a function of man's existential consciousness of self, and thereby explicitly rejects the mechanist's notion that man is a product of environmental forces ..." Ibid., p. 51.

60. Ibid., p. 38.

61. Ibid., p. 53.

62.   *Ibid*., p. 55.

63.   *Ibid*., p. 58.

64.   *Ibid*.

SELECT BIBLIOGRAPHY

Adams, F. W., Songs of the Army of the Night, London, 1894.

Addis, H., Essays on the Social Problem, San Francisco, 1898.

Adler, M. J., The Idea of Freedom, New York, 1958.

The Adult, 1892-98.

Aldred, G. A., Michael Bakunin: Communist, Glasgow, 1920.

Aldred, G. A., Bakunin, Glasgow, 1940.

Aldred, G. A., At Grips With War, Glasgow, 1932.

Aldred, G. A., A Call to Manhood and Other Essays in Social Struggle, Glasgow, 1944.

Aldred, G. A., For Communism, Glasgow, 1935.

Aldred, G. A., No Traitor's Gait, II Vols., Glasgow, 1955-60.

Aldred, G. A., Convict 9653 – America's Vision Maker: A Story of Eugene V. Debs, Glasgow, 1942.

Aldred, G. A., Socialism & War, London, 1915.

Aldred, G. A., Communism: Story of the Communist Party, Glasgow, 1944.

Aldred, G. A., Historical & Traditional Christianity, London, 1907.

Aldred, G. A., The Devil's Chaplin, Glasgow, 1942.

Aldred, G. A., John McClean: Martyr of the Class Structure, Glasgow, 1932.

Aldred, G. A., ed., Bakunin's Writings, Glasgow, 1963.

Aldred, G. A., The Possibility & Philosophy of Communist Anarchism, London, 1907.

Aldred, G. A., Studies in Communism, London, 1940.

Aldred, G. A., The Two Nations: A May Day Message, Glasgow, 1968.

Aldred, G. A., Dogma's Discarded: An Autobiography of Thought 1886-1908, Glasgow, 1940.

Aldred, G. A., Richard Carlile: Agitator, London, 1912.

Aldred, G. A., Pioneers of Anti-Parliamentarianism, Glasgow, 1940.

Aldred, G. A., Sown in Dishonour, Glasgow, 1945.

Aldred, G. A., The Logic & Economics of Class Struggle, London, 1906.

Aldred, G. A., Socialism & Parliament, Glasgow, 1942.

Aldred, G. A., Militarism & Revolution, London, 1909.

Aldred, G. A., From Anglican Boy-Preacher to Anarchist Socialist Impossiblist, London, 1908.

Aldred, G. A., Communism & Religion, Pt. 1, London, undated.

Aldred, G. A., Friedrich Nietzche, London, undated.

Aldred, G. A., Towards the Social Revolution?, Glasgow, 1934.

Alsberg, H. G., Alexander Berkman Sixtieth Birthday Celebration, New York, 1930.

Anarchism, 6 Essays, 1965.

Anarchist Federation Equity, The Struggle in the Factory: History of a R, Ordinance Factory, Glasgow, 1945.

The Anarchist, Glasgow Weekly, 1912-13.

The Anarchist Labour Leaf., London Monthly, 1890.

Anarcho-Syndicalist Union Spain, Anarchism, London, 1937.

Andrews, J. A., A Handbook of Anarchy, n.pl., n.d.

Anshen, R. N., ed., Freedom: Its Meaning, London, 1942.

Apter, D. E. & Joll, J., eds., Anarchism Today, London, 1971.

Arendt, H., Between Past and Future, New York, 1961.

Armand, E., ed., Divers Aspects De L'Anarchisme, Paris, 1933.

Arnold, M., Culture and Anarchy, London, 1889.

Arnot, R. P., William Morris: The Man & The Myth, London, 1964.

Arshinov, P., L'Histoire du Mouvement Makhnoviste: 1918-1921, Paris, 1924.

Arytage, Ed., Heaven Below: Utopian Experiments in England 1560-1960, n.pl., n.d.

Associated Anarchists, Manifesto, n.pl., 1895?

Associated Anarchists, Aims & Objects etc., n.pl., 1895?

Aveling, E. B., God Dies - Nature Remains, London, 1881.

Aveling, E. B., Darwinism & Small Families, London, 1882.

Aveling, E. B., The Creed of an Atheist, London, 1881.

Aveling, E. B., (trans.), Marx, K., Capital, London, 1886.

Aveling, E. B. & E. M., The Woman Question, London, 1886.

Aveling, E. B. & E. M., The Factory Hell, London, 1885.

Aveling, E. B. & E. M., Shelley's Socialism, London, 1888.

Aveling, E. B. & E. M., The Chicago Anarchists, London, 1888.

Avrich, P., An American Anarchist, Princeton, 1978.

Avrich, P., The Russian Anarchists, Princeton, 1967.

Bagehot, Walt, The English Constitution, London, 1963.

Bailie, W., Josiah Warren - The First American Anarchist, Boston, 1906.

Bakunin, M., Marxism, Freedom & the State, London, 1950.

Bakunin, M. A., The Pol. Phil. of Bakunin: Scientific Anarchism, Glencoe, Ill., 1953.

Bakunin, M., Oeuvres, Paris, 1895-1913.

Bakunin, M., God and the State, Tunbridge Wells, 1883.

Bakunin, M., La Commune de Paris et la Notion de l'etat, Paris, 1899.

Barber, B. R., Superman and Common Man: Freedom, Anarchy & The Revolution, 1972.

Barrett, Geo., The Anarchist Revolution, London, 1920.

Barrett, Geo., An Appeal to Socialists, n.pl., n.d.

Barrett, G., The Last War, Bristol, n.d.

Barrett, Geo., Objections to Anarchism, London, 1921.

Bax, E. B., Reminiscences & Reflections of a Mid & Late Victorian, London, 1918.

Bax, E. B., et al., A Short Account of the Commune of Paris, London, 1895.

Bax, E. B., A Short History of the Paris Commune, London, 1885.

Bax, E. B. & Morris, W., The Manifesto of the Socialist League, London, 1885.

Bax, E. B., J. P. Marat: A Historico-Bibliographical Sketch, London, 1882.

Bax, E. B., Jean Paul Marat: The People's Friend, London, 1900.

Bax, E. B., The Story of the French Revolution, London, 1890.

Bax, E. B., The Last Episode of the French Revolution, London, 1911.

Bax, E. B., The Ethics of Socialism, London, 1889.

Bax, E. B., Essays in Socialism: Old & New, London, 1906.

Bax, E. B., Outlooks from the New Standpoint, London, 1891.

Bax, E. B., The Students' Marx, London, 1892.

Bax, E. B., The Social Side of the Reformation in Germany, 3 vols., London, 1894-1903.

Bax, E. B., The Legal Subjugation of Men, London, 1908.

Bax, E. B., The Fraud of Feminism, London, 1913.

Bax, E. B., Problems of Men, Mind & Morals, London, 1912.

Bax, E. B., The Problem of Reality, London, 1892.

Bax, E. B., A Handbook of the History of Philosophy, London, 1886.

Beecher, J., ed., The Utopian Vision of Chas. Fourier, London, 1972.

Bell, T. H., Edward Carpenter: The English Tolstoi, Los Angeles, 1932.

Benn, S. I., & Peters, R. S., Social Principles and the Democratic State, London, 1959.

Berkman, A., What is a Communist-Anarchist, New York, 1929.

Berkman, A., ed., Selected Works of V. De Cleyre, New York, 1914.

Berkman, A., Prison Memoirs of an Anarchist, London, 1926.

Berkman, A., The Russian Tragedy (a review and an outlook), Berlin, 1922.

Berkman, A., & Goldman, E., Deportation: Its Meaning and Menace, New York, 1919.

Berkman, A., The Bolshevik Myth (Diary 1920-1922), London, 1925.

Berkman, A., A.B.C. of Anarchism, London, 1942.

Berkman, A., Anarchism on Trial, New York, 1917.

Berkman, A., What is Communist Anarchism?, New York, 1929.

Berkman, A., The Kronstadt Rebellion, Berlin, 1922.

Berkman, A., The Anti-Climax, Berlin, 1925.

Berkman, A., The Blast, Vols. 1 & 2, San Francisco, n.d.

Berkman, A., ed., Mother Earth, New York, 1906-17.

Berlin, I., Four Essays on Liberty, Oxford, 1971.

Berneri, Marie-Louise, Journey Through Utopia, London, 1950.

Berneri, Camille, Peter Kropotkin: His Federalist Ideas, London, 1942.

Bernstein, J., Pacifism and Rebellion in the Writings of Herman Melville, The Hague, 1964.

Besant, A., Why I Am A Socialist, London, 1886.

Binning, T., Organized Labour: The Duty of the Trades Unions in Relation to Socialism, London, 1886.

Black Rose Books Editorial Collective: Quebec Labour: The Confederation of National Trade Unions, n.pl., n.d.

Bookchin, M., Post Scarcity Anarchism, Berkeley, 1971.

Bookchin, M., The Ecology of Freedom, Palo Alto, 1982.

Borghi, A., Enrico Malatestra, 1947.

Borovoi, Alexi, Anarchism and Law.

Bosanquet, B., The Principle of Individuality and Value, London, 1912.

Bosanquet, B., The Value and Destiny of the Individual, London, 1923.

Bose, A., A History of Anarchism, Calcutta, 1967.

Bowman, Guy, Syndicalism: Its Basis, Methods & Ultimate Aim, London, 1913.

Briggs, A., Victorian People, London, 1954.

Briggs, A., ed., The Nineteenth Century: The Contradictions of Progress, London, 1970.

Briggs, R. C. H., A Handbook of the Public Addresses of William Morris, Kew, 1961.

Brinton, C., English Political Thought in the Ninetenth Century, New York, 1962.

Brooks, J. G., American Syndicalism: The IWW, New York, 1913.

Brown, K. D., Essays in Anti-Labour History, London, 1974.

Brown, Tom, The Social General Strike, London, 1948.

Bryant, A., English Saga – 1840-1940, London, 1948.

Bunzel, J. H., 'Liberal Ideology and the Problem of Power', Western Political Quarterly, June 1960.

Burke, E., A Vindication of Natural Society, Dublin, 1766.

Burns, J. H., 'J. S. Mill & Democracy 1829-61', Political Studies, Vol. 5.

Burns, John, Brains Better than Bets or Beer, London, 1902.

Burns, J., The Man with the Red Flag, London, 1886.

Burns, J., Labour & Free Trade, London, 1903.

Burns, J., The Tragedy Of Toil, London, 1899.

Burns, J., The Unemployed, London, 1893.

Burns-Gibson, J., Essays in Communist-Anarchism, n.pl., n.d.

Burrow, J. W., Evolution & Society: A Study of Victorian Social Theory, Cambridge, 1966.

Burrows, H., Zola, London, 1899.

Burrows, H., Emerson's Centenerary: His Thought & Teachings, London, 1903.

Burrows, H., The Future of Women, London, 1909.

Burrows, Herbert, Darwinism & Development Through Mutual Aid, London, 1915.

Burrows, H., & Hobson, J. A., eds., Wm. Clarke: A Collection of His Writings, London, 1908.

Bury, J. B., A History of Freedom and Thought, London, 1952.

Calder-Marshall, A., Lewd, Blasphemous & Obscene, London, 1972.

Calder-Marshall, A., "Lewd, Scandalous, Obscene", Encounter, 1971.

Carpenter, E., The Village & the Landlord, London, 1907.

Carpenter, E., Homogenic Love and Its Place in a Free Society, Manchester, 1894.

Carpenter, E., Cooperative Production: with reference to the experiment of Le Claire – A lecture, 1883.

Carpenter, E., Angel's Wings, London, 1898.

Carpenter, E., ed., Forecasts of the Coming Century. By a Decade of Writers – A. R. Wallace, Tom Mann, etc., London, 1897.

Carpenter, E., The Drama of Love & Death. A Study of Human Evolution and Transfiguration, London, 1912.

Carpenter, E., Prisons, Police & Punishment. An inquiry into the causes and treatment of crime and criminals, London, 1905.

Carpenter, E., The Religious Influence of Art, London, 1870.

Carpenter, E., The Art of Creation. Essays on the Self & Its Powers, London, 1904.

Carpenter, E., British Aristocracy & the House of Lords, London, 1908.

Carpenter, E., Iolaus. An Anthology of Friendship, London, and Boston, 1902.

Carpenter, E., Desirable Mansions: A Tract, London, 1883.

Carpenter, E., Social Progress & Individual Effort, London, 1886.

Carpenter, E., The Healing of Nations & the Hidden Sources of their Strife, London, 1915.

Carpenter, E., Woman and her Place in a Free Society, Manchester, 1894.

Carpenter, E., Vivisection - An Address, London, 1904.

Carpenter, E., Englands Ideal & Other Papers on Social Subjects, London, 1902.

Carpenter, E., Civilization: Its Cause & Cure & Other Essays, London, 1921.

Carpenter, E., Towards Democracy, London, 1907.

Carpenter, E., Towards Industrial Freedom, London, 1917.

Carpenter, E., Sex-Love & Its Place in a Free Society, Manchester, 1894.

Carpenter, E., The Intermediate Sex: A Study of Some Transectional Types of Men and Women, London and Manchester, 1908.

Carpenter, E., Intermediate Types among Primitive Folk. A Study in Social Evolution, London and Manchester, 1914.

Carpenter, E., Loves Coming of Age. A series of papers on the relations of the sexes. Manchester, 1896.

Carpenter, E., Modern Money-Lending & the Meaning of Dividends, London, 1883.

Carpenter, E., Marriage in a Free Society, Manchester, 1894.

Carpenter, E., My Days & Dreams. Being Autobiographical Notes , London, 1916.

Carpenter, E., Modern Science: A Criticism, Manchester, 1885.

Carpenter, E., A Bibliography of E. C. A Catalogue of books, manuscripts, letters, etc., by and about E. C. in the Carpenter Collection in the Dept. of Local Hist. of the Central Library Sheffield, Sheffield, 1949.

Carpenter, E., A Letter Relating to the Case of the Walsall Anarchists, London, 1892.

Carr, E. H., The Romantic Exiles, London, 1933.

Carter, A., Political Theory of Anarchism, London, 1971.

Cary, E. L., Wm. Morris: Poet, Craftsman Socialist, New York, London, 1902.

Chamberlain, J., "Blueprints for a New Society – Dream of Anarchism" in New Republic September 1939.

Champion de Crespigny, A., ed., Contemporary Political Theory, New York, 1970.

Chapelier, E., & Gassy, Marin, Anarchists & The International Language: Esperanto, London, 1908.

Chesterton, G. K., Wm. Morris: An Appreciation, Walthamstow, 1934.

Christie, S. & Meltzer, A., Floodgates of Anarchy, London, 1970.

Clutton-Brock, Art., Wm. Morris: A Study in Personality, New York, 1913.

Clutton-Brock, Art., Wm. Morris: His Work & Influence, London, 1914.

Cohn-Bendit, D. & G., Obsolete Communism: The Left Wing Alternative, London, 1968.

Cole, G. D. H., Socialist Thought: Marxism & Anarchism 1850-1890, London, 1954.

Cole, G. D. H., A History of Socialist Thought – 3 vols., New York, 1965.

Collins, F. H., Epitome of the Synthetic Philosophy, London, 1889.

Comfort, A., Authority & Delinquency in the Modern State, London, 1950.

Comfort, A., Delinquency, London, 1951.

The Commonweal, Vols. I-VII 1885-1892, Vols. I & II 1892-3 1893-4.

Compton-Rickett, A., The London Life of Yesterday, London, 1909.

Compton-Rickett, A., Wm. Morris: A Study in Personality, London, 1909.

Confino, M., La Violence dans la Violence: le debat Bakounine-Necaev, Paris, 1973.

Confino, M., ed., Daughter of a Revolutionary, London, 1974.

350

Craig, E. T., An Irish Commune. The History of Ralahine, Dublin, 1920.

Cranston, M., Freedom: A New Analysis, London, 1967.

Cranston, M., The Mask of Politics, London, 1973.

Crosby, E. H., Edward Carpenter: Poet & Prophet, London, 1905.

Crosby, E. H., How the United States Curtails Freedom of Thought, New York, 1904.

Crosby, E. H., Tolstoy As A Schoolmaster, London, 1904.

Dahl, R. A., After the Revolution, New Haven, 1970.

Dahl, R., Modern Political Analysis, New Jersey, 1970.

Dave, Victor, M. Bakounine et K. Marx, Paris, 1900.

Dave, Victor, Pacifisme et Anti-Militarisme, Paris, n.d.

Dave, V., Louis Buchner, Paris, 1910.

Dave, V., Fernand Pelloutier, Paris, 1909.

Dave, V., Eugene Vermersch, Paris, 1911.

Dave, V. & Others, A Short Account of the Commune of Paris, London, 1886.

David, Henry, A History of the Haymarket Affair: A Study in American Social & Revolutionary & Labour Movements, New York, 1936.

Davidson, J. M., Anarchist Socialism Versus State Socialism at the London International Labour Congress (1896), London, n.d.

Davidson, J. M., Second Chambers, London, n.d.

Davidson, J. M., Scotland for the Scots, London, 1902.

Davidson, J. M., Scotia Rediviva, London, n.d.

Davidson, J. M., The Wisdom of Winstanley, London, 1904.

Davidson, J. M., The New Book of Kings, London, 1884.

Davidson, J. M., The Book of Lords, London, 1907.

Davidson, J. M., The Annals of Toil, London, 1899.

Davidson, J. M., Politics for the People, London, 1892.

Davidson, J. M., The Dangerous Classes, London, n.d.

Davidson, J. M., The Gospel of the Poor, London, 1893.

Davidson, J. M., Eminent Radicals in Parliament, London, 1879.

Davidson, J. Morrison, Bluffing the Foreign Devils, or Dear-Bread
     Imperialism, London, n.d.

Day, J., 'Authority' in: Political Studies, October 1963.

De Cleyre, V., The Dominant Idea, New York, 1910.

De Cleyre, V., The Worm Turns, Philadelphia, 1900.

De Cleyre, V., The Mexican Revolt, New York, 1911.

De Cleyre, V., Direct Action: A Lecture, New York, 1912.

De Cleyre, V., Anarchism & American Traditions, Chicago, 1932.

De Cleyre, V., Selected Works (Edited by A. Berkman), New York, 1914.

De Cleyre, V., In Defence of Emma Goldman, Philadelphia, 1894.

De Cleyre, V., The Gods & The People, New York, 1897.

De Grazia, S., The Political Community, Chicago, 1948.

De Grazia, S., 'Authority & Rationality' in: Philosophy, Vol. 27, 1952.

De Jouvenel, B., Power: The Natural History of its Growth, London, 1952.

De Jouvenel, B., 'A Discussion of Freedom' in: Cambridge Law Journal,
     September 1953.

Delavenay, E., D. H. Lawrence & Edward Carpenter: A Study in Edwardian
     Transition, London, 1971.

Dolgoff, S., Bakunin on Anarchy, New York, 1972.

Dolgoff, S., The Anarchist Collectives: Worker's Self Management in the
     Spanish Revolution 1936-39, New York, 1974.

Dolleans, E., Proudhon, Paris, 1948.

Donisthorpe, W., Socialism and Individualism, London, 1883.

Donisthorpe, W., Individualism: A System of Politics, London, 1889.

Donisthorpe, W., Individualism: A Lecture, London, 1884.

Donisthorpe, W., Democracy: A Lecture on State Structure, London, 1886.

Donisthorpe, W., The Claims of Labour - or - Surfdom, Wagedom & Freedom,
     London, 1880.

Donisthorpe, W., Empire & Liberty: A Lecture on the Principles of Local

Government, London, 1886.

Donisthorpe, W., Labour Capitalization, London, 1887.

Donisthorpe, W., Law in a Free State, London, 1895.

Donisthorpe, W., Liberty or Law, London, 1885.

Donisthorpe, W., Love & Law: An Essay on Marriage, London, 1894.

Dos Passos, J., Facing the Chair: Sacco and Venzetti.

Drachkovitch, M., The Revolutionary International, 1864-1943, Stanford, 1966.

Drinkwater, J. et. al., Speeches in Commemoration of Wm. Morris, Walthamstow, 1934.

Drinkwater, J., Wm. Morris: A Critical Study, London, 1912.

Drinnon, R., Rebel in Paradise, Toronto, 1970.

Dubofsky, M., We Shall Be All, Chicago, 1969.

Edwards, S., ed., Selected Writings of Pierre-Joseph Proudhon, London, 1970.

Eidelberg, Paul, 'Intellectual & Moral Anarchy in American Society' Review of Politics, 1970.

Ellis, H. H., My Life, London, 1940.

Ellis, H. H., The 19th Century: A Dialogue in Utopia, London, 1900.

Ellis, H. H., Marriage Today & Tomorrow, San Francisco, 1929.

Ellis, H. H., The Erotic Rights of Women, London, 1918.

Ellis, H. H., The Criminal, London, 1901.

Eltzbacher, P., Anarchism: Exponents of the Anarchist Philosophy, London, 1960.

Ellis, Edith M. O., Personal Impressions of Edward Carpenter, London, 1921.

Emerson, R. W., Basic Selections from the Writings of Ralph Waldo Emerson, New York, 1963.

Emerson, R. W., Works of Ralph Waldo Emerson, London, 1889.

Eshleman, L. W., A Victorian Rebel: The Life of Wm. Morris, New York, 1940.

Fairchild, E. C., The Failure of Radicalism: A Socialist View of Working Class Politics, London, 1911.

Faure, S., L'Anarchie en Cour d'Assises, Paris, 1891.

Finifter, Ada W., 'Dimensions of Political Alienation', APSR, June 1970.

Fishman, W. J., East End Jewish Radicals 1875-1914, London, 1974.

Fishman, W. J., 'Rudolf Rocker: An Anarchist Missionary to the Jews', History Today, 1966.

Fleming, M., The Anarchist Way to Socialism, London, 1979.

Foner, P., ed., Autobiographies of the Chicago Martyrs, New York, 1969.

The Fortnightly Review, 1865-1951.

Fourier, Chas., De l'anarchie industrielle et scientifique, Paris, 1847.

Fourier, Chas., Design for Utopia, Paris, 1857.

Fowler, R. B., "The Anarchist Tradition of Political Thought", Western Political Quarterly, December 1972.

Fox, J., Trade Unionism & Anarchism - A Letter to a Brother Unionist, Chicago, 1908.

Fox, J., The Free Speech Case, New York, 1912.

Fox, J., Roosevelt, Czolgosz & Anarchy, New York, n.d.

Freedom: A Journal of Anarchist Communist Work and Literature, from October 1886.

Freedom Group, Mankind is One: Selected Articles of Freedom, Vol. 1, London, 1951.

Freedom Group, Postscript to Posterity: Selected Articles of The Anarchist Journal Freedom. Vol. 2, 1952, London.

Freedom Pamphlets, Anarchism & Outrage, London, 1893.

Friedman, R., 'A New Exploration of Mill's Essay on Liberty', Political Studies, Vol. 14.

Friedrich, C. J., 'The Political Thought of Neo-Liberalism', A.P.S.R., June 1955.

Friedrich, C. J., Tradition and Authority, London, 1972.

Friedrich, C. J., ed., Authority, Cambridge, Mass., 1958.

Friends of Freedom Press, London, n.d.

Fromm, E., Man for Himself - An Inquiry into the Psychology of Ethics, New York, 1969.

Fromm, E., The Sane Society, New York, 1955.

Fromm, E., Escape From Freedom, New York, 1967.

Fromm, E., The Art of Loving, London, 1957.

Garnett, D., The Golden Echo, London, 1954.

George, Henry, Progress & Poverty, London, 1882.

Gilmour, Wm., The Creed of Liberty, London, 1895.

Glasier, B. J., Wm. Morris & the Early Days of the Socialist Movement, London, 1921.

Glass, R., et. al., London: Aspects of Change, London, 1964.

Glasse, H., Socialism: The Reality, London, 1901.

Godwin, W., An Enquiry Concerning Political Justice, 3 Vols., Toronto, 1946.

Goldman, E., Anarchism: What It Really Stands For, Trace made available by the University of Toronto, undated.

Goldman, E., Anarchism & Other Essays, New York, 1969.

Goldman, E., My Further Disillusionment in Russia, New York, 1924.

Goldman, E., Living my Life, New York, 1931.

Goldman, E., Patriotism: a Menace to Liberty, New York, 1908.

Goldman, E., The Place of the Individual In Society, Chicago, 1933.

Goldman, E., The Social Significance of the Modern Drama, Boston, 1914.

Goldman, E., Trotsky Protests Too Much, 1938.

Goodman, Paul, Drawing the Line, New York, 1946.

Goodwin, Michael, Nineteenth Century Opinion: An Anthology of Extracts from the first 50 Vols. of "The Nineteenth Century, London, 1951.

Grave, J., Anarchy on Trial, London, 1901.

Grave, J., Association & Organization, London, 1921.

Grave, J., Moribund Society & Anarchy (trans. by V. de Cleyre), San Francisco, 1899.

Grey, E. L., Wm. Morris: Prophet of England's New Order, London, 1949.

Guerin, D., Anarchism: From Theory to Practise, New York, 1970.

Guillaume, J., Etudes Revolutionaires, Paris, 1908-9.

Guyau, J. M., A Sketch of Morality Independent of Obligation or Sanction, London, 1898.

Hamon, A., Les Hommes et les Theories de l'Anarchie, Paris, 1893.

Handcock, W., 'The Function & Nature of Authority in Society' in: Philosophy, Vol. 28, 1953.

Hare, Rich., Portraits of Russian Personalities Between Reform & Revolution, London, 1959.

Harris, Frank, Oscar Wilde, London, 1938.

Harris, Frank, The Bomb, London, 1908.

Harris, Frank, Contemporary Portraits, New York, 1920.

Harris, Frank, Frank Harris: His Life and Adventures, London, 1947.

Harris, F., Lies & Libels of Frank Harris, New York, 1929.

Harris, Frank, My Life, New York, 1925.

Harris, F., Frank Harris on Bernard Shaw, London, 1931.

Harrison, F., The Modern State: An Anarchist Analysis, Montreal, 1983.

Harrison, R., ed., Radical Action, Cambridge, 1977.

Hart, W. C., Confessions of An Anarchist, London, 1906.

Hayek, F., The Constitution of Liberty, Chicago, 1960.

Hayek, F., The Road to Surfdom, Chicago, 1944.

Hearnshaw, F. J. C., The Development of Political Ideas, London, 1927.

Hecht, John W., Russian Radicals & America, Cambridge, Mass., 1945.

Helmholtz-Phelan, A. A., The Social Philosophy of Wm. Morris, Durham, 1927.

Henderson, Philip, Wm. Morris: His Life Work & Friends, New York, 1967.

Henderson, P., ed., The Letters of Wm. Morris, London, 1950.

Henry, Agnes, Anarchist-Communism in Its Relation to State Socialism, London, 1896.

Herbert, A. E. W. M., Taxation and Anarchism, London, 1912.

Herbert, A., The Right & Wrong of Compulsion by the State: Anti-Force Paper No. 2, London, 1885.

Herbert, A., The Free Mind in the Free Body: A Statement of Principles & Measures: Anti-Force Paper No. 1, London, 1885.

Herbert, A., _A Politician in Trouble About His Soul_, London, 1884.

Herbert, A. E. W. M., _The Rights of Property_, London, 1889.

Herbert, A. E. W. M., _The Free Mind in the Free Body_, London, 1885.

Herbert, A. E. W. M., _Some Reasons Why We Object to Compulsory Taxation_, n.p., 1893.

Hewetson, J., _Mutual Aid & Social Revolution_, London, 1946.

Hewetson, J., _Italy After Mussolini_, London, 1945.

Hewetson, J., _Ill-Health, Poverty & The State_, London, 1946.

Hintox, J., _The First Shop Steward's Movement_, London, 1973.

Hobsbawm, E., _Labouring Men_, London, 1964.

Hobsbawm, E., _The Lesser Fabians_, London, 1962.

Hobsbawm, E., _Bandits_, London, 1969.

Hofstadter, R., _Social Darwinism in American Thought_, Boston, 1955.

Hofstadter, R., _Anti-Intellectualism in American Life_, New York, 1963.

Honderich, T., ed., _Essays on Freedom of Action_, London, 1973.

Horowitz, I. L., ed., _The Anarchists_, New York, 1964.

Horowitz, I. L., _Radicalism & The Revolt Against Reason_, London, 1961.

Hospers, J., _Libertarianism: A Philosophy for Tomorrow_, Los Angeles, 1971.

Hoy, T., ed., _Politics & Power: Who Should Rule_, New York, 1968.

Hubbard, E., _Little Journeys to the Homes of Great Business Men_, n.p., 1909.

Hubbard, E., _A Message to Garcia_, New York, 1899.

Hubbard, E., _Jesus Was An Anarchist_, n.pl., n.d.

Huggan, J., _Libertarian Readings_, n.pl., n.d.

Hughes, N. Stuart, _Consciousness & Society: The Reorientation of European Social Thought_, London, 1959.

Hulse, James W., _Revolutionists in London: A Study of Five Unorthodox Socialists_, London, 1970.

Hunter, E. E., _The A.B.C. of Socialism_, London, 1912.

Hunter, R., _The Enemies of Anarchy_, Toronto, 1970.

357

Huxley, Thomas, Evolution & Ethics, London, 1947.

Hyndman, H. M., England For All, London, 1881.

Hyndman, H. M., & Others, Liberalism & Labour, London, 1903.

Hyndman, H. M., & Morris, W., A Summary of the Principles of Socialism, London, 1884.

Iaroslayaskii, E., The History of Anarchism in Russia, London, 1937.

'Icarus', The Wilhelmshaven Revolt, London, 1944.

International Anarchist Conference - Amsterdam, August 26-31, 1907, London, 1907.

International Anarchist Manifesto on the War, n.pl., 1915.

The International Review: formerly - TO-DAY: The Monthly Magazine of Scientific Socialism, formerly - A Monthly Gathering of Bold Thoughts: 1844-1889 Nos. 1-70, London.

Ishill, J., ed., Free Vistas, 2 vols., Berkeley Heights, N.J., 1933-37.

Jack, H. A., ed., The Wit & Wisdom of Ghandi, Boston, 1951.

Jackson, Holbrook, William Morris, London, 1926.

Jackson, Holbrook, Wm. Morris: Craftsman-Socialist, London, 1926.

Jackson, Holbrook, The Eighteen Nineties: A Review of Art & Ideas At The Close of the Nineteenth Century, 1950.

Jackson, J., Dreamers & Dreams: The Rise & Fall of 19th Century Idealism, London, 1948.

Jackson, John H., Marx, Proudhon & European Socialism, London, 1957.

James, C. L., Anarchy, Eau Claire, Wisc., 1886.

James, C. L., Anarchism & Malthus, New York, 1910.

Joll, J., The Anarchists, London, 1964.

Joll, J., The Second International, 1889-1914, London, 1956.

Jones, P. d'A., The Christian Socialist Revival, 1978-1914, Princeton, 1968.

Kanter, R. M., Commitment and Community: Communer and Utopias in Sociological Perspective, Cambridge, Mass., 1972.

Kenworthy, John C., From Bondhood to Brotherhood, London, 1894.

Kenworthy, John C., The Anatomy of Misery, London, 1893.

Kidd, Benjamin, Social Evolution, 1894.

King, P. T., Fear of Freedom: An Analysis of Anti-Statism in Three French Writers, London, 1967.

Kolakowski, L., ed., Toward a Marxist Humanism, New York, 1968.

Krimerman, L. I., Perry, L., eds., Patterns of Anarchy: A Collection of Writings on the Anarchist Tradition, New York, 1966.

Kropotkin, P., Law, The Supporter of Crime, London, n.d.

Kropotkin, P., Law & Authority: An Anarchist Essay, London, 1886.

Kropotkin, P., The Wage System, London, 189?

Kropotkin, P., Memoirs Of A Revolutionist, London, 1908.

Kropotkin, P., Ethics: Origin & Development, London, 1922.

Kropotkin, P., Selected Writings on Anarchism & Revolution, Ed., Martin A. Miller, Cambridge, Mass., 1970.

Kropotkin, P., The Coming Revival of Socialism, London, 1903?

Kropotkin, P., The Conquest of Bread, New York, 1960.

Kropotkin, P., Mutual Aid: A Factor of Evolution, London, 1903.

Kropotkin, P., Anarchist Morality, London, 189?

Kropotkin, P., The Place of Anarchism in Socialist Revolution, London, 1886.

Kropotkin, P., Kropotkin's Revolutionary Pamphlets, Ed., Roger N. Baldwin, New York, 1927.

Kropotkin, P., The Terror in Russia, London, 1909.

Kropotkin, P., Modern Science & Anarchism, London, 1912.

Kropotkin, P., Anarchism: Its Philosophy and Ideal, London, 1897.

Kropotkin, P., The State: Its Historic Role, London, 1946.

Kropotkin, P., In Russian & French Prisons, London, 1887.

Kropotkin, P., The Great French Revolution: 1789-93, London, 1909.

Landauer, Carl, European Socialism: A History of Ideas & Movements, Los Angeles, 1959.

Landauer, G., Social Democracy in Germany, London, 1896.

Lane, Joseph, The Anti-Statist Communist Manifesto, London, 1887.

Lasswell, H. D., Power & Personality, London, 1952.

Latouche, P., Anarchy, London, 1908.

Laurence, Dan. H., G. B. Shaw: Collected Letters (1874-1897), London, 1965.

Leftwich, J., What Will Happen To The Jews, London, 1936.

The Legitimation League, 'The Rights of Natural Children - Proceedings Inaugural 1893', Leeds 1893.

Leval, G., Social Reconstruction in Spain, London, 1938.

Lewis, C. S., 'Studies in Words', Freedom, Cambridge, 1960.

Libertarian Movement National Committee, Three Years of Struggle in Spain, n.p., n.d.

Lippincott, B. E., Victorian Criticism of Democracy, Minneapolis, 1938.

Lockwood, G. B., The New Harmony Movement, New York, 1905.

Lowi, T. J., The End of Liberalism, 2nd ed., New York, 1979.

Lukes, S., Power: A Radical View, London, 1974.

Lum, D. D., The Economies of Anarchy. A Study of the Industrial Type, New York, 1890.

Mabbott, J.D., The State & The Citizen, London, 1970.

Malatesta, Errico, Anarchy, London, 1949.

Malatesta, E., Vote: What For!, London, 1945.

Malatesta, E., A Talk About Anarchist Communism Between Two Workers, London, 1892.

Mallock, W. H., Aristocracy & Evaluation, London, 1898.

Manifesto-Independent Union of Direct Actionists, London, 1907?

Mann, T., 'All Hail, Solidarity' The Industrial Syndicalist No. 4, 1910.

Mann, T., Memoirs, London, 1923.

Mann, T., 'Forging the Weapon', The Industrial Syndicalist No. 3, September 1910.

Mann, T., From Single Tax to Syndicalism, London, 1913.

Mannheim, K., Freedom, Power & Democratic Planning, New York, 1950.

Manuel, Frank, Utopias & Utopian Thought, Boston, 1966.

Manuel, Frank, French Utopias, New York, 1966.

Marillier, H. C., The Morris Movement, privately printed, n.d.

Martin, Chas., Towards a Free Society, London, 1960.

Martin, James J., Men Against the State, De Kalb, Ill., 1953.

Meijer, J. M., Knowledge & Revolution: The Russian Colony in Zurich 1870-1873, Amsterdam, 1955.

Michel, L., Memoires, Paris, 1886.

Michel, L., La Commune, Paris, 1898.

Mill, J. S., On Liberty, London, 1863.

Mill, J. S., Utilitarianism, London, 1863.

Mill, J. S., The System of Logic, London, 1843.

Mill, J. S., Principles of Political Economy, London, 1848.

Mills, C. W., Power, Politics & People, New York, 1963.

Meredith, I. (pseud. for Olivia Rossetti) A Girl Amongst The Anarchists, London, 1903.

Money-Kyrle, R. E., Psychoanalysis and Politics, London, 1951.

Montefiore, D., Position of Women in the Socialism Movement, London, 1909.

Montseny, F., Militant Anarchism and the Reality in Spain, Glasgow, 1937.

Morel, E. D., Will You Make War Again?, London, 192?

Morris, May, Wm. Morris - Artist, Writer, Socialist, 2 vols., Oxford, 1936.

Morris, W., The Collected Works of Wm. Morris, 24 Vols., London, 1910-15.

Morris, W., Art, Labour & Socialism, London, 1907.

Morris, W., The Aims of Art, London, 1887.

Morris, W., Art & Socialism, London, 1884.

Morris, W., Hopes & Fears for Art, London, 1882.

Morris, W., How I Became A Socialist, London, 1896.

Morris, W., Love Is Enough, London, 1873.

Morris, W., Letters on Socialism, London, 1894.

Morris, W., The Labour Question From The Socialist Standpoint, (True & False Society), London, 1888.

Morris, W., Labour & Pleasure Vs. Labour & Sorrow, Birmingham, 1880.

Morris, W. & Bax, E. B., Socialism: Its Growth & Outcome, London, 1893.

Morris, W., A Talk With Wm. Morris on Socialism, London, 1885.

Morris, W., Useful Work Vs. Useless Toil, London, 1902.

Morris, W., The Tables Turned, London, 1887.

Morris, W., The Story of the Glittering Plain, London, 1891.

Morris, W., Statement of the Principles of the Hammersmith Socialist Society, London, 1890.

Morris, W., Signs of Change: Seven Lectures, London, 1888.

Morris, W., The Reward of Labour, London, 1892.

Morris, W., Unpublished Letters, London, 1951.

Morris, W., The Pilgrims of Hope & Chants for Socialists, London, 1915.

Morris, W., A Dream of John Ball and a King's Lesson, London, 1892.

Morris, W., News From Nowhere: or, an Epic of Rest, London, 1891.

Morris, W., Monopoly or How Labour is Robbed, London, 1890.

Morris, W., Communism, London, 1903.

Morris, W., A Factory as It Might Be, London, 1907.

W. Morris Society, The Journal of, Vol. 1, No. 4.

Morrow, F., Revolution & Counterrevolution in Spain, New York, 1938.

Morton, A. L., Political Writings of Wm. Morris, London, 1973.

Most, Johann, "Science of Revolutionary Warfare: A Manual in the Use and Preparation of Nitrogylcerine Dynamite, Gun-Cotton, Fulminating Mercury, Bombs, Poisons, etc. etc., Pamphlet, n.p., 1885.

Motler, L. A., Anarchist Communism (in plain English), London, n.d.

Maccoby, S., The English Radical Tradition 1763-1914, London, 1952.

McBriar, A. M., Fabian Socialism & English Politics, 1884-1918, London.

McCabe, J., 1825-1925: A Century of Stupendous Progress, London, 1925.

McCabe, J., The A.B.C. of Evolution, London, 1920.

McCabe, J., The Bankruptcy of Religion, London, 1917.

McCabe, J., A Bibliographical Dictionary of Modern Rationalists, London, 1920.

McCabe, J., Can We Save Civilization?, London, 1932.

McCabe, J., The Evolution of Mind, London, 1910.

McCabe, J., Modern Rationalism, London, 1897.

McCabe, J., The Martyrdom of Ferrer, London, 1909.

MacFarlane, L. J., 'Justifying Political Disobedience', Ethics, Oct. 1968.

MacKail, J. W., The Life of Wm. Morris, (Official Biography), Vols. I & II, London, 1899.

MacKail, J. W., Wm. Morris & His Circle, Hammersmith, 1903.

MacKay, Thos., ed., A Plea For Liberty: An Argument Against Socialism & Socialistic Legislation, London, 1891.

MacKay, J. H., The Anarchists: A picture of civilization at the close of the 19th century, Boston, 1891.

McKay, T., The English Poor, London, 1889.

MacMurray, J., Freedom in the Modern World, London, 1941.

Nash, V., & Llewellen-Smith, H., The Story of the Docker's Strike, London, 1890.

Negley, G., Political Authority & Moral Judgement, Durham, 1965.

Negley, G. R., ed., The Quest for Utopia, New York, 1952.

Nettlau, M., Responsibility & Solidarity in the Labour Struggle, London, 1900.

Nettlau, M., Sidelights on Errico Malatesta, Stroud, 1932.

Nettlau, M., Sabotage, Berlin, 1923.

Nettlau, M., Errico Malatesta: The Biography of An Anarchist, New York, 1924.

Nettlau, M., Elisee and Elie Reclus, In Memorium, Leipzig, 1928.

Nettlau, M., "Anarchism In England 50 Years Ago", Freedom, Nov.-Dec. 1905.

Nevinson, H. W., Essays in Freedom and Rebellion, New Haven, 1921.

Nevinson, Henry W., England's Voice of Freedom, London, 1929.

Nevinson, H. W., <u>Visions & Memories</u>, London, 1944.

Nevinson, H. W., <u>Essays in Rebellion</u>, London, 1913.

Nevinson, H. W., <u>The Growth of Freedom</u>, London, 1912.

Newman, S. L., <u>Liberalism at Wit's End: The Libertarian Revolt Against the Modern State</u>, Ithaca and London, 1984.

Nicoll, D. J., <u>The Sheffield Outrages</u>, Sheffield, 1896.

Nicoll, D. J., <u>Anarchy At The Bar</u>, London, 1893.

Nicoll, D. J., <u>The Ghosts of Chelmsford Jail</u>, Sheffield, 1896.

Nicoll, D. J., <u>The Walsall Anarchists</u>, London, 1895.

Nicoll, D. J., <u>The Featherstone Massacre</u>, n.p., n.d.

Nicoll, D. J., <u>The Greenwich Mystery</u>, London, 1898.

Nieuwenhuis, F. D., <u>The Pyramid of Tyranny</u>, London, 1909.

<u>The Nineteenth Century</u> (Now: <u>The Twentieth Century</u>) (1887-1954)

Nordhoff, C., <u>The Communistic Societies of the United States</u>, New York, 1960.

Norton, S. F., <u>Ten Men of Money Island</u>, Chicago, 1892.

Noyes, John H., <u>Strange Cults & Utopias of the Nineteenth Century</u>, n.pl., n.d.

Nozick, R., <u>Anarchy, State and Utopia</u>, New York, 1974.

Oakeshott, M., ed., <u>Hobbe's Leviathan</u>, Oxford, 1955.

Oakley, H., <u>Liberty Through Communist Anarchism</u>, London, 1920.

O'Brien, M. D., <u>The Natural Right to Freedom</u>, London, 1893.

O'Brien, M. D., <u>Socialism Tested by Facts</u>, London, 1892.

O'Brien, M. D., <u>Socialism & Character</u>, London, 1910.

O'Brien, M. D., <u>Socialism & Infamy</u>, London, 189?

Oppenheimer, F. E., <u>Dimensions of Freedom</u>, New York, 1961.

Orwell, G., <u>Homage to Catalonia</u>, London, 1938.

Osborn, R. (pseud. Reuben Osbert), <u>Humanism & Moral Theory</u>, London, 1959

Ostergaard, G., 'George Bernard Shaw - Anarchist', <u>The New Statesman & Nation</u>, Nov. 21, 1953.

"Our Corner", London Monthly, 1883-1888, Vols. 1-12.

Owen, W. C., The Anarchist Revolution, London, 1920.

Owen, W. C., Objections to Anarchism, London, 1921.

Owen, W. C., Set My People Free, London, 1925.

Owen, W. C., Anarchy Versus Socialism, New York, 1908.

Owen, W. C., et al., Les Differents Visages de Anarchisme, Paris, 1927.

Owen, W. C., Anarchism Versus Socialism, London, 1922.

Owen, W. C., The Economics of Herbert Spencer, New York, 1891.

Owen, W. C. (Senex), England Monopolized or England Free, London, 1920.

Paine, T., The Rights of Man, Dublin, 1791.

Parsons, A. R., Anarchism, Chicago, 1887.

Peaceful Anarchist Group, Peaceful Anarchism, n.p., n.d.

Pearson, K., The Moral Basis of Socialism, London, n.d.

Pease, E., The History of the Fabian Society, London, 1963.

Pease, E., The Diaries of Edward Pease, London, 1907.

Pelling, H. M., The Origins of the Labour Party - 1880-1900, London, 1932.

Perlin, T. M., Anarchist-Communism in America (1890-1914), Boston, 1970.

Phillips, W. R., 'Why Are The Many Poor?' Fabian Tract No. 1.

Plamenatz, J. P., Consent, Freedom & Political Obligation, London, 1938.

Plamenatz, J., The English Utilitarians, Oxford, 1958.

Planche, F. & Delphy, J., Kropotkine, Paris, 1948.

Plechanoff, G., Anarchism & Socialism, Minneapolis, 1912.

Pouget, E. & Pataud, E., Syndicalism & The Cooperative Commmonwealth, Paris, 1909.

Pouget, E., L'A.B.C.D. de la Revolution, Londres, 1894.

Pouget, E., The Basis of Trade Unionism, London, 1908.

Pouget, E., Les Bases du Syndicalisme, Paris, 1895.

Pouget, E., La Confederation General du Travail, Paris, 1908.

365

Pouget, E., *Le Sabotage*, Paris, 1911?

Pouget, E., *Le Syndicat*, Paris, 1895.

Proudhon, P. J., *What is Property: An Inquiry into the Principles of Right and of Government*, New York, 1891.

Proudhon, P. J., *System of Economical Contradictions ... or the Philosophy of Misery*, Boston, 1888.

Quail, J., *The Slow Burning Fuse*, London, 1978.

Quelch, H., *Trade Union. Cooperation & Social Democracy*, London, 1892.

Quelch, H., *The Social Democratic Federation: Its Objects*, London, 1907.

Quelch, H., *Social Democracy and the Armed Nation*, London, 1900.

Quelch, H., *The Cooperative Snare*, London, 1913?

Quelch, H., *Economics of Labour*, London, 1908.

Quinton, A., ed., *Political Philosophy*, Oxford, 1971.

Read, H., *Anarchy & Order - Essays in Politics*, London, 1954.

Read, H. E., *Existentialism, Marxism & Anarchism: Chains of Freedom*, London, 1949.

Read, H. E., *A Coat of Many Colours*, London, 1945.

Read, H. E., *Education Through Art*, London, 1943.

Read, H. E., *Art & Society*, London, 1945.

Read, H. E., *The Education of Free Men*, London, 1944.

Read, H. E., *The Contrary Experience: Autobiographies*, London, 1963.

Read, H., *The Philosophy of Anarchism*, London, 1947.

Reclus, Elisee, *An Anarchist on Anarchy*, London, 1894.

Reclus, Elisee, *Evolution & Revolution*, London, 1886.

Reclus, Elisee, *The Great Kinship*, Berkeley Heights, N.J., 1933.

Reclus, Elisee, *Education & Revolution*, London, n.d.

Reclus, J. J. E., *Do Not Vote (and) The Parliamentary Elections*, N. W. Tchaykowsky, 1900?

Rees, J. C., *Equality*, Swansea, 1971.

Rees, J. C., 'Rereading Mill on Liberty', Political Studies, Vol. 14.

Reichert, W. O., 'Anarchism, Freedom & Power', Ethics, January 1968.

Reichert, W. O., 'Toward a New Understanding of Anarchism', Western Political Quarterly, 1967.

Reid, G. W., The Natural Basis of Civilization, London, n.d.

Remus, P., Why Does Anarchism Progress So Slowly?, San Francisco, 1935.

Renard, G., Guilds in the Middle Age, London, 1919.

Renard, G., Socialisme Libertarie et Anarchie, Paris, 1895.

Renard, G., La Valeur de la Loi, Paris, 1928.

Reuss, C. T., The Matrimonial Question From An Anarchist Point of View, London, 1887.

Reynolds, T., Non-Competition and Perfect Social Equality Versus Anarchism, n.pl., 1896.

Rhodes, C. O., Authority in a Changing Society, London, 1969.

Richards, V., Lessons of the Spanish Revolution, London, 1972.

Richards, V., ed., Errico Malatesta: His Life and Ideas, London, 1965.

Robertson, A. H. M., Independence or Cooperation in Education, London, n.d.

Robinson, Jack, Leo Tolstoy: His Life & Work, London, 1968.

Rocker, R., Pioneers of Am. Freedom, Los Angeles, 1949.

Rocker, R., Nationalism & Culture, London, 1938.

Rocker, R., Anarcho-Syndicalism, London, 1938.

Rocker, R., The London Years, London, 1956.

Rogers, James A., Prince Peter Kropotkin Scientist & Anarchist, Harvard, 1957.

Roller, R., The Social General Strike, New York, 1905.

Rossetti, W. M., Some Reminiscences, London, 1906.

Rothbard, M., For a New Liberty, rev. ed., New York, 1978.

Ruskin, J., The Nature of Gothic, London, 1854.

Russell, B., Authority & the Individual, London, 1949.

Russell, B., Roads to Freedom - Socialism Anarchism & Syndicalism, London,

1966.

Russell, B., _Power: A New Social Analysis_, London, 1967.

Ryan, A., ed., _The Idea of Freedom_, Oxford, 1979.

Sampson, R. V., 'Culture, Power & Knowledge', _Current_, June 1969.

Sampson, R. V., _Tolstoy: The Discovery of Peace_, London, 1973.

Sampson, R. V., _Equality & Power_, London, 1965.

Sampson, R. V., 'Power - The Enshrined Heresy' in _The Nation_, Jan. 4, 1971.

Samuels, H. B., _What's to be Done?_, London, 1892.

Sansom, T. R., Unpublished manuscript, 1971.

Scalapino, R. A. & Yu, G. T., _The Chinese Anarchist Movement_, 1961.

Schaar, J., 'Notes on Authority', _New American Review_, New York, No. 8.

Schuster, E. M., _Native Am. Anarchism: A Study of Left Wing American Individualism_, Northampton, Mass., 1932.

Seed-Time, No. 1 'The Sower', Nos. 1-34, July 1889-Feb. 1898.

'Senex', _England Monopolized or England Free_, London, 1920.

Seymour, H. J., _The Fallacy of Marx's Theory of Surplus Value_, London, 1897.

Seymour, H., _Michael Bakounine - A Biographical Sketch_, London, 1888.

Seymour, H., _The Monomaniacs: A Fable in Finance_, London, 1895.

Seymour, H., _Anarchy: Theory & Practice_, London, 1888.

Seymour, H., _An Examination of the Malthusian Theory_, London, 1889.

Seymour, H., _Anarchy: Theory & Practice_, London, 1888.

Seymour, H., _The Anarchy of Love: or the Science of the Sexes_, London, 1888.

Seymour, H., _P. J. Proudhon: A Biographical Sketch_ ... Reprinted from _The Anarchist_, London, 1887.

Seymour, H., _Physiology of Love: A Study in Stirpiculture etc._, London, 1898.

Seymour, H., _The Two Anarchisms_, London, 1894.

Seymour, H., _The Philosophy of Anarchism_, London, 1888.

Seymour, H. ed., _The Anarchist_, 1885-87, 1887-88.

Seymour, H. ed., The Revolutionary Review, 1889.

Seymour, H., Reproduction of Sound: Being a description of the Mechanical Appliances and Technical Processes Employed in the Art. London, 1918.

Shaw, G. B., 'Impossibilities of Anarchism', Fabian Tract No. 45, London, 1911.

Shaw, G. B., Anarchism versus State Socialism, London, 1889.

Shaw, G. B., Wm. Morris as I Knew Him, London, 1966.

Shaw, G. B., 'The Fabian Society - What It Has Done and How It Has Done It'. Fabian Tract No. 41, London, 1892.

Shklar, J. N., 'Rousseau's Images of Authority', A.P.S.R., Dec. 1964.

Silverian, Henry J., American Radical Thought: The Libertarian Tradition, Lexington, Mass., 1970.

Sime, A. H. M., Ed. Carpenter: His Ideas and Ideals, 1916.

Simon, S. F., 'Anarchism & Anarcho-Syndicalism in South America', Hispanic American Historical Rev., Feb. 1946.

Simons, A. M., Socialism vs. Anarchism, Chicago, 1901.

Smith, Sir Hubert Llewellyn, The History of East London From the Earliest Times to the End of the Eighteenth Century, London, 1939.

Smith, J. Blair, Direct Action versus Legislation, London, 1909.

Sorel, G., Reflections on Violence, Glencoe, Ill., 1950.

Spencer, H., The Right to Ignore The State, London, 1913.

Spielmann, M. H., John Ruskin: A Sketch Of His Life, London, 1900.

Sprading, C. T., Liberty & The Great Libertarians: An Anthology of Liberty, San Francisco, 1913.

Stafford, D., From Anarchism to Reformism, London, 1971.

Stansky, P., Redesigning the World, William Morris, the 1880's and the Arts and Crafts, Princeton, N.J., 1985.

Stephen, L., The English Utilitarians, 3 vols., London, 1900.

Stirner, M., The Ego and His Own, London, 1921.

Strachey, L., Eminent Victorians, London, 1948.

Swan, Tom, Edward Carpenter: The Man And His Message, London, 1929.

Talmon, J. L., Political Messianism: The Romantic Phase, London, 1960.

Tarn, A., A Free Currency: What It Means, London, 1889.

Tarn, A., The Individual and the State, London, 1891.

Taylor, M. T., Anarchy and Cooperation, London and New York, 1976.

Taylor, M. T., Community, Anarchy, and Liberty, Cambridge, 1982.

Thompson, E. P., Wm. Morris; Romantic to Revolutionary, London, 1955.

Thompson, E. P., The Communism of Wm. Morris, London, 1965.

Thompson, P., Socialists, Liberals and Labour, London, 1967.

Thoreau, H. D., Anti-Slavery & Reform Papers, London, 191?

Thouless, R. H., Authority & Freedom, London, 1954.

Tilley, C., The Redemption of Labour, Paterson, N.J., 1879.

Tolstoy, L., The Kingdom of God is Within You, New York, 1905.

Tolstoy, L., Rule by Murder, London, 19--?

Tolstoy, L., The Law of Love & the Law of Violence, London, 1970.

Tolstoy, L., The Slavery of Our Times, Maldon, 1900.

Torch Group, Anarchist May Day Manifesto, London, 1895.

Townshend, P., 'William Morris and the Communist Ideal', Fabian Tract No. 167, London, 1912.

Tsuzuki, C., Edward Carpenter, Cambridge, 1980.

Tuchman, B. W., "The Anarchists", The Atlantic, Vol. 211, No. 3, May 1963.

Tuchman, B., The Proud Tower: A Portrait of the World Before The War, 1890-1914, New York, 1966.

Tucker, B. R., Instead of a Book: a fragmentary exposition of philosophical anarchism, New York, 1897.

Tucker, B. R., Individual Liberty, Boston, 1896.

Tussman, J., Obligation & the Body Politic, New York, 1960.

Vallance, A., Wm. Morris: His Art, His Writings & His Public Life, London, 1898.

Venturi, F., The Roots of Revolution, London, 1960.

Vizetelly, E. A., My Adventures in the Commune of Paris - 1871, London, 1914.

Vizetelly, E. A., The Anarchists, London, 1911.

Voice of Labour: A Weekly Paper for those who Work and Think, London, 1907.

W. B., Freedom, London, 1916.

W. H. C., Confessions Of An Anarchist, London, 1911.

Wakeman, J., Anarchism & Democracy, London, 1920.

Wallace, A. R. et al., Forecasts of the Coming Century by a Decade of Writers, Manchester, 1897.

Walters, N., Three Essays on Anarchism, Sanday, Orkney, 1979.

Ward, Colin, Anarchy in Action, London, 1973.

Warren, G. O., Anarchism (and Politicians), n.p., 1890.

Warren, G. O., Freedom, Rent, Interest Profit & Taxes the True Causes of Wage Slavery discussed & Exploded, London, 1893.

Watt, I., ed., Conrad, The Secret Agent: A Casebook, London, 1973.

Webb, S., 'Facts For Londoners', Fabian Tract No. 8, London, 1889.

Weiner, The Labour Party Illusion, New York, 1961.

Weinstein, W. L., "The Concept of Liberty in Nineteenth Century Political Thought", Political Studies, 1963.

Weintraub, S., Four Rossettis, London, 1978.

Weldon, T. D., The Vocabulary of Politics, London, 1953.

Wexler, A., Emma Goldman: An Intimate Life, New York, 1984.

White, Ida, The Banner Red, London, 1894.

Wilde, O., 'The Soul of Man Under Socialism', The Fortnightly Review, Feb. 1891.

Willey, B., Nineteenth Century Studies: Coleridge To Arnold, London, 1949.

Wills, J., The Case For Amalgamation, London, 19--?

Williams, R., Culture and Society, 1780-1950, London, 1967.

Wilson, C. M., 'Women & Prisons', Fabian Tract No. 163, London, 1912.

Wilson, C. M. & Others, 'What Socialism Is", Fabian Tract No. 4, London, 1886.

Wilson, C. M., Social Democracy & Anarchism, London, 1886.

Wilson, C. M., The Principles & Aims of Anarchism, London, 1886.

Winstanley, Gerrard, The Works ... New York, 1941.

Winstanley, Gerrard, Law of Freedom & Other Writings, London, 1973.

Wishart, A. W., The Case of Wm. MacQueen, Trenton, N.J., 1909.

Withington, L., Constructive Murder, London, 1887.

Wolff, R. P., In Defense of Anarchism, New York, 1970.

Wood, C. E. S., Too Much Government, New York, 1931.

Woodcock, G., Pierre Joseph Proudhon, New York, 1972.

Woodcock, G., Anarchy or Chaos, London, 1944.

Woodcock, G., Anarchism: A History of Libertarian Ideas & Movements, 1962.

Woodcock, G., 'Anarchism Revisited', Commentary, 1968.

Woodcock, G., New Life to the Land, London, 1942.

Woodcock, G., A Hundred Years of Revolution: 1848 & After, London, 1948.

Woodcock, G., Anarchism & Morality, London, 1945.

Woodcock, G., Railways & Society, London, 1943.

Woodcock, G., Civil Disobedience, Toronto, 1966.

Woodcock, G., The Basis of Communal Living, London, 1947.

Woodcock, G., What Is Anarchism?, London, 1945.

Woodcock, G., Wm. Goodwin: A Biographic Study, London, 1946.

Woodcock, G., 'Bakunin: The Destructive Age', History Today, July 1961.

Woodcock, Geo. & Avakumovic, I., The Anarchist Prince: A Biographical Study of Peter Kropotkin, London, New York, 1950.

Worker's Circle Friendly Society, 1909-59.

Wrekin Anarchist Voice: Wrekin Libertarians, 1972.

Yarros, V., Anarchism: Its Aims & Methods, Boston, 1887.

Yarrows, V. S., 'Philosophical Anarchism: Its Rise Decline & Eclipse', American Journal of Sociology, 41 (1936) 470-483.

Yelensky, B., In The Struggle for Equality: the Story at the A.R.C., pp. 96, Chicago, 1958.

Young, G. M., <u>Victorian England: Portrait Of An Age</u>, London, 1937.

Zenker, E. V., <u>Anarchism</u>, London, 1898.

For Product Safety Concerns and Information please contact our EU
representative GPSR@taylorandfrancis.com
Taylor & Francis Verlag GmbH, Kaufingerstraße 24, 80331 München, Germany